Novelistic Love
in The Platonic Tradition

Fielding, Faulkner and the Postmodernists

JENNIE WANG

ROWMAN & LITTLEFIELD PUBLISHERS, INC.
Lanham. Boulder. New York. Oxford

ROWMAN & LITTLEFIELD PUBLISHERS, INC.

Published in the United States of America
by Rowman & Littlefield Publishers, Inc.
4720 Boston Way, Lanham, Maryland 20706

12 Hid's Copse Road
Cummor Hill, Oxford OX2 9JJ, England

British Library Cataloguing in Publication Information Available

Library of Congress Cataloging-in-Publication Data

Wang, Jennie, 1952–
    Novelistic love in the platonic tradition : Fielding Faulkner,
and the postmodernists / Jennie Wang.
        p. cm.
    Includes bibliographical references and index.
    ISBN 0-8476-8622-1 (cloth : alk. paper). — ISBN 0-8476-8623-X
(paper : alk. paper)
        1. English fiction—History and criticism. 2. Love stories—History and criticism.
3. Platonic love in literature. 4. American   fiction—20th century—History and
criticism. 5. Postmodernism   (Literature) 6. Fielding, Henry, 1707–1754   Tom
Jones. 7. Faulkner,   William, 1897–1962 Go down, Moses. 8. Plato—Influence.
9. English fiction—Greek influences. I. Title.
PR830.L69W36 1997
823.009'3543—dc21   97-25282
                                                                                 CIP
ISBN 0-8476-8622-1 (cloth : alk. paper)
ISBN 0-8476-8623-x (pbk. : alk. paper)

Printed in the United States of America

∞™ The paper used in this publication meets the minimum requirements of
American National Standard for Information Sciences—Permanence of Paper
for Printed Library Materials, ANSI Z39.48–1984.

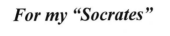

For my "Socrates"

For liberation—not less of love but expanding
Of love beyond desire, and so liberation
From the future as well as from the past. Thus, love of a country
Begins as attachment to our own field of action.

—T. S. Eliot, "Little Gidding"

Contents

Acknowledgments

I wish to thank my colleague Jerry Klinkowitz for reading and editing an early version of this manuscript; Professor Marc Blanchard at the University of California, Davis, for his valuable comments and suggestions in his review of this manuscript; Michelle Harris and Robin Adler at *Rowman & Littlefield* for their editorial assistance; and Paul Plisiewicz, my student and editorial assistant for *The North American Review*, for his help in preparing the manuscript. Without their happy assistance, this book probably would never have been published.

Since this project began as my dissertation work at the State University of New York, Buffalo, where I enjoyed five happiest years in my life (1987-91), in publishing this book, my most affectionate gratitude goes to Professors Neil Schmitz, Henry Sussman, and Roy Roussel. I thank these learned wits at Buffalo for their Socratic wisdom and Platonic understanding in directing this project. Neil's paternal demand was always a challenge, his feminine humor a nourishment, his minimalism my discipline, his political correctness my affirmation. In my nifty grasp of the heart's truth in literary "lies," I have learned, however clumsily, a great deal from him. I am most indebted to Henry Sussman for his decisive guidance of my project from research to revision. His polymathic knowledge, creative methodology, and philosophical erudition have certainly begotten the best part of this work. I am grateful to Roy Roussel for his initial interest in my subject. His serious reading opened new perspectives in my reordering the chapters. Even his well-known sadism was a liberating force, which freed my mind from the routines of academic convention.

I also would like to take this opportunity to thank my professors and friends whose instruction directly and indirectly informed and influenced my work. Professor Raymond Federman taught me the aesthetics of postmodern fiction from a fictionist's perspective. The original idea of my thesis came into being when I was translating his award-winning novel *Smiles on Washington Square: A Love Story of Sorts* (1986). This translation project was directed by Professor Constantine Tung, who was my "Santa Claus" at Buffalo, as his family hosted many a Christmas to keep me out of the snow. Professor Leslie Fiedler's instruction on the American novel of the 1930s made me aware of the historical discontinuity between modernism and postmodernism. Professor Marcus Klein's seminar on twentieth-century American literature, in a rigorous way, opened my eyes to the politics of interpretation. Professor Joseph Conte directed my reading of Pynchon, Barth, Hawkes, and Sorrentino. Professor Mark Sheckner provided very informative instruction on *Finnegans Wake* in our reading group.

Among my friends in graduate school, I shall always remember the warmth and generosity of Linda Reinfeld and Kandace Lombard. Linda shared her library of critical theories with me, patiently helped me to understand deconstruction, postmodern theories, and Greek philosophy; and Kandace, with her wonderful hospitality and cross-Atlantic emigre experience, engaged my interest in women's writing and French feminism. It was the scholarship and support of my beloved friends, above mentioned or not, that nourished my intellect while I was composing this work.

The book is dedicated to "my Socrates"—those who taught me and gave me the wisdom of love. My earliest indebtedness goes back to my tutor in China, Professor Frank Zhou at Shanghai International Studies University, who taught me English and literary translation, and more important, the value of love and learning as a way of life. Such a way of life became my American dream. My pursuit of that dream, since my undergraduate years at San Francisco State University in the early 1980s, had never been separated from the bounteous library, love and learning of Professor John Hamilton Edwards, who remained a friend until he passed away in 1994. His death left me with the ultimate knowledge of love beyond life.

A large section of Chapter One was originally published in *Critique: Studies in Contemporary Fiction* 34 (1992): 63-79 under the title of "To Wielderfight His Penisolate War: 'The Lover's Discourse' in Postmodern Fiction." Another section from the Faulkner chapter was first presented at "Voice of Diversity: The Third International Conference on the Short Story in English" at the University of Northern Iowa in 1991, and subsequently published under the title "Romantic Love and Its Repudiation of Cultural Legacy: Faulkner's Silver Horn in 'Delta Autumn'" in *Short Story* 4 (1996): 85-103. To the editors of *Short Story*, Dr. Mary Rohrberger and Dr. Farhat Iftekharuddin, I wish to express my appreciation for their Southern interest in my work.

Finally, thanks to the support of David Walker, two project grants from the Graduate College at the University of Northern Iowa in 1997 helped to cover the cost of copyright permissions and the preparation of the book manuscript. Permissions for quoting from Plato, Fielding, Faulkner, Lanier and Eliot were respectively granted by Penguin, Random House, the Johns Hopkins University Press, and Harcourt Brace & World.

Introduction

Love, the eternal theme in world literature, has been only a marginal subject in the study of the English and the American novel. In American literary criticism, the study of love stories has been an exotic subject, either a continental game, Irish humor, Greek mythology, or Oriental fantasy. Seldom has love been treated as an aesthetic or philosophical subject for academic inquiry, or studied in a cultural or historical context beyond the pleasure principle, beyond sensual materialism. Leslie Fiedler's *Love and Death in the American Novel* remained on the margin of American literary criticism. Not until the late 1970s, under the influence of the French poststructuralists—Barthes, Derrida, Foucault, Lacan, and Kristeva did the conversation of a "lover's discourse," to borrow the title of Barthes's book, take place in academic criticism. Yet still love as a literary subject has been studied mostly by Freudian psychoanalytic critics in terms of human sexuality, eroticism, or sentimental romance. Few have explored the relationship between aesthetics and ideology beyond the pleasure principle. Book-length publications on the subject of love are mostly studies in medieval and Renaissance literature, Victorian domestic novels, or popular romance. Relatively few have been written across literary periods from a contemporary postmodern perspective, examining twentieth-century American fiction in its relation to the classics.

Along with the development of poststructuralist theories, a lover's discourse has been invented in postmodern fiction. In postmodern fiction, the language of love stories becomes highly hyperbolic, allusive, and metaphorical. There is an ideological discourse embedded in the eroticism of sensational "love stories" which, remarkably, marks its difference from pornography and functions as a counter rhetoric of cultural criticism. The study of this ideological discourse provides an intriguing subject that opens the possibility for linguistic and philosophical investigations in novelistic love.

This book is a postmodern study of Socratic "love stories" in the English and the American novel. It is not concerned with the love relationship between men and women or the sexual and textual politics of human desire. Instead, its subject is the political economy of literary love—its modes of production, distribution, representation, and historical transformation. It studies novelistic love as a rhetorical tradition derived from Plato's love panegyrics in *The Symposium*, and it traces the presence of such a tradition in the eighteenth-century English novel and twentieth-century American modernist and postmodernist fiction. Its goal is to deconstruct the myth of "love stories" and reconstruct their historicity.

Novelistic love, I argue, is neither real love nor ideal love; it is a language, a rhetoric, a way of writing. Great novelists are literary seducers, who impregnate their "love stories" with pretty ideas. Novelistic "love making" procreates and projects ideological arguments. Such a rhetorical tradition can be traced to Plato's *Symposium*; but the Platonic tradition of novelistic love has not been well identified and well defined in literary studies. According to my study, in the Platonic tradition, the construction of "love stories" is often a dramatization of the author's idea—either his historical vision, philosophical speculation, cultural criticism, or political ideology. As often as not, the most provocative arguments the individual novelist has with history and society are conceived in the most sensational scenes, deeply embedded in the text of pleasure. The use of pleasure, due to its seductive power, functions as an effective "internal persuasive discourse," in Bahktin's words, that dialogizes with the public discourse of a social-linguistic hierarchy. By entertaining the reader in an "amusement park," or in the "funhouse" of language, novelistic love produces a power of free speech that enables the novelist to speak the unspeakable and include the excluded subjects under hard historical circumstances. The lover's discourse in the novel opens the space for ideological debates.

My study begins with postmodernist fiction. In postwar American fiction writing, explicit sexual presentation has become a popular norm. The language of sexual love, which used to be a private discourse in serious fiction, is externalized stark nakedly to entertain a popular audience; meanwhile, the ideological discourse is repressed and silenced. Ideology itself has lost its momentum in postwar America. In postmodernist fiction, nevertheless, the ideological text survives on the margin. The serious message, though suppressed, is now internalized in a double narrative, intertwined with the text of pleasure. As Nabokov conceives in *Lolita*, "Sex is but the ancilla of art." In the hands of postmodern fictionists, the language of sexual love has been masterfully controlled, subverted, and effectively recreated as a power of free speech. The bedroom scene has become a political platform to deliver the "issues" of ideological differences and cultural criticism.

The political use of pleasure, as I further pursue, is a Platonic tradition and a Swiftian gesture, revived by James Joyce and a generation of postmodernists—"the pen is mightier than the sword." Plato's invention of "Greek" love stories, the love panegyrics in *The Symposium*, is an archive of literary love, which has informed the lover's discourse in prose and poetry throughout the ages. With a postmodern literary sensibility, I read *The Symposium* as a series of metafictive "love stories," or love stories of sorts. Exploring Plato's philosophical implications, as well as rhetorical strategies, as Derrida did with Plato's *Pharmacy*, I differentiate the conceptual meaning and ideological values in his various panegyrics. I find that from the master narrative of Plato's *Symposium*, various modes and models of literary love, the epic, courtly, romantic, modern, postmodern, aesthetic, philosophical, can be identified, derived, and disseminated. Platonic love is not simply spiritual love or homosexual love as commonly understood; it embodies a political philosophy—the great lover as the ideal ruler in government. Thus my reading of Plato deconstructs Platonic love while it demystifies love as a human desire, a natural subject, or a universal signifier. I suggest that novelistic love is a language, a rhetoric, a way of writing. As a way of writing, Platonic love offers a system of representations that informs the history of novelistic writing in world literature.

The presence of such a Platonic tradition in the English and the American novel is pervasive, from Sterne's *Tristram Shandy* to Kurt Vonnegut's *Slaughterhouse-Five*. It is powerfully exemplified in Fielding's *The History of Tom Jones, a Foundling* and Faulkner's *Go Down, Moses*. In both Fielding's and Faulkner's novels, I find that there is a Platonic subtext deeply embedded in the construction of "love stories." Its "naked charms," as Fielding alludes to it, once seen in a Platonic spirit, lay bare the philosophical truth of the novel. Such philosophical truth, or the truth/beauty of such "love stories," as Joyce suggests in *Finnegans Wake*, lies in the "rare" of a text, in what he calls the "feminine fiction in Tory tales." A close inspection of bedroom scenes in such Tory tales or Socratic "love stories" not only opens the reader's eyes to the artistic intentions of the novelists and the deep structure of the novel; but also, and even more significant, it opens the door to the ideological propositions the novelists painstakingly conceive "in the rare" of their texts.

Therefore, it is my presumption that since novelistic love touches the heart of the matter in a novel; the study of novelistic love may offer a productive new approach in the study of the novel. I recommend such an approach, first, because it is truthful and pleasurable and, second, because it most effectively bridges the gap between aesthetics and ideology in the current development of critical methodology. For this approach does not abandon the close reading of the primary text, while the critic is engaged in interdisciplinary studies of the novel, examining its relation with history and philosophy. Nor does it impose any preconceived theoretical formula or ideological dogma upon the specific cultural and historical context in a work of art or upon the novelist. It only helps to explicate, as I shall demonstrate in the study of Fielding and Faulkner, the most controversial critical ambiguities in regard to both the aesthetics of the novel and the ideology of the novelist.

I choose Fielding and Faulkner for a number of reasons. First, in the English and the American novel, Fielding and Faulkner are nationally representative figures. Second, *Tom Jones* and *Go Down, Moses* respectively deal with large issues of national politics. The historical material and subject matter involved in these two novels—legitimacy, national leadership, government ethics, war, class and race relations—have been critical issues in contemporary history, especially during the Bush years while I was working on this project and speculating upon the intertextuality of history, philosophy, politics, literature, and the media. They are still crucial issues under the Clinton administration even after the 1996 presidential election. Third, there is a shared Platonic subtext in the deep structure of these two novels and a shared conservative positionality with a radical cultural critique. Thus they are chosen for their literary and aesthetic, as well as their ideological values.

My approach is informed by poststructuralist and deconstructive theories but open to cultural and historical inquiries. It explores the ideological implications of "love stories" and the politics of novelistic design. Through contextual and intertextual readings, it demonstrates that certain fictive constructs and rhetorical strategies are necessitated by historical circumstances. In other words, while this book offers a detailed reading of specific texts, it nevertheless addresses a number of critical interests: cultural studies, aesthetics and ideology, public and private discourses, fiction and history, philosophy and the novel, love and the novel, epic and romantic love, the problem of language, metalanguage, and the reinterpretation of classic novels. Above all, I find myself sharing the contemporary interest in opening up a lover's discourse in American literary criticism by investigating the literary, linguistic, and philosophical meanings of love as an academic subject.

In developing a theory of the novel, I am concerned with the position and reposition of means and end in literary study, the interconnection between novelistic art and political philosophy. Therefore, to end with the proposition that novelistic love is a power of free speech is still as good as to end with a means without end, for power, as I contend at the conclusion of this work, is only a tool; it is but neutral. The ideas delivered in those Socratic "love stories" are of equal value and importance in the study of the novel today, as they inspire our speculation upon history and philosophy. Contemporary critical theories have revived our interest in the politics of aesthetics; yet the task of how to locate and ground a political argument in the art of fiction and in the center of current critical interests remains a challenge in literary study.

Studying Joyce and the French poststructuralists at once makes me aware of the dialectical relationship between theory and literature. The philosophers undertake the task of theorizing the technical experiments that have already taken place in modernist and postmodernist literature. They seek to appropriate the philosophical, historical, and political arguments raised implicitly in literary texts. Their theories seek to establish the legitimacy of these arguments, which in turn empowers the literary critic to reexamine and reinterpret literature from new perspectives. The philosopher in a sense is doing the work of the literary critic except for one thing: As Karsten Harries reminds us, "the metaphysician's descriptions are essentially inadequate in that he has to content himself with abstract ideas. . . . For the sake of clarity and distinctness he surrenders the concrete and sensuous" (Harries 74). This is a sacrifice the metaphysician has to make in order to make theories. The literary critic in making literary theory may want to escape such a sacrifice, avoiding the dryness of a philosophical discourse.

Plato's *Symposium* provides a rare model that escapes such a "sacrifice." He marvelously dramatizes "abstract ideas" with "the concrete and sensuous," filling up the "inadequacy" of a philosophical discourse with delightful invention of "love stories." His is an ideal model for making a theory. For my purpose, I hope to avoid the tendency of making literary theory a philosophical discourse or a linguistic textbook, on the one hand; and, on the other, I wish to step aside from the pitfalls of turning ideology and cultural criticism into political propaganda. Therefore, in my style and method, I learn from Plato and the novelists I study. The intimacy I have gained through investigating the "private parts" of their "love stories" has suggested the most useful literary strategies that I apply in this text. Mainly, novelistic love serves as an agency mediating between aesthetics and ideology, fictional fabrications and historical reality. It performs a postmodern genre—tragicomedy. In a way, this book can be read as many "love stories" of sorts.

The first chapter is a cultural study of the economics of postmodern love stories. It explores the cultural mechanism that influences and produces the lover's discourse in postmodern fiction in the works of later Joyce, Beckett, Nabokov, Vonnegut, Pynchon, Coover, Barth, Hawkes, Federman. The hyperbolic use of "love stories," it argues, marks the change of a style from modernism to postmodernism. In postwar American culture, stark naked representation of sex, violence, and mystery is a cultural norm, a privileged language as it appears in TV commercials and Hollywood romance. Postmodern "love stories" can be read as a stylization of such a culturally privileged language; but at the same time, they are a reverse translation of a popular form, a subversive form of writing. Underneath sensational "love stories" there lies an ideological discourse. Borrowing from Barthes, Bahktin, Chomsky, and Starobinski, this chapter discusses the mystification of sensual materialism in bourgeois society, the problems in popular reception of postmodern fiction, and the economics of its textual reproduction.

The second chapter is an analytical speculation of the invention of "Greek" love stories in Plato's *Symposium*. Treating Plato's narrative drama as metafiction, this chapter investigates Plato's philosophical implications, as well as his rhetorical strategies, to establish a convention of Socratic "love stories" and identify the "feminine fiction" within. It disseminates from the master trope of Plato's narrative the various modes and models of literary love—the epic, courtly, romantic, modern, postmodern, aesthetic, philosophical—that inform the history of world literature. By pointing to their differences, the differences of their conceptual meanings and ideological values, it demystifies Love as a universal or natural subject.

Chapter Three identifies the model of epic love (a model derived from Phaedrus's panegyric) as a canonical model in the English novel established by Richardson's *Pamela*. Epic love celebrates marriage;

conceptually, it deals with the issue of legitimacy in social distribution and redistribution of wealth and power. The legitimacy of the Crown is a disturbing factor in eighteenth-century England when the English novel rises; in a manner, novelistic love entails the political gossip of national life. This chapter discusses the political situation, the historical drama in eighteenth-century England. Reconsidering the theories of Ian Watt and Michael McKeon, it suggests that royal marriages, court politics, and party lines might have determined the politics of "love stories" in the works of Defoe, Swift, and Fielding in their representation of male and female virtue.

Chapter Four demonstrates Fielding's subversion of epic love in *The History of Tom Jones, a Foundling*. It offers an allegorical reading of "The Legitimate Lover of 'Sophia' and the Rightful Ruler: Fielding's *The History of Tom Jones, a Foundling*," as the chapter is entitled, based on rhetorical studies and historical research. It demonstrates that Fielding's most provocative argument of legitimacy is abstrusely conceived in the feminine fiction of sensational "love stories"—stories such as Bridget's sexual comedy, Mrs. Waters's highway rape scene, the Upton seduction scene, Jenny Jones's incest charge, and the beauty of Sophia. Fielding's hidden political agenda, his historical vision of the Hanoverian regime, and his pre-Jeffersonian democratic political ideal are well conceived in the politics of these "love stories." This chapter reassesses Fielding's politics around 1745 by reconstructing Tom's parenthood, his lineage, and his legitimacy as the future ruler of Paradise Hall.

The final chapter on Faulkner's *Go Down, Moses* projects romantic love (a model derived from Diotima's account in Plato) as an antithesis to the epic. Romantic love functions in Faulkner's text as an interrogative power, a controlling idea to measure the happiness in a society, the legitimacy of its ruler, and the promise of a Jeffersonian democratic ideal. This chapter is an intertextual study of Keats, Plato, and Faulkner's idea of love and happiness as philosophical concepts. It reveals, while the Keatsian reference yields its lyric romanticism to question the balance of power in race relations, that it is Plato's notion of a happy state (his critique of "imperfect societies" in *The Republic*) that underlines Faulkner's novelistic conception of love's dynastic decay. The loss of love upon the land, in a downward narrative movement from the first tale "Was" to the final tale, "Go Down, Moses," from timarchy to tyranny, embodies Faulkner's vision of the past, present, and future. The "love stories" are the heart of the matter, that provides a soft structure to what is generally regarded in Faulkner criticism as a "formless" and "loveless" novel.

Chapter One

The Lover's Discourse in Postmodern Fiction: From *Finnegans Wake* to *Smiles on Washington Square*

Extracts

This is jinnies cry. Underwetter! Goat strip Finnlambs!

Sir Tristram, violer d'amores, fr'over the short sea, had passencore rearrived from North Armorica on this side the scraggy isthmus of Europe Minor to wielderfight his penisolate war.

> —Joyce, *Finnegans Wake*, 9, 3

Sex is but the ancilla of art.

> —Nabokov, *Lolita*, 261

It's not a question of going to bed, but being there.

> —Calvino, *Cosmicomics*, 9

Half a century younger she might have been taken for pregnant.
. . . It wasn't true love, true love was in another. Molloy, or life
without a chambermaid.

—Beckett, *Trilogy*, 265, 59

It was a gesture of superb contempt. . . . I learned that I too had
a sadistic capacity. . . . Furthermore it illustrates that I am indeed
a specialist on the subject of dead passion.

—Hawkes, *Travesty*, 74

The traditional material for the artist is the passions of men and
women; in handling his material, i.e., writing fiction, he must
make the fatal choice between sadism and satiety. While Sadism
leads to pathological boredom and ends with the desire for death
and nothingness—"the Romantic syndrome," satiety may be
extended to a larger measure of "vicariousness," which he thinks
undeniably applies to himself and his work.

—Barth, *Lost in the Funhouse*, 123-24

"Come back," said Metzger, "Come on."
After awhile she said, "I will." And she did.

— Pynchon, *The Crying of Lot 49*, 43

Oh I know why she's late you warn her and it does no good I
know who's got her giddy ear with his old death-cunt-and- prick
songs haven't I heard.

—Coover, *Pricksongs & Descants*, 16

Yes ham and eggs. Well, the chicken is involved, the pig is
committed.

—Federman, *Smiles on Washington Square*, 136

"Ahab Has His Humanities!": The Story and the Idea

The telling of "love stories" is the essence of novelistic writing. In the history of the English and the American novel from Defoe's *Moll Flanders* (1722) to Kingston's *Tripmaster Monkey* (1987), one can think of few novels written without telling a "love story" or two. Not to mention the novels of manners, even what Leslie Fiedler calls the "womanless" novel, "the great Romantic Unroman"[1]—Melville's *Moby-Dick*—begins with a shocking bedroom scene, Ishmael's bedding with a cannibal: "In our heart's honeymoon, lay I and Queequeg—a cozy, loving pair." Toward the end of the novel, Ahab, doomed to death, tells his "love story":

> "Away, whole oceans away, from that young girl-wife I wedded past fifty, and sailed for Cape Horn the next day, leaving but one dent in my marriage pillow—wife? wife?—rather a widow with her husband alive! I widowed that poor girl when I married her . . . Tis my Mary, my Mary herself!"[2]

The dramatic presentation of a "love story" or two, however incidental and sparingly seasoned, is not to be neglected. Its effect may be as deep as the "one dent" in Ahab's marriage pillow and as far-reaching as the old man's last cry "whole oceans away." Novelistic love bespeaks the heart's truth of a novel; it is an interesting subject to observe.

The two "love stories" in *Moby-Dick* can be read as the "tail" of the tale, which entails the richest irony of Melville's tale—"Ahab has his humanities!" (*M-D* 77). The first "love story" gives us an idea of the profundity of Ishmael's humanities; the last illustrates, tragically and comically, the failure of Ahab's humanities. The first foreshadows, thematizes the novelist's idea; the last echoes, cries out his message. It is the "love cries" that make sound sense of the unspeakable truth unspoken. Read in the way the novel is read within the literary convention of the day, or in ordinary perception of reality, there is no pronounced connection along the plot line between the two "love affairs." However, the connection is metaphysically constructed beyond the story, linked with the same idea, Melville's projection of H—.

Ironized against his "Heroism," the question of Ahab's humanities stands silently, a latent subject in the narrative. It is first inscribed in the opening page of "Etymology," where Melville indirectly calls his reader's attention to the letter H, its mute presence in the naming of the whale:

> While you take in hand to school others, and to teach them by
> what name a whale-fish is to be called in our tongue, leaving out,
> through ignorance, the letter H, which almost alone maketh up
> the signification of the word, you deliver that which is not true.
> Hackluyt. (*M-D* "Etymology")

Melville is self-consciously speaking of his dilemma in telling the truth of his whaling tale. To tell the history of whaling without addressing the subject "H" is to speak "that which is not true." Yet "in our tongue," in modern English, in the way the language is spoken within its system of the day, the letter H is habitually left out, unspoken, unspeakable—a suppressed word. Hence his difficulty in speaking. Hence his challenge in writing.

In spite of the difficulty, truth is still discernible depending on literacy. Melville does not bring up the subject without making a remarkable effort to suggest that it is "through ignorance" that the original truth of H is left out, or rather, subverted and suppressed. The truth lies in that in terms of "Etymology," H— stands in the first place in its original form of the word, either in Old English—"Hwael," or in the languages of whaling peoples—"hval" in "Sw." and "Dan." "It is more immediately from the Dut. and Ger. Wallen; a.s. Walw-ian," also *wal, whale,* that the sign of that overwhelming creature, a sign of supreme power, takes its present form, in which the H is either removed or reversed (*M-D* "Etymology").

Thus the question of Ahab's legitimacy and that of his humanities are at once inscribed in the very beginning. Although this significant subject, identical with the letter H—, is never explicitly spoken in the public discourse of the novel, repressed in the narrative, it is embedded in its "love stories" of sorts. In such Socratic "love stories," it is the idea beyond the story that silently makes up the signification of the word, the truth of the story.

One wonders where the novelists draw their ideas when they write their "love stories." Faulkner was said to be reading *Moby-Dick* to his stepdaughter at the time he was writing *Go Down, Moses.* In a strange way, before I end this study with Faulkner's novel, the reader shall encounter another Mary, who widowed her unmarried widower in another "love story." As far as novelistic love goes, it is a small world, for novelistic writing still operates within the boundaries of cultural and literary convention. Staged in the drama of "love stories," the world is large, anything may happen, once the reader discerns the idea beyond the story.

"To Wielderfight His Penisolate War": The Joycean Word

What is the narrative status of such "love stories" in a novel? How does it function, for what purpose? In other words, what is the idea? I propose my questions as such, so that I may approach the subject from multiple critical perspectives, examining not only the rhetorical, and formalistic questions of "how," but also the political and ideological questions of "why?" and "what for?"

These questions can be interestingly explored if we begin by examining the economics of the lover's discourse in postmodern fiction. In postmodern fiction, Joyce's *Finnegans Wake* is the end of a beginning; the end of modernism and the beginning of postmodernism. The book opens with a central metaphor of "home is the sailor, home from the sea."[3] The modernist theme of exile and expatriation fades into a preoccupation of repatriation and homecoming. Instead of the Greek hero or the English laureate, the "bygmester" chooses to wear the persona of a national hero, an Irish noble, Sir Tristram (Tristan; Sir Amory Tristram; Trismegistus the sad one), who has come home, not for retirement, but to "wielderfight his penisolate war." He lays himself down by the River Liffy, reflecting upon History and coming to terms with Reality. He is content that after the night's love-making with Liffy, which is also the process of writing the whole book, he will have by daylight created "the uncreated conscience of his race," as Joyce willed it decades ago.

Thus the prospective expatriate in "The Dead," the mythic artificer in *The Portrait of the Artist as a Young Man*, the prodigal son with a guilty conscience wandering through the night town of Dublin unsettled with his identity in *Ulysses*, is finally comfortable to identify himself with Everyman in Ireland, from legendary figures to bartender, a tragicomic married man. From isolation to homecoming, from aesthetic disinterestedness to political commitment, from the sense of alienation to the sense of communion, from detachment to attachment, from "non-serviam" to "penisolate war"—the thematic concern in experimental fiction and poetry has changed after 1929. A generation of modernists passed beyond "the age of innocence" into a new phase with a new historical consciousness that I regard as postmodernist.

From modernism to postmodernism, novelistic love changes, too, stylistically. The postmodern style appeals to the intellect instead of the instinct; its experimentation invites metaphysical speculation instead of free association, metaphorical imagination instead of symbolic abstraction. If Molly Bloom's bed is sensual, exotic, naturalistic, the center of the mundane, then the bed of A.L.P. is lofty but local, inexhaustible and metaphysical, proliferate with ancient learning and the sound of Celtic origin, the center of eternity. Joyce's rhetoric has transcended the stream of consciousness to metaphysics. It has transformed the body language into a metalanguage, which marvelously restores love to immateriality. The prevailing techniques in modernist experiments such as Eliot's "objective correlative," or Lawrence's "blood consciousness," or Joyce's and Woolf's "stream of consciousness," basically work through sensory experience to reveal the presence of the unconsciousness, and the subjective consciousness is often identified with natural sexual energy or repressed human sexuality. *Finnegans Wake* displays a whole set of new subjects and techniques that clearly break away from modernism, and that inform, by and large, the modes and motifs in postmodernist fiction. The sensational elements in the Joycean "love story" are more and more colored with black humor (which becomes more apparent later in the works of Beckett and Vonnegut). With black humor, these sensational elements provoke thought more than emotion. The comprehension of meaning no longer depends upon the fuse of emotion that Eliot's "catalyst" may synthesize, but resorts to speculative faculties, syllogism, geometry, rational knowledge, and the recognition of foreign accents, remote historical events, and dialectic oppositions that contradict but reconcile with one another, synthesized in a different kind of chemical element—"antimony" (not antinomy). The linguistic innovations are arbitrary combinations. One might call them "subjective correlatives" instead of objective correlatives.

Most important of all is the political economy that Joyce transmits into the text of pleasure. Words of pleasure such as "Goat strip Finnlambs," "Gricks may rise and Troysirs fall," "this whorl world," "Her Madesty," and "royal divorsion" are used to express political sentiment with a postcolonial gesture. To put it simply, dirty words economically serve the purpose of political gossip, well conceived in a private discourse of the text. Other sexy puns even more economically produce a three-dimensional subject joined in a single adventure. Wellington's horse "Copenhagen," for instance, bears the royal color in the battlefield of textual engagement. The "thing" appears within manageable context in three different forms—Cokenhape, Capeinhope, Culpenhelp. The phallic sign, the battlefield, and the pen in hand form a new "Trinity," which empowers the writer's political gesture in telling "love stories."

Writing is warring, as Joyce conjures it, "the war is in words and the word is the world" (FW 90). Michael J. O'Shea has written a fascinating book on Joyce's use of heraldry and suggests that heraldic blazon is the "official" language in the heroic age and that heraldry precedes the genesis of articulate speech. It makes perfect sense that by creating a seemingly inarticulate and incomprehensible discourse in *Finnegans Wake*, Joyce is claiming the legitimacy as well as the authenticity of his language. That heroic language has heralded all the exotic, marginal, alien linguistic elements in the development of postmodern literature, high and low. The linguistic experiment in Maxine Hong Kingston's *China Men*, for example, carries on so much Joycean verve that one could almost hear an echo. It is *Finnegans Wake*, rather than *Ulysses*, that restores the "political unconsciousness" in the writing of the postmodern fictionists, and of the poststructuralists as well.

Joyce in *Finnegans Wake* has found the lost Word Eliot was searching for when he wrote "Ash Wednesday" (1930):

If the lost word is lost, if the spent word is spent
If the unheard, unspoken
Word is unspoken, unheard,
Still is the unspoken word, the Word unheard
The Word without a word, the Word within
The world and for the world . . .
And the light shone in darkness and
Against the Word the unstilled world still whirled
About the center of the silent Word.

O my people, what have I done unto thee.

Where shall the word be found, where will the word
    Resound? . . .
                . . . .
No place of grace for those who avoid the face
No time to rejoice for those who walk among noise and deny the
voice

And let me cry unto thee. [4]

The Word is the Greek word "logos." In Eliot, the original Word, the Lost Word, the Word unspoken or usurped, the omnipotent Word of God became the Word of Love and Speech. In *Finnegans Wake*, Joyce re-created that

Word, and I shall return to that word at the end of this chapter. Here, I would like to conclude with the most significant change in the transition from modernism to postmodernism: The modernists believed in art as salvation, the postmodernists hold the omnipotent power of language as hope of rebirth and re-creation, the power of "God." Fictionists in the wake of the *Wake* have found a new mode of production; they recycled the text of pleasure and reproduced a text of bliss, just as Love procreates the life of a new generation. "Loving, warring, writing"—the Joycean mode—defines the postmodern condition.

"Sex Is But the Ancilla of Art":
The Political Use of Pleasure

In the works of Beckett, Nabokov, Pynchon, Barth, Hawkes, Calvino, Coover, and Federman (see epigraphs), a general style can be discerned: The language of love and sex appears to be highly allusive and metaphorical. While the language of "I-love-you" is employed to evoke sensual pleasure, it is rhetorically treated as a hyperbole, inflating and undermining at once the very substance of its presentation. In effect, the signification embedded in the text of pleasure literally involves another discourse, another subject, a metalanguage, a gossip, a sound track at the back of the text. In Joycean terms, this sound track is "the echo in the wodes," the "feminine fiction" that lies underneath the "Tory tales."

Since the textual revolution of *Finnegans Wake*, the post-structuralists have developed, along with Bahktin's theory, various theoretical concepts, so that today we may call the text "inside" or "outside" a text "the carnivalesque discourse," "the double voice," "the hybrid construction," "the imaginary," or "the trace."

Whatever theoretical names we may ascribe to this metalanguage beyond the body language, it is rather important to hear what it says—"the jinnies cry" and "being there" (see *Extracts*). The symbolic message entailed in the language of sexual love turns out to be either an unutterable or outrageous political slogan, as in the quote from Joyce: "Storm! God punish England!"; or a Heideggerian philosophical concept of "being there," as in the quote from Calvino; or a metafictional argument in the quote from Barth. In the works of Beckett, Hawkes, and Coover, it is a cultural criticism, cursing "the great cunt of existence." In Pynchon, the identity of the subject "she" is deliberately made indistinguishable from the image and voice of the TV screen; a stereotyped character is created for the purpose of satire, not upon the character herself, but metaphorically upon the seductive manipulation and potential violence of the media system. Federman's breakfast of "ham and eggs" serves both sides of the table talk with a plateful of sarcasm, which is aimed at his characters' halfhearted commitment in politics, as well as in love. Overall, what is said may be outside of the printed, visual text; yet listening to the voice, the "orchestra," "the mute eloquence of love," one discovers that the metalanguage of Love deals with a subject that is more serious than the story of love and sex. It reveals the fictionists' political gestures, philosophical speculations, and cultural criticism—a wide range of issues that, generally speaking, belong to the realm of ideology.

These issues, that otherwise would have bored the "giddy ear," now luckily gain a hearing through these "pricksongs and descants"—a bliss, an intellectual "jouissance." "That there is thus a politics and a historicity of *jouissance* seems clear, as does its fundamental ambiguity as a socially symbolic experience," as Fredric Jameson recognizes in his essay "Pleasure: A Political Issue" (1988). "The point, however, is not to awaken some scarcely dormant Left tendency to moralize such experiences, but rather to draw the lesson of what might be a radically different political use of pleasure as such." Thus Jameson suggests "that the proper political use of pleasure must always be *allegorical*."[5]

It is certainly not my intention either to "moralize" or "utilize" the production of pleasure, but rather, to examine the economics of such production. While Jameson is speaking from a strategic viewpoint of leftist criticism, what I have just revealed is the "artistic intentions" of the fictionists, who appear to have their own political agenda already inscribed in the text of pleasure. One ought to recognize that the historicity of erotic art is never absent in postmodern fiction. Rather, it is the presence of this ideological metalanguage that distinguishes serious fiction from pornography and popular romance.

In serious fiction, "Sex is but the ancilla [chambermaid] of art," as Nabokov states in a crystal metaphor. Art, as he displays in *Lolita*, is the dagger to "murder and create."[6] In the hands of a true artist, the use of pleasure is always handled as a weapon. As such, it generates an effective power of free speech, a political platform, that enables the fictionist to speak the unspeakable and include the excluded, as we have just heard.

The polyphonic or ambivalent nature of this platform might be easily derived from various poststructural theories; the question I wish to ask here is rather practical: What endows the language of love with this kind of political power? The question invites some historical speculations. The Dionysian power of Love as a source of all artistic creation, if there still is any, exists only within the individual consciousness of the artist and is reduced from tragedy to the form of parody or parodic sadism (as in Nabokov or Hawkes). Its transcendental power has gradually lost its potential to evoke a universal tragic sentiment among a reading public in postwar era. Only in the form of self-parody, black humor, or schizophrenia the romantic sentiment does still linger in the air and hang on breathlessly. So Beckett presents his Molloy, crutches in hands, making a last-ditch effort to grasp the withered "grassroots," the alienated transcendental self, on a nightmarish bleak "Waste Land." Opposed to sadism and its "romantic syndrome," as Barth proposes, there is likely a more popular mode to the taste of the comic spirit of the age, that is, "satiety"—the epic reservoir of love and war. Its mythic power is so inexhaustible that it dynamically stirs the desire for power.

The presentation of the explicit sexual "talking cure" or pornographic eroticism in serious fictions, as one must acknowledge, is but a post-modern literary "fashion" (as one could easily call it a post-Freudian intellectual exercise of masturbation among the "learned wits" who wrote fictions for a generation of sexually "well-educated" college readers). In literary history, the subject of sexual love in serious fiction has been mostly a private discourse. Even in the modernist novel, sexuality is still presented to a large extent through symbolic motifs, and it remains an inexpressible subject, which holds an instinctual and mystic attraction to the artist. In postmodern fiction, the situation is interestingly reversed: The subject of love and sex is externalized, the text of pleasure becomes a legitimate public discourse—"a skin dialogue," as Hawkes calls it.

The forces that affect such change are rather tangible, though more complex than mere "anxiety" of literary influence. The social, economic, historical, and cultural dynamics are all at work in the transformation of a literary style. The emergence of a substantial middle class in the postwar period—with it, a tremendous economic power—has generated a stark naked need for pleasure. It might be commonplace to say that the market value determines the mode of production in postmodern fiction. The fact is that since sex, violence, mystery become three indispensable elements, the basic motif, to make a best-seller in the postwar period, explicit sexual remarks serve as an ornament, a decorative art, the repartee of salon talk, that even serious writers cannot do without. In order to go out into the world for a show, the subject of the naked body is the proper "party dress" or, in a

Joycean word, the "uniform." It is the fashion.

"Je-t'aime/I-Love-You":
The Myth of Bourgeois Democracy

How does it become a fashion? The language of "I love you," which used to be an expression that lovers uttered in the dark recess of their private chamber, or which disturbed Mr. J. Alfred Prufrock ("Do I dare? Do I dare?") as an inner voice, now in the great democracy of Western society is at last "liberated"—the Word is spoken in daylight. It is soon manufactured through the assembly line of the culture industry in liberal industrial nations from London via Paris to New York and Los Angeles. It becomes an open voice everywhere—the singsong of radio, TV commercials and soap operas, movies, and magazines, a public "how are you," that salutes us from shop windows, cartoons, the painted lips under neon lights. It becomes "the significant better half" for the alienated city dwellers. It is the first phrase of American English that a five-year-old girl from China learns to speak; and the second is "I am free." It is the myth of free speech in the free economy of the free world. It is the mind's fancy, the children's toy. Yet in the economy of social linguistics, the sign of I-love-you is the most popular currency that circulates and inflates freely in the compartmentalized "u. of d." (universe of discourse)[7] in our high-tech professional life, and in our leisure life as well. The sign might be only play money that tosses and turns on the playground and in the nursery, but in the world of commercial competition and advertisement, it is the sterling—its phallic power forging the forever desirable and forever illusive Other.

It is Roland Barthes who cleverly demystifies the commercial label of "je-t'aime/I-love-you." In a frustrated effort and with a disparaged desire to rescue, to affirm, the subject (substance) of the lover's discourse that today has been "ignored, disparaged, derided" by "thousands of subjects, but warranted by no one," he denounces the label: "The figure refers not to the declaration of love, to the avowal, but to the repeated utterance of the love cry." He points out:

> The "signs" of love feed an enormous reactive literature: love is represented, entrusted to an aesthetic of appearances (it is Apollo, ultimately, who writes every love story). As a counter-sign, I-love-you is on the side of Dionysus: suffering is not denied (nor even complaint, disgust, resentment), but by its

proffering, it is not internalized: to say I-Love-You (to repeat it) is to expel the reaction-information, to return it to the deaf and doleful world of signs—of the detours of speech.

Moreover, the myth of love prospers in a consumer culture:

> As proffering, I-love-you is on the side of expenditure. Those who seek the proffering of the word (lyric poets, liars, wanderers) are subjects of Expenditure: they spend the word, as if it were impertinent (base) that it be recovered somewhere; they are at the extreme limit of language, where language itself recognizes that it is without backing or guarantee, working without a net.[8]

In a linguistic hierarchy, wherein the signified is usurped, signifiers proliferate. These "self-conscious" and "self-reflective" signifiers lean on one another, compete and collide through bargains, deals, cash exchange, public auction, and private negotiation, to generate "by itself and for itself" a text with "infinite" opportunities and freedom for Trade.

Penis Envy: The Middle-Class Syndrome

The eternal, persuasive, entertaining, seductive power that is nature inherent in the text of pleasure, is an aspect that we will have to consider later. But I am not going to dwell on the narrativity of "desire" in Freudian or humanistic terms. When it comes to Freud, I am always amused with Nabokov's nonchalant statement: "Let the credulous and the vulgar continue to believe that all mental woes can be cured by a daily application of old Greek myths to their private parts, I really do not care."[9] Having lived in different cultures and different societies, I personally do not believe there is a universal "human nature" or universal "desire" that we can talk about, either in love or war.

Take the use of novelistic love in two war fictions for example—Vonnegut's *Slaughterhouse-Five* and Mishma's short story "Patriotism," one about Dresden, the other about Hiroshima; the political implications embody two extreme attitudes toward World War II. There is a vast cultural, religious, and historical difference in the representation of erotic desire. In Vonnegut, the desire that appeals to a fourth-generation German-American veteran now living in easy circumstances on Cape Cod embraces a non-teleological worldview. Billy's fantasy of running away with a sexy Hollywood star to an imaginary world has its special appeal to the postwar generation in a hedonistic American culture. Whereas, in Mishima, the erotic desire that obsesses a newly wed Japanese lieutenant who takes his conjugal bed as battlefield to build up his martial spirit, masculine strength, a narcissistic image of triumph and glory, which only urges him to commit suicide, demands absolute personal loyalty, self-discipline, and self-denial. It is medieval in its moral structure and fascist in its spirit. As the title suggests, it stands for Japanese patriotism, an equivalent of which or its alliance, is Nazi nationalism. The erotic desire, as it is presented to its immediate reading public, first appeals to Japanese nationalism; and second, its ecstasy is obviously intended to ease the sense of guilt, to rebuild a wounded national conscience by suicidal heroism. It is projected to help both sexes in the nation come to terms with death's "sublime immortality" after Japan's defeat in World War II. Ironically, Mishima's eroticism glorifies what Vonnegut laments as "the children's crusade."

So one can see how erotic desire can be manipulated for political propaganda to achieve the persuasive effect advocating either pacifism or patriotism with equal "success." But the power of its appeal, to achieve its purpose and intent, works effectively only within a specific cultural milieu, within the boundary of a social and racial consciousness. If we recognize the representation of erotic desire as a cultural construct, then what Saussure discovers about "the Nature of the Linguistic Sign" also applies to the language of "love story":

> The arbitrary nature of the sign alone explains in turn why the social fact alone can create a linguistic system. The community is necessary if values that owe their existence solely to usage and general acceptance are to be set up . . . The value of just any term is accordingly determined by its environment.[10]

I am far from saying, however, that the desire of love is solely determined by racial or class consciousness. I only presume that the persuasive power of love and sexual appeal always rely to a considerable degree on the value system within a shared cultural and historical milieu. The traditional dogmatic practice of Marxist theory, which holds that an individual's "class consciousness" is fatally determined by one's class origin, family background, in my opinion, needs to be reconsidered, deconstructed and reconstructed, because it fails to account for the rapid social mobility in modern society that the individual may have. In other words, the individual's own social economic status may change under the change of historical circumstances far more drastically, and sometimes dramatically, than Marx could have anticipated in his time. Thus it is the discontinuity of the historical status of the lover's discourse that I would like to address here.

The emergence of a substantial middle class after the 1950s in this country—and with it a tremendous economic power—has generated a consumer need that places the physical, sensational, and surface values in human life prior to any other educational, recreational, or spiritual well-being; hence the market demand of pornography in the culture industry. The text of pleasure is forged under the pressure of the economics of a prevailing social linguistic code, the festival parade of an economic power that I diagonose as "the middle-class syndrome" or "penis envy." "Penis envy" really describes accurately the symptom of a class distinction instead of a sex or gender distinction.

My understanding of such a syndrome is inspired by Starobinski's study of pleasure and liberty in relation to art history in eighteenth-century France. In *The Invention of Liberty, 1700-1789,* he offers an analysis on the distinct correlation between the social phenomenon and the aesthetic climate during the ascendancy of the rococo style, providing us with a critical insight into the nature of the middle class' desire for sensual pleasure. Starobinski finds that the need for liberty thrives on opposition during a period when the middle class rises to power.[11]

According to Starobinski's analysis, for the upper class, wealth is meant as a mere symbol of the status quo. When material comfort and well-being become ends in themselves, entirely dissociated from all the religious, spiritual, and symbolic values structured in the feudal order, hedonism arises as an escape from boredom, despondency, inertia, melancholy. Hedonism provides a sensational experience to feel alive and to be in touch with the private self. At the same time, however, sensual indulgence indicates a failure of status and social responsibility. This is because when a nobleman lives apart in his own pleasure, which comes to constitute the sole end of his existence, when his pleasures are no longer just an incidental pastime but come to constitute the sole end of his existence, the whole spiritual structure which justified his rank is repudiated. In other words, the privilege becomes an abuse; race and blood become superstition. "In his flickering pleasures the solar myth of royalty disintegrates and fades away" (Starobinski 15).

For the middle-class well-to-do, pleasure doesn't imply any negligence of duty or proper function. A middle-class man regards pleasure as a right to exercise his freedom based on the wealth he has obtained, a right equal to the power of the aristocracy. Self-love and a taste for pleasure are the first principle of his morality, the foundation of a new social life that he builds with his economic success one step up the social ladder.

But Starobinski further prescribes a very interesting "class difference" in the use of pleasure. According to his theory, what I call "penis envy" is only a typical middle-class syndrome, not necessarily applicable to the noble:

> The bourgeois who had just made his fortune was akin to the aristocrat who had nothing left but his fortune. . . . Whereas the genuine noble tends to restrict his pleasures to himself, the self-made parvenu tries to hide his origins by assuming an openly "noble way" of life; while his real aim is financial profit, he wants to resemble the noble who ruins himself in the name of honor or pleasure. (Starobinski 15)

From Starobinski I derive three conceivable symptoms of penis envy in the middle-class syndrome: the anxiety for publicity; the problem of identity; sensual materialism in the use of pleasure.

First, the anxiety for publicity: One is given to understand that when the noble loses his distinction by indulging himself in sensual pleasure, he castrates himself. It is the parvenu who gains his status by an anxious display of his penis. Therefore, what the noble tends to keep private—"restrict his pleasures to himself" in fear of losing his name—the parvenu makes every effort to show openly in public. It is not that he has nothing to lose, but that the public style of a libertine only gains him social recognition—the legitimacy of his love for his "mother." It also eases his envy of his "father" and upgrades him to the equal status of his progenitor for a "royal" room in a brothel. It is indeed a break-through from his Oedipus complex with the fortune he has made himself. But sooner or later, he'll find himself in that brothel occupying the very room used by his father. Under such circumstances, his Oedipus complex will be compounded with a "castration anxiety," from which the middle class shall have no escape later in its day. Then and there, the power and the worth of his fortune will become questionable. (So Jake Barnes in Hemingway's *The Sun Also Rises* anxiously keeps questioning his money's worth and the value of things, while he pays for a good time involved with the British aristocracy.)

Second, the problem of identity: Even though pleasure is identified with "the power of aristocracy," still there is a substantial discrepancy in such an identity. When the nouveau riche assumes a stylish "imitation of life" as a noble, "to ruin himself in the name of pleasure," fortune is his only means of identity. He is often unaware that the real identity, the substance of nobility of the noble whom he imitates, is already dissolved into nothingness because of pure sensual dissolution. (This is the revelation Nick Caraway achieves at the end of *The Great Gatsby.*) Starobinski decomposes the essence of such imitation; when the noble character is "disintegrated," the spiritual status of his privilege is already "repudiated." What the egoist imagines himself to be in the mirror of the noble libertine might be an illusive Other at face value, but in substance, a skeleton, a ghostly shadow. It has no reality at all.

Third, materialism in the use of pleasure: What may appear to be an "unreal" identity with its latent narcissism and its lamentable absence of spiritual substance is simply not a concern for the middle class in its practice of pleasure. Its desire identifies pleasure only with all the public ostentation and social privilege that one's fortune can obtain. Its aim is not, as in the case of the noble, to escape the established social status quo, but the establishment of it. Its morbid consciousness of materialism in sexual desire stubbornly argues for itself that power and freedom and equality are attainable with the mechanic function of the penis; and that only physical possession of the object of beauty in society has the power to substantiate legitimacy in the existing social hierarchy. Hence the middle class' penis envy.

Starobinski explains for me both the motive of desire in the middle-class syndrome and its morbid obsession with sensual freedom. Even on the symbolical level, pleasure is also reduced to materialism. It symbolizes the power of economic success, democratic franchise, political autocracy at home, but global expansion abroad—all the material forces in the world. Thus pleasure serves as the motivation of economic competition, as well as the reward of economic success. To obtain the object of desire, economic power becomes the means and end in itself.

In a society that encourages economic competition and success above everything else, as in American society, the practice of pleasure is naturally encouraged by the system itself. It only helps to articulate and express the desire of the middle-class economy and its irresistible power. The love cry is no longer a revolt against repression, at least not against twentieth-century American capitalism, but the expression of it.

The need for pleasure during the postwar era in America also thrives on an opposition. For the well-established ruling class, the puritanical spirit, or the New England conscience of Lambert Strether, is eventually dissolved into the schizophrenia of Billy Pilgrim. Strether's fascination with that impressionistic boat carrying Chad and Madame Vionnet on the lake of a Parisian countryside (which marks the moment of "first love" in American modernism) is reduced to boredom and a "dead passion." It is on the subject of dead passion that Hawkes declares to be a "specialist," and he treats it with masochism. So in *Travesty*, also on a country road in "Southern France," we watch a beige sports car that Papa drives 149 kilometers per hour bringing Henri, his shadow, and Chantal "the porno-brat" to willed death and destruction. Masturbation and rape fantasy have outmoded bear-hunting and trout-fishing.

On the mass level, economic boom and social mobility produce a new class of well-to-do, as mentioned before, and, with it, the middle-class syndrome—the desire to demonstrate its wealth and power, to argue for freedom and equality through the practice of libertinism. "The anxiety of publicity" manifests itself in the popularization of sexual education, the sexual revolution, and a high divorce rate. Sexual freedom becomes a high priority on the political agenda of social reform. Materialism in the use of pleasure finds its expression in the representation of such freedom in mass media, in popular entertainment and economic consumerism, as many cultural critics have observed. Abroad, the attraction of "American democracy" is often associated with the sign of bikinis on California beach. At home, "the beautiful and the damned" is still the dream and the promise for the young and the successful—a stale, old eighteenth-century Richardsonian tale.

As Charles I. Glicksberg criticizes in his study *The Sexual Revolution in Modern American Literature*,"In American public life sex has become a form of big business, a veritable industry and profitable mode of exploitation, as well as a national obsession. Sex is now a mental intoxicant, an end in itself." [12] Few might disagree with him. However, the problem of such criticism lies in that it easily backs up the Ancient's stance of humanism. What puzzles him is still the mechanic function of sexual freedom, not the economic system itself. He makes his judgment with a moral pitch: "What is wrong is the ever increasing emphasis placed on the mechanics of sex, the technology of sex" (241-42). In my opinion, I am not saying it is right or wrong. I am just pointing to the fact that there exists a class difference in the use of pleasure. The three symptoms of the middle-class syndrome explain that the mechanism, which sustains such stark naked use of pleasure, runs hand in hand with the middle-class social interest and economic power. "Ostentation," as Starobinski puts it, is "the expression of power externalized" (14). So for the middle class, it is perfectly "right," whereas, at the bottom of the social ladder, the need for love and liberty is different. What the pregnant teenagers and raped working-class women are in need of, at this stage of American civilization, probably is not freedom, but security in sexual relationships; not the exposure of the body, but the respect of it; not "a loaded gun" to seek a "Master's hand," but self-esteem, sense of identity, and self-preservation. Penis envy, after all, is symptomatic of a class distinction, not a gender distinction.

"The Change of Philomel": Freedom of Speech in the Culture Industry

Since sexual freedom is seen as a class privilege, the lover's discourse in postmodern fiction is a stylization of a contemporary socially privileged language. The text of pleasure, with all its ostentatious symbolic power, has become a dominant language in a capitalist economy. It is the dominant sign in Western democracy, the dominant discourse in everyday life, which the avant-garde fictionist must claim and disrupt at once with novelistic art.

As Bakhtin pointed out in the 1930s (a time when economic depression brought hedonism to a halt and Russian formalism was purged by socialist realism): "In the history of literary language, there is a struggle constantly being waged to overcome the official line with its tendency to distance itself from the zone of contact, a struggle against various kinds and degrees of authority."[13] This is also the idea Kristeva later assimilated into poststructuralist theory: the historicity in a novel lies in the interaction of the two novelistic linguistic codes—"the official linguistic codes" and "the carnivalesque word." The latter functions as a social political protest against the former, and as such, it protests against the hierarchy of the official law as well. Significantly, the social function of the experimental writers, I would assume, is often masked in the "carnival." As Kristeva suggests, the writer participates in history by reading/writing through the practice of a signifying structure, in relation or opposition to another structure. But the question remains: When the body is put on as the mask, unless it is living dead, what keeps the ball rolling at the masquerade?

In authoritarian Russia, Bakhtin would call the dominant privileged language the "authoritative" or "official" discourse that the novelist dialogizes with an "internal persuasive discourse." In democratic countries, I suppose the dominant privileged language is the popular language of the majority. Fictionists must use the popular language for public speech, if they want to locate themselves in history or participate in the masquerade. Those whose private minds disagree with the majority voice in a democracy are often compelled to write fiction instead of making public speech, because in fiction, they can at least create a "double voice" with "double irony" beyond the speech by inventing a private discourse, which dialogizes with the public discourse.

Ironically, in Russia, the authoritative discourse is the political, moral, religious, the word of a father, or a teacher; it is possibly the didactic word. Whereas "the internal persuasive word"—such as the petty bourgeois ego or I-love-you—is denied all privilege, backed up by no authority at all, and "is frequently not even acknowledged in society (not by public opinion, nor by scholarly norms, nor by criticism), not even in the legal code."[14] In Western democratic society, the public discourse is not didactic, but "carnivalesque." It is the sensational, indulgent, undulating I-love-you that Barthes demystifies and, eventually, after he exhausts its sensation, exposes as "a socially irresponsible word" that goes at large, being soothing to the "giddy ear" and popular taste, while the ideological discourse, the serious sober message in the novel, is often silenced into the internally persuasive discourse. The minority's critical voice, being marginal, is denied all the privilege and suffers from almost the same lot as described above in Russia. Even within academia, the internal persuasive discourse is seldom acknowledged, if not deliberately ignored.

Theodor Adorno observed, as early as 1944 that "in the public voice of modern society accusations are seldom audible; if they are, the perceptive can already detect signs that the dissident will soon be reconciled."[15] Why is this so? Those "culture monopolies" have the power to merge all individual voices and regulate them to the standard of common market needs and popular taste. "Anyone who resists can only survive by fitting in" (132). Surely in a democracy, censorship takes a much softer measure because it is inlaid in the "soft structure" of the assembly line. The boundary of freedom of speech is drawn with an elegant white lace in the hands of those culture monopolies, such as a certain critical school or a literary canon.

Within the literary canon, the critics are the legislators, attorneys, and sometimes the state police who have the licence and authority to speak in the courtroom (or classroom) because they are in control of the public rhetoric. Being well versed in "mass psychology," they are knowledgeable not only of the law, but also of what the judge, the jury, and the auditors respectively care to hear. It is their job to make sure the "right" things be heard in order to make a good case for the prisoner at the bar. The audience in the courtroom is actually three times removed from the original truth through the mediation and interpretation of these legal "bodyguards." Even though the prisoner at the bar has intended to challenge the official codes or break the law at his own will, he will find himself, in the hands of his attorney, well defended in perfectly legal terms, as Nabokov, Joyce, Faulkner, and Melville were in the hands of their complacent critics.

Noam Chomsky, in his book *Necessary Illusions: Thought Control in Democratic Societies* (1989), discovers that "the propaganda model" in Russia functions surprisingly well in American mass media. He proposes that the media makes predictions at several levels, predictions that set the limit of our freedom of speech. Prediction I: What enters the mainstream will support the needs of the established power. Prediction II: Media debate will be bounded in a manner that satisfies the external needs and thus will be limited to the question of the alleged adversarial stance of the media. Prediction III: Any inquiry or study of the media that escapes these bounds and reaches unwanted conclusions will be ignored or bitterly condemned, for it conflicts with the needs of the powerful and privileged.[16]

Now the problem in postmodern writing becomes evident and rather understandable. The self-interest of the "powerful and privileged" reading public (critics included) sets the bounds of "the external needs" or "the official linguistic codes" for the novelistic discourse. Whatever runs into conflict with the narcissistic desire of the powerful and privileged will be easily "ignored or bitterly condemned." Or as often as not, if the novel is truly well made in its design, the culture monopolies always have a democratic "seat" for it, and through various misinterpretations, it will, at any rate, survive and serve the established power in its own egocentric terms (the public reception of Nabokov's *Lolita* in the 1950s and 1960s, especially with the Freudian interpretations, is a typical "case history," a critical joke). On the other hand, the floor is always open to talk about love and sex, if not the cold war or race relations.

The genius of experimental writers, one should say, still lies in their discovery of the literary strategies to overcome such difficulties and disrupt the dominance of a public discourse. Joyce in *Finnegans Wake* literally demolishes the official linguistic codes, though until recently his political intentions have always been ignored in Joycean criticism. Dream work, sexual fantasies, incestuous desire, sexy puns and allusions, pornography, and body language preoccupy much of Joycean critical inquiry. The phenomenon ironically suggests that the masquerade in a fashionable society easily passes for the text of pleasure, just as "Disneyland mentality" rules over "the land of opportunity."

When the modernists—Conrad, Woolf, Ford, Lawrence, Eliot,

Forster—revolted against the Victorian mentality and therefore disrupted the discursive and mimetic mode of artistic production, they were more than aware of the difficulty in speaking truth to a middle-class audience, whose "desire" had no depth beyond the phantom of that "Unreal City." Appealing to myth, symbolism, and poetic metaphors, Eliot in "The Waste Land" registers such a change of style in human communication, the same as Adorno criticizes in his above-mentioned theoretical treatise:

> The change of Philomel, by the barbarous king
> So rudely forced; yet there the nightingale
> Filled all the desert with inviolable voice
> And still she cried, and still the world pursues,
> Jug Jug to dirty ears.[17]

Here, as Bakhtin might agree, the public discourse is the audible speech "Jug Jug" that "the world pursues," and the internally persuasive discourse is the inviolable voice of the raped Philomela, bitter, despairing, furious, and persistent. The nightingale's tongue, having been cut by the barbarous king, "Treuth," is alienated from the world. But the voice is still there and inviolable. Still there is a trace discernible in the tension retained by her persistent repetition of "still . . . still" and "Jug, Jug." Only those, as Faulkner claims, who have heard "the best of all talking, the best of all breathing and forever the best of all listening," and thereby cared to trace the sound and fury of ancient wisdom and primitive truth, may still be able to distinguish Philomela's voice from her speech and lend her cry a justful hearing. (When we come to Faulkner's *Go Down, Moses*, we'll "darkly listen" to the cry of a "Nightingale.")[18]

A justful hearing indeed "The Waste Land" has gained from a far wider audience than the theory of the Frankfurt School. Yet, in fact, by discovering a new form of artistic expression, Eliot finds means to convey forcefully what Bakhtin was theorizing and Adorno was criticizing. It only proves that literary language, thanks to its inherent persuasive power of pleasure, may have its special mechanism that could be more appealing to the public ear than direct cultural criticism. Therefore, the power of literary language can be said to be by itself a kind of "internal persuasive discourse" juxtaposed against the structure of the ideological discourse of history. In times when the popular sentiment prefers rococo art to political idealism, the mock-heroic, the "Rape of the Lock," the comic mode, and the suave witty satirical "soft" rhetoric surpass the power of serious theoretical discourse and radical indoctrination.

The truth is that in a capitalist society poets and novelists are deprived of the phallic power to influence mass consciousness, and freedom of speech finds its expression in the "Jug Jug." In a sense the serious ones are all Philomelas who are not free to speak the truth but nevertheless speak with a voice. They might be less brave, but possibly more sensible, than political advocates and social radicals. Under disappointing historical circumstances, knowing their own limit and the limit of human possibilities in general, they retreat into literary language and literary imagination, not to give up their battle, but to preserve their intelligence for a better company, better times, and hopefully, a better hearing.

In postmodern fiction, the interaction between the externalized public I-love-you and the internally persuasive lover's discourse opens a space of ambivalence, whereupon Novelistic Love functions. The "love story," which is deliberately thinned out by digressions in most of these fictions, much in the vein of Sterne's *Tristram Shandy*, serves as a rhetorical medium for such dialogical interaction. The subject of Love bridges the gap between the public and the private in a carnivalesque discourse. Interestingly, Bakhtin had speculated such a possibility:

> Both the authority of discourse and its internal persuasiveness
> may be united in a single word—one that is simultaneously
> authoritative and internally persuasive—despite the profound
> differences between these two categories of alien discourse.
> (342)

If there is such a "single word" in postmodern fiction, I should think it is the Joycean word: his "penisolate" war (or the lover's discourse reproduced from "love stories"). As said before, I-love-you is the authoritative word, a socially privileged word during the postwar period. Because of its "mute eloquence," its sensational, seductive, and private communicative power, it is simultaneously the internally persuasive word. Joyce, as always, has the right word. He actually does more than unite a dual system as Bakhtin proposes; he disseminates it into a three-dimensional and even multi-referential word. Philosophers are often tempted to theorize on the basis of a dual system; but in practice, reality is always more complex and yet promises more unpredictable possibilities. As fictionist, Joyce is able to create, or more precisely, re-create, a linguistic system, down to earth and close to nature, that is not dual but multiple—a system of international pluralism, "Plurabilities" (FW 104).

The Joycean word "penisolate" (war), like the rest of the text, is semireferential but with infinite possibilities of signification. Read as "penis" war, the word provocatively evokes a sense of pleasure. It does not appear in official annotations, but one who reads it hears it. As a postmodern reader, I bring it up not to pursue the "Jug, Jug," but to make the point that Joyce's use of pleasure is at once economic and political as it is sensational. In public discourse, the word refers to the Napoleonic Peninsular War. Since the word is not capitalized in the text, it is not restricted to the Napoleonic War, but to all Imperialist wars fought on the peninsular past and present that Joyce might have had in mind at the time he wrote the book. It is also the "pen-isolated" war that the novelist chooses to fight in exile. Without joining the military force or armed uprising in Ireland, Joyce is nevertheless fighting a metafictionist's war (a "peninsular/an almost island/Ireland war") on behalf of his nation, and of all the colonized nations as well, against the dominance of imperialism. His nationalistic sentiment, or his "laughtears" over "Irish independence," protests loudly throughout the carnivalsque text of *Finnegans Wake*. His political gossips seldom appear to be a scholarly interest in the Joycean canon. As late as 1980, canonical critics held that James Joyce had no politics. In fact, isolated as he is in the prison house of language postponing death by writing (as a generation of postmodern metafictionists is to follow in his wake), Joyce writes from start to finish with a deep and enduring love for his moherland—"a way a lone a last a loved a long the . . . riverrun." As Henry Sussman puts it, "Anna Livia Plurabella is a woman and a river, a geological river and a river of language. She is the river of language in which the writer delves, according to a venerable tradition of gentrification, the matter formed."[19] For the Irish warrior, the river is the source of his language, his "mamafesta," the nourishment of his native culture to which he eventually returns as a postmodernist.

> The interpretation of any phrase in the whole, the meaning of every word of a phrase so far deciphered out of it, however unfettered our Irish daily independence, we must vaunt no idle dubiosity as to its genuine authorship and holusbolus authoritativeness. (FW 117-18)

It is Love that sustains his "penmight" and writing that fulfills his duty as Tristan. In short, by way of comic re-creation, phallic power in the hands of the "bygmester" is wielded as a weapon to fight epistemological, linguistic, and textual "world wars." Joyce gossips:

To whom the headandheelless chickenstegg bore some Michelangiolesque resemblance, making use of the sacrilegious languages to the defect that he would challenge their hemosphores to exterminate them but he would cannonise the b---y b---r's life out of him and lay him out contritely as smart as the b---r had his b---y nightprayers said. (FW 81)

That Joycean phrase "to wielderfight his penisolate war" on the opening page of *Finnegans Wake* is historically significant. It marks a fundamental change of style in novelistic writing and novelistic love from modernism to postmodernism. It redefines the historical position of the novelist by reviving the Swiftian tradition that "the pen is mightier than the sword." It is the sperm seed of deconstruction, the source of Derrida's theory of dissemination. It is the declaration of novelistic love as "writing."

In the wake of the *Wake*, the postmodernists have expertly reinvested their literary talent in that power plant of pleasure, reinvestigated its mode of production, recaptured the mechanism of mass psychology, so that they are the ones who have regained control of the phallic power as a linguistic capital. Mocking and parodying "the great cunt of existence" they have exhausted its mystic attraction. Exposing the penis envy to its worst extremity, they've turned the table around to ruin it—"to weilderfight" what Joyce announced as the "penis(is)olated war."

"Persuasive eloquence (peitho) is the power to break in, to carry off, to seduce internally, to ravish invisibly." [20] Apparently well versed in the *Wake*, Derrida in his own writing self-consciously resorts to sexual metaphors and heavily relies on its persuasive power. When he writes in *Of-Grammatology* that "the silent language of love is not a prelinguistic gesture, it is a 'mute eloquence,'"[21] he actually locates the text of pleasure in what Bakhtin has proposed as the internally persuasive discourse; thus he opens a postmodern theoretical perspective of novelistic love. That "mute eloquence" is not a simple expression of love, but something else, a trace, a musical text, a language by itself.

What he proclaims beyond modernism and structuralism, beyond the sensational and private nature of communicative power inherent in the word of pleasure, is its power of sophistry. The fact that sophistry becomes a prevailing mode of writing in the postmodern period, in criticism as well as in fiction, is by no means incidental; it is only a literary correlative of the prevailing mode of communication in a media society. It borrows from two major modes of production in late capitalist economy: advertisement and stock market exchange. In the former, presentation is constantly undermined; in the latter, value is never stable.

We live in an age of mass media, the economy of which is dominated by the function of commercial advertisement. The mechanism of its rhetoric has already developed a contemporary form of sophistry to its full maturity. Its language takes a form that is highly metaphorical, arbitrary, seductive, unpredictable, inflating and fluctuating all the time, speculative, and ruinous of itself. The rapid programming on the TV screen has altered, if not completely erased, our sense of time and reality with its sensational but far-fetched temporal and spacial juxtapositions of images and topics. In other words, the linguistic hierarchy in a media culture is fast developing into a system of sophistry. Its very artificiality has become not only an acceptable and pleasurable way of entertainment, but also a desirable, challenging, and stimulating mode of communication that fits the tempo of a high-tech society, and its boredom as well.

That mode of communication is a literary form of consumerism. The laissez-faire of proliferate signifiers is characteristic of capital circulation in the stage of a finance economy in which surplus must be spent not for necessities (such as education and health care), but for ornaments and publicity; or it must be exported, reinvested in the Other. As a result, the natural need of the original producer of that capital, the worker, is discounted, alienated, ignored, and unfulfilled. Consciously or unconsciously, the fictionist borrows rhetoric from the advertiser who uses excessive body images and sexy voices to sell a commodity. But remarkably, there is a fundamental difference between the fictionist and the commercial advertiser: The fictionist has more serious stuff to sell than the advertiser. Instead of mouthwash or hair spray, the novelist sells ideology—historical arguments and philosophical debates. Novelistic love works as the advertisement of cultural criticism and political gossip. John Barth might call this kind of rhetorical strategy the "reverse translation" of a popular form.

I hope I have suggested that sophistry has its economic roots in the American soil when it blossoms, just as Freudism has its psychological roots in the middle-class syndrome when it rises.

Notes

1. "But our great Romantic Unroman, our typical ant-novel, is the womanless *moby-Dick*." Leslie Fiedler, *Love and Death in the American Novel*, rev. ed. (New York: Scarborough House,1982), 25.

2. "'Tis, my Mary herself!' She promised that my boy, every morning, hsould be carried to the hill to catch the first glimpse of his father's sail!" Herman Melville, *Moby-Dick*, Norton Cdritiacl Edition (New York: W. W. Norton & Co., 1967), 54, 443-44. Subsequent references will be indicated as *M-D*.

3. James Joyce, *Finnegans Wake* (New York: Penguin, 1984), 3. Subsequent references will be indicated as *FW*.

4. T. S. Eliot, "Ash-Wednesday" (1930), *The Complete Poems and Plays 1909-50* (New York: Hartcourt Brace & World, 1971), 65.

5. Fredrid Jameson, "Pleasure: A Political Issue," in *The Ideologies of Theory, Essays, 1971-1986* Vol. 2: *Syntax of Hitory* (Minneapolis: University of Minnesota Press, 1988), 73.

6. Vladimir Nabokov, *The Annotated Lolita*, Ed. Alfred Appel Jr. (New York: McGraw-Hill, 1970), 261.

7. The phrase comes from Donald Barthelme's *Snow White* (New York: Atheneum, 1986), 45-46, in Jane's letter to Mr. Quistgaard.

8. Roland Barthes, *A Lover's Discourse: Fragments*, trans. Richard Howard (New Yor k: Hill & Wang, 1985), 1, 147.

9. Nabokov, *The Annotated Lolita*, 327.

10. Ferdinand de Saussure, "Course in General Linguistics," in *Critical Theory Since 1965*, ed. Hazard Adams and Leroy Searle (Tallahassee: Florida State University Press, 1986), 649.

11. For the following discussion, please, see Jean Staronbinski, *The Invention of Liberty, 1700-1789* (Cleveland, Ohio: World Publishing Co., 1964).

12. Charles I. Glicksberg, *The Sexual Revolution in Modern American Literature* (Hague, Netherlands: Martinus Nijhoff, 1971), 241-42.

13. M. M. Bakhtin, "Discourse in the Novel," *The Dialogical Imagination*, ed. Michael Holquist, trans. Caryl Emerson and Michael Holquist (Austin: University of Texas Press, 1981), 345.

14. Ibid., 342.

15. Theodor W. Adornor and Max Horkheimer, "The Culture Industry: Enlightment as Mass Deception" in *Dialectic of Englightenment*, trans. John Cumming (New York: Continuum, 1969), 132.

16. See Noam Chomsky, *Necessary Illusions: Thought Control in Democratic Societies* (Boston: South End Press, 1989), 153.

17. T. S. Eliot, "The Waste Land," *The Complete Poems and Plays*, 40.

18. See my reading of "Delta Autumn" in Chapter Five.

19. Henry Sussman, *Afterimages of Modernity* (Baltimore: Johns Hopkins University Press, 1990), 165.

20. Jacques Derrida, *Dissemination*, trans. Barbara Johnson (Chicago: University of Chicago Press, 1981), 116.

21. Jacques Derrida, *Of Grammatology*, trans. Gayatri Chakravorty Spivak (Baltimore: Johns Hopkins University Press, 1976), 236.

Chapter Two

The Invention of "Greek" Love Stories: Plato's Symposium [1]

Out of Plato come all things that are still written and debated among men of thought, great havoc makes he among our originalities. . . . No wife, no children had he, and the thinkers of all civilized nations are his posterity and are tinged with his mind. . . . Calvinism is in his Phaedo: Christianity is in it. Mahometanism draws all its philosophy, in its handbook of morals, the Akhlak-y-Jalaly, from him. Mysticism finds in Plato all its texts. This citizen of a town in Greece is no villager nor patriot. An Englishman reads and says, "how English!" a German, —"how Teutonic!" an Italian, —"how Roman and how Greek!" As they say that Helen of Argos had that universal beauty that every body felt related to her, so Plato seems to a reader in New England an American Genius. His broad humanity transcends all sectional lines.

—Ralph Waldo Emerson, "Plato: Or the Philosopher"[2]

"There Is Truth in Wine": Literary Procreation

In the last chapter, I explored the economics of "love stories" in postmodern fiction in relation to the cultural climate during the postwar era. Beyond the external forces that influence the change of a literary style, the intrinsic law and the nature of literary love also have to be considered. As discussed before, novelistic love functions similarly to the mechanism of TV commercials, where the seduction of sexy voices and beautiful blondes is intended for another subject, another discourse. Its rhetoric, also like the language of advertisement, relies heavily on the persuasive power of sophistry. Yet sophistry is but a way of speaking, a method, a rhetoric, not truth itself. Similarly, novelistic love is a way of writing, a medium, rather than the message itself. As a way of writing, novelistic love develops out of a system—the convention of literary love. It is, to a considerable extent, generated and governed by its momentum, its models and motifs, too. Literary love is open to literary imagination, but subject to literary laws—literary conventions.

Literary love is neither real love nor ideal love, but the art and archive of love, that since the time of Homer and Plato, has supplied the literary and literate people with the idea of love. While Homer's poetry establishes the epic tradition in literary love, Plato's *The Symposium* invents a philosophy of love that has throughout the ages informed the lover's discourse in prose and poetry. "For whom the funhouse fun? Perhaps for lovers," writes John Barth in *Lost in the Funhouse*; and Barth names his hero Ambrose after Plato—"a swarm of bees lit on Plato's mouth when he was a kid. They say that's where he got his way with words."[3]In the Platonic tradition, the construction of "love stories" are not necessarily real, based on real-life experience, but divine fabrication, designed to entertain the reader's fancy with thoughts that are only too serious. Most often, the fabrication of fabulous "love stories" is nothing but a dramatization of the novelist's ideas—a historical vision, philosophical speculation, political gossip, or cultural criticism.

In this chapter, I will offer a postmodern rereading of Plato's narrative, much in the spirit of his dinner party, in order to show that Plato's invention of "love stories" is a pure artifice, a rhetoric, a language, and that his love stories are impregnated with philosophical ideas and novelistic conceits. First, I will examine his rhetorical strategies by way of discovering the artistic designs and philosophical implications in his narration. Then I will analyze Plato's idea of literary procreation and its deliverance of truth.

When I come to Socrates' panegyric, I hope to show how the ultimate truth of Love is framed in a feminine fiction, the voice of Diotima, which makes a difference and thereby disrupts the rational discourse of philosophy. Finally I will disseminate the master narrative of Platonic love and reveal the various models of literary love that have been developed into the novel. I will point out the differences and distinctions in each model as the basic form, or idea.

The *Symposium*, presented in the form of dramatic dialogue, is actually composed of a series of "Greek" love stories, which eventually leads to a theory of Platonic love. From a postmodern perspective it can be read as a metafiction of Love, or at least a metadiscourse among "Greek" lovers. All the accounts of Love, either personified as one of the oldest and most honorable and powerful gods, or as two Aphrodites, the Common and the Heavenly, are purely mythic and fictive constructs. In addition, the work contains a plot, some digressions, and a thematic progression carefully designed in its narrative framework and narrative sequence. Some of the narrative strategies Plato employs are highly self-conscious dramatic and fictive devices. For instance, Aristophanes's hiccups are used to delay his speech until he can launch an argument to negate Eryximachus's theory. Socrates' presentation of Diotima stages "a play within a play," a moment of aporia in the text. Alcibiades' self-parodic, tragicomic farce, which eventually dissolves the myth of Socrates, is a moment of catharsis releasing the intensity of philosophical truth. So the form of Plato's *Symposium* is not only a dramatic dialogue but also a structured drama and a dramatic narrative by itself.

Realism is deliberately discounted from the very beginning. When the narrator, Apollodorus, is asked to relate Socrates' story at Agathon's party, which actually took place in Athens "while we were still boys," as he says, he has to recall from a distant memory and an unreliable account twice removed from the original (that of Aristodemus). Such a narrative framework sets the narrator free from the authority of the original authors of these love stories, and thereby adds to his account a picturesque touch of fictionality. In spite of his failure to account for the "real thing," which is irretrievable anyway, he is highly self-conscious of his artistry in his narrative performance. He tells his audience that he is not "unrehearsed" and that he has told the story a couple of days before, so that the audience is expected to view his presentation as his own design—a refined, restructured, and therefore re-created work of art by itself, a dramatic "rehearsal" beyond "recollection."

Such a narrative strategy is as good as what we now consider to be a metafictive device that deliberately destroys the reader's illusory sense of reality. Truth, especially literary truth, does not necessarily partake of reality. Sterne warns us in the chapter "Sleep" in *Tristram Shandy*: "But remember, *'La Vraisemblance . . . n'est pas toujours du Cote de la Verite.'* And so much of sleep."[4] Joyce in *Finnegans Wake,* too, insinuates a syllogism to pinpoint where literary truth dwells: "Where the possible is the improbable and the improbable the inevitable" (FW 19). In *The Symposium,* when one reaches the last panegyric, that of Alcibiades, one is surprised to see that "the improbable" becomes "the possible." It becomes possible only through a manipulation of language, a deployment of literary tropes. In the beginning of his story, Alcibiades explains his choice of language: "It isn't easy for a man in my condition to sum up your extraordinary character in a smooth and orderly sequence"; so he proposes to praise Socrates "by using similes." "I declare," the debauchee says, "he bears a strong resemblance to those figures of Silenus in statuaries' shops, represented holding pipes or flutes; they are hollow inside, and when they are taken apart you see that they contain little figures of gods" (S 100).

What "improbable" yet "inevitable" truth of Socrates can one logically expect other than what is conveyed here through Alcibiades' seemingly illogical speech with its absurd similes? But when Alcibiades finally puts the "flute" of Socrates together after he has taken it apart, it is through reflection and recollection that one begins to realize that there is indeed such improbable and inevitable truth "in wine," in a pleasurable simile, although the moment he spoke, it had been indeed impossible to take his words seriously.

"There is, as the proverb says," claims the intoxicated lover, "truth in wine" (S 104). The wine flows in the world of fiction, and intoxication is the expression, not of ordinary reality, but of extraordinary truth. In the mind of metaphysicians East and West, as Arthur Christy once said, "the tavern was the call to contemplation, and wine the intoxication of the spirit."[5] For the storyteller, literary tropes come from the stimuli of wine, or spirit. Whether such hobby-horsical truth, or what we call self-conscious and self-reflective mode of writing, characterizes metafiction as a postmodern phenomenon, as critics have claimed, is questionable. I'd assume rather, it is part of the Platonic tradition revived in postmodern fiction. This is not to say that there is nothing new under the sun. On the contrary, as Plato himself knows, anything that recapitulates the past is never the same thing as the past event; but the present becomes meaningful only through a second thought of the past events and experiences. Such an aesthetic principle intentionally underlines Plato's fictive devices. It is even more revealing toward the end of work, when Socrates summons Diotima's lesson of Love from memory, which immortalizes artistic procreation through the art of recollection and memory. Diotima says to Socrates:

> When we use the word "recollection" we imply by using it that knowledge departs from us; forgetting is the departure of knowledge, and recollection, by implanting a new impression in the place of that which is lost, preserves it, and gives it a spurious appearance of uninterrupted identity. It is in this way that everything mortal is preserved; not by remaining for ever the same which is the prerogative of divinity, but by undergoing a process in which the losses caused by age are repaired by new acquisitions of a similar kind. . . . So do not feel surprise that every creature naturally cherishes its own progeny; it is in order to secure immortality that each individual is haunted by this eager desire and love. (S 89)

Proust's *Remembrance of Things Past*, for example, is a recapitulation of Diotima's theory, with "new acquisitions of a similar kind." Now as I recall this passage from the perspective of the postmodern Joycean mode (it is only fair to say that such a mode is preconceived in Plato), in which literary creation is conceived in the simile of love and procreation, my intention is to still "repair" some impaired concepts of literary love and literary transformation. On the one hand, literary love exists as a discourse independent from ordinary reality, because it has its own "unrealistic" legitimacy in its formation and its mechanism of function. On the other, forms and motifs are not constant fixed models, but organic evolutionary artistic creations propelled by the progeny of each story.

Whatever is recollected from memory, be it a story or "history," is a departure from reality. Mimesis in the Platonic tradition is only a "spurious" appearance of uninterrupted identity. This is because, first of all, literary reminiscence depends upon mortal memory and cannot escape mortality; second, artistic "recollection" is open to artistic invention. A story cherishes "its own progeny," represents a new stage of being, a higher level of reality. To reach that higher level of being, as Plato believes, is the ultimate goal of Love, that is, "Immortality." In this sense, literary invention is never out of touch with history; it is always "eager" to secure a place and a presence in history with its desire for progeny. The relationship between literature and history in a larger sense is less a temporary whimsical love affair than a long-range serious commitment of marriage, because the process of artistic creation aims not at mechanic function, but at generic immortality. At the same time, however, since it is generic, a creative work is unlikely to be completely free of its "origin." What is at work between the past and the present, reality and fiction, a love affair and a love story, is the author's living hand, the progenitor's artistic consciousness and creative desire. What the author's hand produces is writing, writing that makes the difference from original reality. When a love story enters into a literary discourse, it lives in a linguistic hierarchy, subject to literary forms and lyric laws.

In order to recognize the role that language plays in the way we think of love and speak of love, it might first, be helpful to consider the difference between animal love and human love. The beasts in the jungle are unable to tell the difference between rape and love, because they have not made that distinction yet through legislature, and they do not have a language to appeal to the court in case of a rape. Maybe they do, but we have no means to know since we do not know their language. As a result, we have no idea of what Love is in the jungle.

On the other hand, educated people write love letters, tell lies of love, seduce or deceive each other with "sweet words," court with a song, or swear with a vow, reject by reasoning, or protest by moralizing. Without language, love may hardly exist in Western civilization. Furthermore, the songs and vows, the reasoning and moralizing, are not only linguistic expressions, but also more or less modeled on the basis of a theory, a law, a morale, a religion, a code of ethics, a literary motif within a certain literary tradition. After all, only human love can be reenacted, re-presented, recollected through memory by means of art and language to be communicated to an audience and posterity. Nietzsche defines "the phenomenon of love" as "what is called love in all the *languages* and silences of the world."[6]

Is there anything that can be called "natural love"? I suppose there is, as long as one does not "call" it. When one can speak of it, one has already lost it. As D. H. Lawrence argues in *Women in Love* (a philosophical novel it is): "How can I say 'I love you' when I have ceased to be, and you have ceased to be. . . . Speech travels between separate parts. But in the perfect one there is perfect silence of bliss."[7] The plain truth is that the one who knows how to make love does not necessarily know how to speak of love, write a love poem or tell a love story. In *The Symposium*, the physician Eryximachus observes such a discrepancy between the physical practice of love and its literary form:

In the actual constitution of a harmony there is no difficulty in perceiving the principle of love at work, and the question of the double nature of love does not so far arise; but when one has to deal with the effect upon human beings of rhythm and harmony, either in their creation by the process known as composition, or in the right use of melodies and verse-forms in what is called education, difficulties occur which demand a skillful artist. (S 56)

As Eryximachus points out, what Love is actually at work is a different matter from what it appears to be in "composition" and "verse-forms." In other words, in literary love, it is not simply a question of decorum or idealization of love for love's sake, but also a question of what can be said of Love within the limit and possibilities of rhetorical tropes and literary convention. Hence the art of Love.

Eryximachus also mentions another complication in literary love that needs to be considered, that is, when it comes to the purpose of "what is called education, difficulties occur which demand a skillful artist." The presentation of Love enters the value system of ethics that intrudes and interferes with the realms of natural and literary love. Thus a work of art depends upon the purpose of "education" and the skillfulness of the poet or the philosopher, who then would have an artificial, as well as an artistic intention in praise of Love. His artistry most likely serves the purpose of his artificiality in praise of Love. The issue is further explored by Socrates, as I will discuss subsequently.

After Eryximachus has spoken of Love from a physician's technical point of view, Plato presents two most skillful artists in verse and theater—Aristophanes the comedian and Agathon the tragedian—to account for Love. Remarkably, even the wise Socrates had no idea of Love until he hears a "love story" from Agathon. It is Agathon, the romantic idealist, who finally figures out the importance of having a "method" in praise of Love. So Socrates, the wisest of all men, acknowledges the power and artistry of literary love:

I was stupid enough to suppose that the right thing was to speak the truth about the subject proposed for panegyric, whatever it might be, and that the truth would provide the material, as it were, out of which one selected the most favorable points and arranged them as artistically as possible. . . . But now it appears that this is not the right way to set about praising anything, and that the proper method is to ascribe to the subject of the panegyric all the loftiest and loveliest qualities, whether it actually possesses them or not; if the ascription is false, it is after all a matter of no consequence. In fact, what was proposed to us was that each of us should give the appearance of praising Love rather than that we should actually do so. That is why, I imagine, you rake up stories of every kind and ascribe the credit of them to Love; that is why you depict his nature and the effects of his activity as you do. Your object is that in the eyes of those who do not know him—for such a description will never pass among experts—he should appear the loveliest and best of all beings, and your panegyric has a very fine and solemn sound. I, not knowing the proper method, agreed in my ignorance to contribute my share, but it was my tongue that gave the promise, not my mind. (S 73-74)

Socrates, at this moment, is actually formulating a "proper method," a theory of panegyric in praise of Love, after he has observed the way in which performing artists account for Love (not unlike the way contemporary philosophers theorize literary experiments). If I understand him correctly this passage, he has gathered from performing art that the subject of a panegyric, Love, doesn't have to be truthful raw material from life. The proper method is to start with an idea—eulogize, fantasize, fabricate a fiction. Whether such a fiction has any reality or not is "a matter of no consequence." All that matters is the art of constructing the fiction—"raking up stories of all kinds" in the name of Love—to depict an imaginary appearance, tell a dramatic story, create an object of desire, and make a strong impression upon the audience.

More explicitly than Eryximachus's hint at the "artificiality" of the author's intention in telling love stories, as mentioned above, Socrates prioritizes such an artificiality: "In fact . . . each of us should give the appearance of praising Love rather than that we should actually do so." It is clear now that there is a difference between the telling and the tale, the appearance and the implications in those round-table discussions. He reveals such a difference by modestly admitting his own ignorance: The telling of love stories (or mimesis) is only intended for "those who don't know" Love, himself included. Presumably, if such an audience should fall in love with the appearance of Love as the author presents, naturally they will love whatever attributes the author attaches to Love. Since love is blind, "love stories" are the most effective persuasive tool to attract a popular readership. As for "the experts," the story will have little effect because they can see through the "appearance" of the author and know what he's "actually doing." Thus Socrates has explained the motivation of the storytellers in praise of Love: Each may have a hidden agenda in their telling of "love stories." (I will look into the agenda in each story later.)

What I have gathered from Socrates' reflection upon the proper method of panegyric is the fake, the drama, the gap in telling Socratic "love stories," which forms a special mode in literary love. The fake is the artificiality or fictionality of love stories. The drama is the presentation and performance of Love. The gap, as Socrates admits— "it was my tongue that gave the promise, not my mind"—reveals the discrepancy, a space of ambivalence, that exists consciously or unconsciously between what is said and what is thought: the story and the idea.

Socrates' Instructress in the Art of Love: A Feminine Fiction

When Socrates begins to speak of the ultimate truth of Love, one wonders whether it is his tongue or his mind that gives his account of truth, the truth he learns from a woman. Walker Hamilton, translator of Plato's text, sensed that "the tone used by Diotima to him [Socrates] is very much that of sage to pupil, and she is even made to express a doubt whether he will be capable of the final initiation into the mysteries of love" (S 20). It puzzles Plato's readers that Socrates should present his ultimate idea of Love to the bachelor party in the persona of a woman of Mantinea, called Diotima. Socrates even calls her the "instructress in the art of love" (S 79). For some critics, Diotima is "a fictitious personage, in spite of the apparently historical statements made about her by Socrates" (S 19). I am not interested in tracing the historical reality of my subject; for me, the character of Socrates in *The Symposium* as well is a "fictitious personage" recreated by Plato in a dramatic fashion through "dimmed memory." Since Plato's presentation of Socrates is opposed to the public charges brought against Socrates' character, Socrates in Plato must be a different figure from what he was reported to be in public, from the history of public record. Socrates in Plato is either an idealized fiction or a fictional ideal—an idol. Yet Socrates, the wisest of all men, is content enough to admit his indebtedness to the "wisdom in a woman," not only for the knowledge of truth that he obtains from Diotima, but also for the rhetoric of speaking truth, which all the men present have not realized so far. Does Plato intend to show, after all, besides "truth in wine" that there is "wisdom in a woman"?

Whether there is or is not wisdom in a woman might not be so much a question for Plato as for some modern Western thinkers. In his political theory, Plato believes that women are unquestionably different from men in certain respects, because they are physically weaker and generally less educated than men of their time as a result of social disadvantage; but among those equally well-educated women, women are equals with men. There are even superior women, wisdom-wise, capable of fulfilling the roles of Guardians; therefore, it is in the state's interest to elevate suitable women to the rank of Guardian.[8]

While most of the characters in *The Symposium* are men, the wisest of all is but a woman. Love as a vivid character appears in Diotima's account, personified in male identity but with feminine features. It might be necessary to mention that in writing *The Symposium*, Plato may not have been as inclined to make the biological distinction between genders as some "male" critics ascertain. Homosexuality is certainly an issue addressed and dealt with in this text; but to read this text as a panegyric of homosexual love is to vulgarize Platonic Love. Here and there, Plato justifies men's love for men; and he did not say that women couldn't love women if they choose to do so. However, the kind of love he has in mind is not limited to sensual materialism, but idealized as intellectual companionship, comradeship, brotherhood, a union against the forces of the world, the government, the rulers, the vulgarity of public opinions. In an ideal sense, Plato wants to believe that men who are capable of this kind of love must be capable of self-control. The physical intimacy between male lovers is not Plato's major concern. It seems that he could not have cared less if it were not for any public scandal or disease. He only warns his reader subtly through Aristophanes' words: "Beware of Zeus' wrath." Plato's personification of Love may have created a model that Beckett is to claim in his fiction: "There is so little difference between a man and a woman, between mine I mean."[9] Metafiction is sledom concerned with biological gender distinction, because characters are only "ideas" or "metaphors." In raking up stories, the metafictionist has philosophical preoccupations, which are beyond the physical and biological (as "meta" means "beyond"). Certain characters are created for an idea, just as stereotypes are created in satire. To come back to my point, I'd rather ask the question from a narrative perspective: Why is the climactic truth in Plato's narrative spoken through the mouthpiece of a woman?

First, I would like to look at the form of narration. When it comes to Socrates' introduction of Diotima, the narrative frame of *The Symposium* has changed from the double structure into a quadruple structure, and the author Plato is five times protected from whatever comes out of the mouth of Diotima. Such a fictive device often appears in the narrative frame of romance novels such as Hawthorne's *Blithedale Romance*, Conrad's *Heart of Darkness*, and Emily Bronte's *Wuthering Heights*. In my perception, the double narrative structure in these novels practically protects the author or the initial narrator from the charge of presenting disturbing pictures and questions that might upset the narrative's immediate audience for speaking against popular beliefs, or a literary canon, or the dominant ideology of the day. Plato, in his design of a feminine fiction may well imply a challenge to philosophical materialism, as well as to the public charges against Socrates' sex life. To what degree Socrates is conscious of such a challenge is a question, and the question is as good as how much Lockwood, Coverdale, and Marlow's friend on board the ship share the intimate truth of their own tales.

The challenge is clearly there once we hear what kind of truth Socrates' "instructress" has to "instruct":

> (Socrates:) "Is Love ugly and bad?" (Diotima:) "Don't say such things," she answered; "do you think that anything that is not beautiful is necessarily ugly?" "Of course I do." "And that anything that is not wisdom is ignorance? Do you know that there is a state of mind half-way between wisdom and ignorance?" "What do you mean?" "Having true convictions without being able to give reasons for them," she replied. "Surely you see that such a state of mind cannot be called understanding, because nothing irrational deserves the name; but it would be equally wrong to call it ignorance; how can one call a state of mind ignorance which hits upon the truth? The fact is that having true convictions is what I called it just now, a condition half-way between knowledge and ignorance." "I grant you that," said I. "Then do not maintain that what is not beautiful is ugly, and what is not good is bad. Do not suppose that because, on your own admission, Love is not good or beautiful, he must on that account be ugly and bad, but rather that he is something between the two." (S 80)

The kind of Love Diotima teaches Socrates the philosopher is the very presence of truth, which is excluded in the binary system of metaphysical reasoning, as deconstruction makes us aware. Now that we have inspected closely the feminine nature of the very truth framed in that "feminine fiction," we understand that maybe men cannot afford their "name" to withstand such an "intoxication" of the real truth (with the exception of Alcibiades, whose name is already ruined). Without "being able to give reasons for them," the masculine mind will not accept irrational convictions, even those "which hit upon the truth." As Hamilton points out, "Plato was most influenced by the mystery religions of his day, whose language is here used by Diotima in describing the ascent of the soul from the sensible to the eternal world" (S 19). In other words, Love is an oracle. "Oracle" in ancient Greece is a "priestess" through whom a deity is believed to speak, a "shrine" in which a deity reveals hidden knowledge or the divine purpose. In Plato's narrative, Diotima plays such a role herself. In other words, abstract, imaginative, irrational, mysterious truth must be conceived with the feminine principle. Such a model seems to have been already established with the invention of these Greek love stories, and it becomes a literary convention we find later in the works of Joyce and other postmodernists. "The Greek, the Turk, the Chinese, the Copt, the Hoterntot," as Joyce is informed, "all admire a different type of female beauty."[10] This different type of female beauty stands for a higher order in human intellect: the embodiment of truth.

By framing truth in the feminine fiction Plato gives this kind of truth, the immaterial truth, a privileged status over Socrates' rational, philosophical discourse; thus we can say that Plato subverts the established order of gender distinction in his society. It is Diotima's account that develops the theme of Love into a final stage where the theory of Platonic Love may stand by itself. In order to explore the status of the feminine fiction, we may want to ask: What is that state of mind that exists "halfway between knowledge and ignorance"? Is it what modern psychology has discovered as the instinctual being and the subconscious mind? Or is it what Lacan defines as the impossible realm of "the Real"? Is it sexuality itself? At any rate, we know from Diotima that it is the world of spirit—Love's bower, the storage of liquor. The spirit of Love dwells in such a state of mind that saintly philosophers are too sober to enter. The feminine fiction opens a window that lets the spirit in. Such a state of being only poetic language may describe. The best description for such a state one may recall from Emily Dickinson's well-known poem 214:

> Till Seraphs swing their snowy Hats—
> And Saints—to windows run—
> To see the little Tippler
> Leaning against the—Sun—!

Thereupon men breathe a heavenly fragrance that refreshes their mortal sense and mortal vision:

"What can Love be then?" I [Socrates] said. "A mortal?" "Far
from it." "Well, what?" "As in my previous examples, he is
half-way between mortal and immortal." "What sort of being is
he then, Diotima?" "He is a great spirit, Socrates; everything that
is of the nature of a spirit is half-god and half-man." (S 81)

Diotima does not conceive the spirit of Love as divinity itself, but rather as
an "agency" that maintains the communication between gods and men,
immaterial truth and mortal understanding. "Being of an intermediate nature,
a spirit bridges the gap between them, and prevents the universe from falling
into two separate halves" (S 81). Love holds the center of the universe;
Diotima seems to perform such a function. The "little Tippler" stands in the
position of a window, which overlooks both inside the room and outside
onto an open space. Such a position may describe the narrative status of
Socrates' feminine fiction. Diotima is his fountain of spirit, from which he
drinks his full, as he keeps asking her for her ideas:

"And what is the function of such a being?" "To interpret and
convey messages to the gods from men and to men from the
gods, prayers and sacrifices from the one, and commands and
rewards from the other." (S 81)

The spirit of Love is possessed with a feminine instinct. She acts like a
soothing mother, singing sweet melodies to appease the wrath of God, while
humming pleasurable lullabies to comfort the agonized desire of man, the
son of God. As she tells us, "God does not deal directly with man; it is by
means of spirits that all the intercourse and communication of gods with
men, both in waking life and in sleep, is carried on" (S 81).

Love himself may not have anything to say. "The artist in drama
forgoes his very self and stands a mediator in awful truth before the veiled
face of God," Joyce once wrote while he was reading Plato.[11] The role of
Love as a "mediator," neutral as it is, is indispensable. Its role is, first, that
of a carrier of messages and second, that of an interpreter between the divine
truth and the mortal will. To play the role of interpreter, Love must be able
to speak two languages and know both sides of the story. In Socrates'
panegyric, Love is dressed up in the form of a "feminine fiction," but
delivered through the philosophical inquiry of a male authority. Thus Love
must have been, imaginably, a bisexual creature. As a carrier, Love is
identical to novelistic love, as I defined before, a medium rather than the

message itself. But as an interpreter, Love is the storyteller personified, s/he has his own progeny, her own artistic and artificial intentions susceptible to our interpretation, too.

Raking up Stories: Nine Stages of "Love Making"

Critics have observed that Plato never gives a full or direct exposition of his theory in his dialogues. "We have to reconstruct it from allusions and from the passages," as Desmond Lee suggests in reading *The Republic*; "Plato never developed a set of technical terminology, whether the forms are referred to or not."[12] It is even more so in *The Symposium*. As I mentioned before, I assume there is a carefully designed narrative sequence and thematic progression in the whole series of these dramatic dialogues. The ideal of Platonic love is gradually expounded throughout the presentation of each panegyric; it reaches its highest level in Diotima's feminine fiction and is then finalized in Alcibiades' anecdote as an endnote. There are seven panegyrics of Love in the whole narrative given by "a handful of wise men who are more formidable than a crowd of fools" (S 66): Phaedrus, Parsanius, Eryximachus, Aristophanes, Agathon, Socrates, Alcibiades. But Socrates' account can be disseminated into two voices and three models; consequently, there are altogether nine stages, with nine "muses" presiding over these stages. Although each presents a specific model of Love, there is an organic structure of "consecutive account" as Socrates takes it (S 79). There exists a chain of being that underlines and develops both the theme and the form of these panegyrics from a lower stage to its higher form, until the theory of Love reaches the Platonic ideal. Each panegyric proposes a unique value system, but in one way or another, each undermines, negates, supplements, or complements the previous version, while leaving room for the subsequent one to unfold what I have observed previously as the mode of generic procreation. In the following pages, I shall reconstruct Plato's system of composition, or the manu of his "dinner party," through a close examination of each panegyric. I shall explicate the varied theories of Love implicit in each model.

Stage I: Phaedrus and Epic Love

Phaedrus is the first speaker, and he opens the topic of Love with a celebration of marital love, which on Plato's scale is but the lowest stage of Love. Phaedrus praises earthly love with a strong sensual quality, though sensual love in his conception is still rational and "firm": "Hesiod tells us that Chaos first comes into existence, but next Broad-breasted Earth, on whose foundation firm Creation stands, and love" (S 42). Love stands "firm" on a foundation, which Chaos secures through his union with Earth under his control. Phaedrus is dealing with the origin of Creation, the foundation of human civilization. In his account, Love "has no parents." Thus Phaedrus denies kindred love, natural bonds, family name, parental authority, and even divine will. He values individual courage, ambition, and heroism. He stresses conjugal fidelity over everything else. But fidelity for him is based on social contract between husband and wife—a public relationship. His figure of speech is regulated by military tropes—"in an army consisting of lovers and beloved." Alcestis is his ideal woman, Achilles his hero. But Orpheus, who is entitled to marry the soul of Alcestis, yet fails in his mission, in Phaedrus's opinion, since he "seemed to lack spirit, as is only natural in a musician; he had not the courage to die for love like Alcestis" (S 44). Phaedrus's despite of Orpheus's love implies his disbelief in the music of love, the kind of love with the lover playing his lute under the window or balcony of his beloved, which we call "Romantic Love." In Phaedrus's theory, the lover must be able to fight for his beloved object. He must prove that he is worthy "to earn the extreme admiration of gods," who in return shall "treat him with special distinction for showing" his fighting power and earning capability. A strong sense of worldly acquisition permeates his diction in his praise of Love.

Phaedrus praises love and war, and idealizes the value of legal marriage. I would identify his model of Love with the model of epic love. Epic love is worldly. Its theme, as in the epic as a genre, is concerned with conserving or restoring the place of the individual within a dynastic consciousness of origins, within a social hierarchy. In other words, it is concerned with the acquisition of an individual's place and right in an existing social order. The epic lover courts for a name—social recognition and acceptance, which are the goals of his love. He usually gains his entrance into society by one of two means: either displaying his valor through fighting a war with the enemies of that society, or proving his virtue as a lawful citizen of that culture. The lover is a social conformist. S/he cares for the established values of a civilization more than the passion of love. The lover is either a "good boy" or a "virtuous woman"—Achilles or Alcestis; Tom Jones or Pamela. Not necessarily so is the beloved, though, who could be Siren or Satan, Helen or Mr. B——. Not personal qualities but the physical beauty of the beloved becomes the object of desire, as it represents the value of a ritual prize or legal property in society. In order to attain the desirable object, the lover must physically possess his beloved in the public eye with authorized legitimacy. That prize or property eventually will be bestowed upon him only by social and public concession. Therefore, epic love stories usually end in ownership and marriage.

Epic love is a dominant mode in the English novel. Only in the English novel love stories are preoccupied with marriage, public morals, social recognition, and material possessions. From *Pamela*, *Tom Jones*, *Pride and Prejudice* to *David Copperfield*, *Jane Eyre*, and *Vanity Fair* it may be argued that the celebration of marriage in love stories is a typical English model. I will examine the transformation of such a model in the next chapter, "Epic Love and the English novel."

Stage II: Parsanius and Courtly Love

Parsanius, the second speaker, begins to distinguish heavenly love from earthly love. He links love with Aphrodite, whom he identifies in two separate parts—the Common and the Heavenly. Thus Love is divided into two types: Common Love—men's love of women for the satisfaction of physical desire; and Heavenly Love—men's love of men for spiritual enlightenment.

Parsanius ascertains that Love has no mother, springs entirely from the male progenitor—Uranus. Heavenly Love is purified of "female strain." But it must be noted that he equates women with young boys. His proposition is obviously based on a naive presumption that, as he puts it, "women, quite as much as young men," are "unintelligent" and "unspiritual"; they fail to satisfy his spiritual love for wisdom (S 46). As for grown-up wise men, he says:

> even among the lovers of their own sex . . . they do not fall in love with mere boys, but wait until they reach the age at which they begin to show some intelligence, that is to say, until they are near growing a beard. (S 47)

Clearly, his gender distinction in its actuality lies in the degree of intelligence rather than biological difference. His discrimination against women might be easily excused for his lack of "a beard"—his boyish inexperience. The bearded one, Socrates, will soon underscore the gender distinction.

The nature of Parsanius' ideal love seeks a lifelong spiritual commitment. The lover fears uncertainty and disputes (whereas the epic lover welcomes disputes as a challenge, as they are occasions for adventure and war). Parsanius desires his beloved object to be "perfect" and self-restrained, also to know better. Once he sees the superiority of the beloved object and accepts its authority, the goal of his love, unlike that in epic love, is not to conquer but to yield, not to possess but to serve. He speaks of his "voluntary submission" and "voluntary servility" in love. He takes pride in the purity of his motive. In his motive there is one thing important for him. He yields only to wisdom and excellence for "the attainment of excellence"; he will not yield to "wealth and power," "material and political advantages," even though his beloved in a powerful position is able to confer these (S 51-53). His is the ideal love, the seed of courtly love, the Italian mode.

Courtly love is idealistic, as we know, developed into the Medieval Italian literature and Renaissance love poetry—Dante's *Divine Comedy*, troubadour poetry, the Petrarchan conceit. Courtly love in its ideology pleads feudal allegiance. The lover stands in a subordinate relationship to his beloved; submission is usually one-sided. The poet or the knight offers unconditioned service and personal royalty to his lady without necessarily possessing her body. Rather often, it is the lover's obligation to protect the lady's chastity and reputation by renouncing his own desire.

So Parsanius earnestly defends the self-control and self-restraint of Socrates, his beloved sage (S 47). The image of the beloved object, like that of the lady in courtly love poetry, beautiful, remote, cruel, chaste, is only a vision. In other words, Beauty is immaterial in the poet's eye. In Parsanius's relation to his beloved, except for the "beard," there isn't any visual depiction of the beloved object, as we have in Agathon's and Aristophanes' accounts. In a sense, courtly love is the love for an idea. The beloved stands for all adorable ideas that the lover believes in his mind's eye. Courtly love ends in renunciation or self-sacrifice. But the lover takes renunciation as an idealization of love, and self-sacrifice as the consummation of his virtue. By proving his virtue he attains the ideal of his love, so that virtue and love become one. "Virtue" in courtly love differs from "virtue" in epic love. It prioritizes the purity in motive; whereas epic love stresses duty in love.

In the novel, the love stories in Conrad's *Under Western Eyes*, Hemingway's *Across the River into the Trees*, and Calvino's *Cosmicomics* are in a way modern transformations of courtly love. In such "love stories," as Kathryn Hume says of Calvino's *Cosmicomics*, "one can make love to the object of one's vision, or can photograph it."[13]

Stage III: Eryximachus and Modernist Love

Aristophanes ought to take the next turn, but here we have a little narrative "fake." "Whether from surfeit or from some other cause," Aristophanes is suffering from a hiccup. He asks Eryximachus, the doctor, either to cure his hiccup or speak in his place. Eryximachus readily accepts his challenge by replying that he will do both. He offers his medical knowledge to teach Aristophanes how to stop a hiccup, which in a way helps to establish the voice of his authority at the dinner party before he opens his speech.

The disruption of the narrative sequence is a common metafictive device: digression. In metafiction, digression arises out of thematic necessity. The progression of Plato's theory of Love still goes steadily undigressed, well-controlled, and well-contained in a vessel of feminine fiction sailing amid the stream of narrative consciousness. The necessity probably arises from the need to redress the balance between the soul and the body at this moment. Now that Parsanius has just elevated Love beyond the physical realm, and Phaedrus has arbitrarily bounded natural passion by social contract, it is high time to address the natural need of the body and its function in matters of Love. In such matters, Eryximachus, with his "professional experience as a doctor," as he claims, serves as the ideal speaker, and he proves wiser than Freud.

For Freud, good appetite brings good health. For Eryximachus, a good appetite is no guarantee of good health; what matters is good taste for good food. He teaches choice, discretion, and quality in matters of Love: "Similarly in my profession it is a matter of no little skill to make the right use of men's appetite for rich food, so that they may enjoy the pleasure it brings without incurring disease" (S 56). What he means by "the right use" is not necessarily restricted by moral principle, but rather by the law of nature that medical science has discovered as professional knowledge.

Eryximachus accepts Parsanius's distinction of Common Love and Heavenly Love, but he modifies the two categories. He designates Heavenly

Love to Urania, muse of astronomy, and Common Love to Polyhymnia, muse of oratory or sacred poetry. By so doing, he places the heavenly design high above the human design. His theory contains the seed of modern scientific thinking. For him, heavenly design is not composed of mythology, but astronomy. He recognizes astronomy as "a department of knowledge" which will inform men of "the function of divination" (S 57). Divinity is neither the absolute heavenly will nor within the soul of man, but knowable through scientific discovery. The human design, in his account, is language. Language for him is also a science, which can be invented through technical experiments. Eryximachus is aware of the gap between words and their meaning, as I mentioned before, and for that matter, he is very careful with language. He knows how to manipulate the signifiers. When he modifies Parsanius's conception of Common Love and Heavenly Love, he actually substitutes the two types of Love with a new set of identities—two muses instead of two sexes.

He views nature as an alien existence outside the language system. The resources of his theory are not limited to literary tropes and literary convention, but extend to primitive arts, music, medicine, and science. He encounters nature in its silence. He adores primitive instincts, "the bodies of all animals and plants which grow in the earth." His theory proposes that a natural harmony between the body and the soul lies in the union between a man and a woman; physical love provides a necessity of balance between natural elements. He believes that the harmony of all elements in the universe depends on the humor of seasons (S 54-55). There is an Oriental touch in his medical theory, his conception of the cosmos, and his philosophy.

Eryximachus hardly mentions conjugal love, in spite of his belief in the physical union between man and woman. Never for a moment in his account does he worship marriage. He only suggests that "Love has other objects in other spheres of action" (S 54). His scientific approach to the theory of Love, his detachment from the divine, social, and linguistic hierarchy that alienates human nature, and his Oriental inclinations shown in both his philosophical attitude and his medical theory turn out to be modernists' rediscoveries through the influence of Freud and Jung. His love of nature plants the seed of German naturalism.

A generation of the modernists is to share his philosophy. The philosophy of "blood consciousness" that D. H. Lawrence develops in *Women in Love* is a typical example; commingled with Nietzsche's Dionysian intoxication, Lawrence turns Eryximachus's theory into the religion of modernist love.

Stage IV: Aristophanes and Postmodernist Love

After the modernist movement is over, the universe "falls into two separate halves." The "bridge" breaks apart. Love "cannot hold," mere alienation "is loosened upon the world." The West takes the role of Aristophanes, the black comedian, an Irish comic mode. Self-love, homosexuality, castration, and "laughteers" dance with Death in the Theater of the Absurd.

"As for what I am going to say, don't watch me too strictly . . . it may be downright absurd" (S 58). "Absurd" happens to be Aristophanes' word. It is with that word that he prefaces his stylistic ambiguity. His Theater of the Absurd turns out to be the most brilliant and sensational panegyric of all, to our postmodern taste. Now that Eryximachus's theory of the inadequacy of language has been laid out, Aristophanes' speech is totally liberated from the rational discourse. He delights in nothing but black humor and mad fantasy. He rakes up fabulous stories about the hermaphrodite as a third sex. The hermaphrodite, he imagines, comes from the moon, partakes of the nature of both sun and earth. In other words, such a creature is self-sufficient in procreation, has no need for the other sex; it contains both sexes in itself. Thus he negates Eryximachus's theory that love between man and woman is a natural necessity. At the same time, he develops Parsanius's theory of men's love for men with a spirit of democracy. He claims that the object of men's love for men is neither a superior being nor a young boy, but his equal, his original self, his lost soul.

> Each of us then is the mere broken tally of a man, the result of a bisection which has reduced us to a condition like that of flat fish, and each of us is perpetually in search of his corresponding tally. (S 62)

One must acknowledge that his narcissism is the great product of a democratic age, and with it comes sterility. If man's love is to search for his "self same thing," Love turns out to be the means and end by itself, and it is impotent.

But the black comedian is not a materialist; he is able to conceive the hermaphrodite as the symbol of the phallic. He describes such a specimen as a gigantic potent race, the most formidable power, a threat to the divine right of gods, the tyranny of Zeus. Then with impressive literary talent displayed in a text of pleasure, which involves all kinds of sexual metaphors—intercourse, ejaculation, castration, masochism, lesbianism, and so on, not unlike Beckett's "Molloy sucking stone"—he exhausts and ruins "the pile of stony rubbish" in "The Waste Land" of Modernism.[14] His ultimate cry of Love is a nostalgic longing:

> It is from this distant epoch, then that we may date the innate love which human beings feel for one another, and love which restores us to our ancient state by attempting to weld two beings into one and to heal the wounds which humanity suffered. (S 62)

These "two beings" reappear in Beckett's "Cartesian Centaur"—Molloy splits himself into two parts through a mystic vision: A and C are lost "in the country, of an evening, on a deserted road"; they know each other "perhaps," but they "don't pass each other by."[15]

Aristophanes is the progenitor of postmodern love. His comic style generates a cock-and-bull story. He describes the Hermaphrodites— "these people could walk upright like us in either direction backwards and forwards"—as though they were riding Uncle Tobby's hobby horse. But unlike Sterne, Aristophanes' humor is black, full of violence and pathos. His Hermaphrodites, with their "circular shape and hook-like method of progression" (S 60), are progenitors of Vonnegut's Tralfamadorians and the "spoon-like" corpses in the battlefields. Vonnegut, in writing his war fiction, sounds as dramatic and philosophical as Aristophanes: "There were five sexes on Tralfamadore, each of them performing a step necessary in the creation of a new individual. They looked identical to Billy—because their sex differences were all in the fourth dimension."[16] Vonnegut the postmodernist speaks Aristophanes' language, as does Beckett, "the black comedian."

Stage V: Agathon and Utopian Love

While the West is "waiting for Godot," the East accepts the fate of Agathon, the romantic tragedian. Agathon fears ruin and flees from everything that belongs to an old age. He walks away from the Homeric tradition, wandering in Love not War. Sensitive, tender, infatuated with youth, he walks barefoot, softly, stepping neither upon the earth nor over men's heads. He embodies a pure ideality. He cares not if there is a food shortage, "for everyone willingly obeys Love in everything, and where there is mutual consent there is also what 'the law, the sovereign ruler of society' proclaims to be right" (S 70). Agathon's world is a utopian "autocracy," a Russian mode. There the ideal of universal comrade love is supposed to be idolized, and Love reigns as the God of a new culture:

> It is Love who empties us of the spirit of estrangement and fills us with the spirit of kinship; who makes possible such mutual intercourse as this, who presides over festivals, dances, sacrifices; who bestows good-humor and banishes surliness, whose gift is the gift of good-will and never of ill-will. (S 72).

Stage VI: Diotima and Romantic Love

Now we are not far from the ideal state of Platonic love, which has been delayed so far: the voice of authority and wisdom of Socrates. Remarkably, the narrative style has changed from a dramatic performance to a philosophical discourse. The language of the philosopher has its cost; as Karsten Harries puts it, "for the sake of clarity and distinctness he [the philosopher] surrenders the concrete and the sensuous."[17] In spite of the fact that Socrates was impressed with the fancy rhetoric exemplified in the style of a dramatist and a poet, he himself speaks in the language of a philosopher. He believes that philosophical truth is nothing but "plain truth." The plain truth style is a privileged rhetoric, wisdom-wise. "Sincerity is the luxury allowed," says Emerson, "like diadems and authority, only to the highest rank, that being permitted to speak the truth, as having none above it to court or conform unto."[18]

Socrates launches his argument in the manner of philosophical inquiry, disarming Agathon by his interrogative mode, which is only appropriate for his master's status. But when he carries over that interrogative mode into his conversation with Diotima, Socrates puts himself in the position of a naive inquisitor and Diotima in the position of a privileged status of wisdom to hold the authority of absolute truth (S 15-16). Both the plain truth style and the interrogative mode prepare the audience to accept an ultimate authority in establishing Plato's theory of Love.

In his interrogation, Socrates establishes two premises that correct the theories of the previous speakers. First, he reaches the argument that "Love is in love with what he [the lover] lacks and does not possess" (S 78), which corrects Aristophanes' theory that Love is love of one's self. Second, he illustrates that "Love exists only in relation to some object" (S 77), which modifies Agathon's proposition that Love is a pure ideality.

When Agathon asks him if he assumes Love does not have beauty and grace as everyone believes, the question sets Socrates out on a project to demystify the common idealization of Love. Since such a project will turn out to be a radical theory, the plain truth style cannot sustain its strength in its argument. Thereupon, Socrates introduces Diotima to speak for him. In other words, Socrates is sagacious enough to know the limit of masculine power in speech. Whenever there is a new theory, or a revolutionary idea, like an infant born into the world, it has to be first conceived in the body of a woman. Not until the woman is ready to take her "maternal leave" can the paternal authority be claimed as the father of the son/sun—the new light.

Diotima's voice varies from the philosophical to the poetic, from that of a sage to that of a beauty, one of the rare voices that we hear in Western literature. Diotima will answer the question for Socrates. But she starts making her point with a feminine strategy appealing to feeling to deconstruct the rational concept of identifying Love as one's "mirror image." She says to Socrates: "You identified Love with the beloved object instead of with what *feels* love; that is why you thought that Love is supremely beautiful" (S 83). This premise undermines, defamiliarizes, and redefines Love as it has been idealized in the previous panegyrics.

Diotima's account of Love contains the initial sketches of romantic love. Diotima tells Socrates that Love is born of noble parentage. Contrivance, the son of Invention, fathers him with Poverty in Zeus's garden. As Poverty is pregnant the day the beautiful Aphrodite is born, her son Love must come into being about eight months after Aphrodite is born. Poverty being Love's "mother nature," Love does not have good fortune; and because of his humble maternal lineage, he becomes an outcast from Zeus's household. Yet by character he is a willing exile. His mother's blood keeps him always in touch with the poor, so that he never minds being "shoeless and homeless." He is stoic enough to endure hard weather. He enjoys his liberty sleeping outdoors or on staircases. But he is neither dull nor vulgar. He has quite a good taste for both wisdom and beauty:

> But, being also his father's son, he schemes to get for himself whatever is beautiful and good; he is bold and forward and strenuous, always devising tricks like a cunning huntsman; he yearns after knowledge and is full of resource and is a lover of wisdom all his life, a skillful magician, an alchemist, a true sophist. (S 82)

It is remarkable that in spite of his talent and huntsmanship, Love does not hunt for fortune. Love is a born anticapitalist: "What he wins he always loses, is neither rich nor poor, neither wise nor ignorant" (S 82). He haunts Zeus' garden not for the inheritance of wealth, but for the beauty of Aphrodite: "He has also an innate passion for the beautiful, and so for the beauty of Aphrodite herself, he became her follower and servant" (S 82). He pursues Aphrodite solely for "the beauty of Aphrodite herself" without any interest in marriage or children. His love is idealistic, but different from the love of Parsanius or Aristophanes; he is neither in worship of wisdom nor longing for the soul. Son of Contrivance, "he is wise already" (S 82), and he has never sold his soul to the devil. His love of Aphrodite is natural, a "desire for the perpetual possession of good" (S 86). "There is indeed a theory," claims Diotima: "Love is not desire either of the half or of the whole, unless that half or whole happens to be good" (S 85).

Diotima's presentation of Love projects the model of romantic love. romantic Love is Platonic. It survives or suspires on an idea—a belief in the goodness of the beautiful Other. The Other is, and is not, the self, but better and more than the self. Take a typical novel of romantic love, *Wuthering Heights*, for example. While contemporary critics take delight in Catherine Earnshaw's declaration "I am Heathcliff," they might have neglected Catherine's deeper understanding of love and of herself: "Heathcliff is *more than* my self." In him, she identifies the wild spirit, one with the cliffs and clouds, which she admires as the ideal consummation of herself; yet she knows herself too well to claim that part as her possessed "self." The romantic lover has highly idealized expectations of the beloved object. As Diotima suggests, love does not exist unless the other half "happens to be good." Once Catherine Earnshaw recognizes a vengeful demon in Heathcliff, she wills her death in a fortnight.

Romantic love dies the instant the heart fails. The reason why romantic love could endure the change of times and circumstances, separation and distance, life and death, lies in that the lovers both believe the heart endures. The lovers' union suspires on the union of the heart alone. Whereas in courtly love, the purity of motive relies on one side only, romantic love demands an equal degree of absolutism. Yet in spite of the lovers' absolute devotion to each other, the physical possession of the beloved object, which is of first importance in epic love, is but the last concern in romantic love. The fact that Catherine Earnshaw has been married to Edgar Linton does not change Heathcliff's love for her. With the conviction of a romantic idea that his Cathy will never love Linton the way she cares for himself, he's not even jealous of Linton. Outside of her bedroom and outside of her wedlock, he loves her all the same, and evermore. Her daughter by Linton does not strike him as an object of resentment but of another idealized self, through which he even fancies that he may accomplish his second project of Love's immortal design. That love does not change because of physical bond seems to be true with other novels of romantic love, such as Fitzgerald's *The Great Gatsby* and Thomas Hardy's *Jude the Obscure*. To Gatsby, the fact that Daisy is married and has a daughter with Tom does not change his love. In Hardy's novel, Jude's love for Sue changes neither before nor after her legal marriage.

In romantic love stories, the physical presence of the beloved seems to matter less than the spiritual affinity that supplies the "innate passion," the food of love. At least, the physical beauty is usually discounted in comparison with that in either epic or courtly love. The beloved does not have to be the most beautiful woman by appearance, or the most handsome man in the eyes of society, as is the case in epic love. The very imperfection of physical appearance, as it were, only removes the beloved object from the visible world and social norm. Actually, the lover's gaze is constantly fixed upon an innate beauty that he knows as well as his own naked self. That is why in romantic love stories, incest love is a more popular motif than love at first sight.

The image of the beloved is conceivably possessed with a metaphysical quality that uplifts the lover's gaze beyond the mortal self and the material world around him. Since the lover's goal is to better himself, to achieve immortality, as Plato teaches, through the union with the beautiful and the good, the Lover is always ready to give up, even destroy, his present self. In his self-destruction, however, the romantic lover is not unequipped with the kind of heroic stature and conquering power as the epic lover is. But his task is not to defend and protect society, but to overthrow or demolish it. By character, the Romantic lover is a nonconformist, uncompromising with the Establishment. Most novels of romantic love address the theme of the insolvable conflict between the individual self and the establishment of law and society. If society has to be preserved, the lovers must die, or the consummation of romantic love will be built upon the ruins of the existing social structure. There is no possible compromise between love and society. In that sense, Romantic love is as revolutionary in its ideology as it is violent and destructive.

Romantic love takes the form of tragedy. The lover almost never ends up in marriage, but in tragic death. The power of death in romantic love cannot be ignored, because death is a positive force that brings fundamental changes to society. Catherine's death castrates the power of Heathcliff's

Satanic revenge. Heathcliff's death brings the hope of a union between Hareton the deprived and Cathy the lost soul. Classic romantic love novels, such as Goethe's *Elective Affinities* (1809) or Matthew Lewis's *The Monk* (1794), often end with a final scene of the grave, as if death is being celebrated. The scene is usually depicted with the images of nature, a penetrating vision of life and death, suggestive of incarnation and rebirth. The narrator shall make a promise of the lovers' reunion through death and a return to nature. This is the way Lockwood ends his story:

> I lingered round them, under that benign sky; watched the moths fluttering among the heath and hare-bells; listened to the soft wind breathing through the grass, and wondered how any one could ever imagine unquiet slumbers for the sleepers in that unquiet earth.[19]

And his promise is sonorous, vibrating, breaking through time and space: "Together they would brave Satan and all his legions." Such is the power of death in romantic love—it aims at future changes.

In its sensibility, romantic love is Eastern. Its uncompromising revolutionary idealism, conceived in the power of willed death, is celebrated in the East more than in the West. Its literary imagination takes roots in natural and rural settings. Romantic love thrives in agrarian society and dies in capitalist economy. It faces insufferable destruction in an age of commercialism and industrialization. On the other hand, the representation of romantic "love stories" such as Fitzgerald's *The Great Gatsby* functions as a powerful challenge to the values of capitalism. I shall return to the topic in Chapter Five, "Romantic Love as an Antithesis to the Epic: Faulkner's *Go Down, Moses*."

Stage VII: Diotima and Aesthetic Love

The essential nature of Love having been presented from a feminine perspective, Socrates' narrative style returns to philosophical inquiry. Diotima still takes the lead in the conversation. She leads Socrates through the gateway of Zeus's garden to the entrance of the India Cave. Meditating upon "the mystery of Love," she ushers him into a far advanced stage, the stage of abstraction. Plato begins to explore the idea of Love's immortality.

Diotima formulates a new theory: "Beauty is the goddess who presides over birth," and Love is the "begetter of ideas." While Beauty has the maternal instinct of giving birth, Love cherishes a strong progeny, a mortal desire, "to procreate and bring forth in beauty" an "immortal renown and a glorious reputation" for them both—the imperishable beauty of immortality (S 87, 90). In order to achieve immortality, those who have "the progeny of wisdom and virtue . . . long to beget spiritually, not physically." Therefore, instead of babies, they beget poetry. So poets are immortal lovers. Diotima mentions Homer and Hesiod, and she proclaims that not only poets but also craftsmen of arts are such begetters—lovers of aesthetic beauty.

Proust's *Remembrance of Things Past* is conceived in such a model, the model of aesthetic love. Proust casts this model in his "Overture," insinuatingly conceiving himself as a begetter of beauty:

> Sometimes, too, as Eve was created from a rib of Adam, a woman should be born during my sleep from some strain in the position of my thighs. Conceived from the pleasure I was on the point of consum-mating, she it was I imagined, who offered me that pleasure. My body conscious that its own warmth was permeating hers, would strive to become one with her, and I would awake. The rest of humanity seemed very remote in comparison with this woman whose company I had left but a moment ago; my cheek was still warm from her kiss, my body ached beneath the weight of hers.[20]

A woman being born from the loins of a man, like a miracle, is produced through the art of sleep and memory, which is consistent with the Platonic philosophy of artistic procreation, as I discussed in the earlier part of this chapter. In his conception of his love story with Albertine, Marcel is incurably in love with an aesthetic object instead of a real woman. Perverted sexuality, as in the case of Proust, is still fruitful, provided the lover is after beauty rather than the body. It produces incredible works of art. The fertility of aesthetic love is a mode of production that Henry Sussman in his philosophical study of Proust calls the mode of the "Pregnant Invert." Sussman interestingly conceives that "Proust fashions both a pregnant discourse and a pregnant narrative structure."[21] As he rightly points out:

> On the highest level of hypothesis, homosexuality becomes a matrix of aesthetic activity, a site of principles and operations that throughout Proust undermine and complicate the surface level of reality.[22]

The "Pregnant Invert" is an immortal being that impregnates

postmodern fiction. The French poststructuralists have reproduced Proust's art with a new aesthetic theory, Barthes' theory of "the Pleasure of the Text." Beyond pleasure there is bliss. A higher stage of Love is yet to come; but when we reaches that higher stage, the rest of humanity appears to be even remoter from the sensual world of aesthetic love.

Stage VIII: Socrates and Philosophical Love

The final stage of Love is love of absolute beauty in oblivion of all physical, moral, scientific, aesthetic, and knowledgeable experiences. It is love of divinity itself, a religious experience, a philosophical stage. Yet to be initiated into the divine world of love, the lover has to make a sacrifice—relinquishing his self-interest and human desire. Not all "lovers" may reach that stage of being—"the perfect revelation" of the ultimate "mystery of Love" (S 92).

As if to emphasize the sacrifice of the lover, Diotima pauses, as if to make sure that Socrates is ready to be initiated into "the India Cave." She issues Socrates a tragic warning as his "guardian angel":

> So far, Socrates, I have dealt with love-mysteries into which even
> you could probably be initiated, but whether you could grasp the
> perfect revelation to which they lead the pilgrim if he does not
> stray from the right path, I do not know. (S 92)

Socrates may still withdraw from his "passage to India." His guardian angel lets him know where he stands:

> The man who has been guided thus far in the mysteries of love,
> and who has directed his thoughts towards examples of beauty in
> due and orderly succession, will suddenly have revealed to him
> as he approaches the end of his initiation a beauty whose nature
> is marvelous indeed, the final goal, Socrates, of all his previous
> efforts. (S 93)

Socrates is positive: "The good man would pursue the right way" (S 92), thus he enters the cave, in which Truth, philosophical truth, shines in its absolute beauty, in eternity. "This above all others, (now close your eyes,) my dear Socrates"—Diotima ushers him in—"this is the region where a man's life should be spent, in the contemplation of absolute beauty."

Socrates is on the point of ecstasy, swooning like a fallen woman; "And then the Windows failed—and then/I could not see to see" (Dickinson 465). So Diotima opens another window, a window of heavenly bliss, to let in some fresh air and help him sustain his vision in the darkness of the cave:

> Once you have seen that, you will not value in terms of gold or rich clothing or of the beauty of boys and young men, the sight of whom at present throws you and many people like you into such an ecstasy that, provided that you could always enjoy the sight and company of your darlings, you would be content to go without food and drink, if that were possible, and to pass your whole time with them in the contemplation of their beauty. (S 94)

Yet still having some fear of man's inability to control his appetite over the feast of pure mystic beauty, unsure "if that were possible," "the woman from Mantinea" boosts Socrates in an exaltation of spirit lest he fall. Over his head, rather than below his knees, she pleads passionately. The love of solitude, she argues, is the privilege of being and becoming God, the lover and the beloved in one. What an irresistible supplication from a "womanhead," from the moon! The persuasive power of a feminine spirit, the spirit of renunciation, the ultimate mystery of Love, makes the "goodman," the philosopher, ready and wanting to quit all earthly desires, because what she promises him is a better world:

> What may we suppose to be the felicity of the man who sees absolute beauty in its essence, pure and unalloyed, who, instead of a beauty tainted by human flesh and color and a mass of perishable rubbish, is able to apprehend divine beauty where it exists apart and alone? Do you think that it will be a poor life that a man leads who has his gaze fixed in that direction . . . ? Do you not see that in that region alone where he sees beauty with the faculty capable of seeing it, will he be able to bring forth not mere reflected images of goodness but true goodness, because he will be in contact not with a reflection but with the truth? And having brought forth and nurtured true goodness he will have the privilege of being beloved of God, and becoming, if ever a man can, immortal himself. (S 94-95)

The ultimate reality of Love is the attainment of Goodness, the attainment of absolute truth, beauty, and wisdom in a Godhead. This Godhead is the immortalized soul of Plato's Philosopher Ruler he had created in *The Republic*; in *The Symposium*, the Philosopher Ruler is crowned the legitimate lover of the divine world. I will further discuss this concept in relation to Plato's political philosophy when I come to Fielding and Faulkner.

With the above quoted remark, Socrates finishes his feminine fiction and reaches the conclusion of his theory. The divinity he has reached "where he sees beauty with the faculty capable of seeing it," procreates Emerson's "Oversoul." Religious sentiments embedded in philosophical inquiry, Oriental mysticism nurtured in transcendental spirit, attainment of eternal truth and beauty through the renunciation of material interest, are seeds of the Emersonian mode, where East and West once had a blind date.

It must be noted that the renunciation of physical contact with women, with the lower order of existence, is neither Greek nor Oriental philosophy. It might be a later addition from Christian theology. In Plato, the renunciation of worldly interest is not as simple a negation of the physical world as Enlightenment thinkers take for granted. A reexamination of Plato's text shows that it is the last stage of human experience, a forgetting of one's past, an obliteration of all human follies one has committed so far, the final accumulation of human knowledge and wisdom, a breakthrough of human consciousness. But in order to reach that stage, one must leave behind solid footprints in various stages of real life. The legitimacy of the philosophical lover, in Diotima's words as I quoted above, is "due to an orderly succession," a legitimate succession to the altar built upon the solid steps of the lover's "all previous efforts" in search for Love. These steps include earthly joy and sensual pleasure to begin with. In Diotima's theory, "the right way of approaching or being initiated into the mysteries of love" is

> to begin with examples of beauty in this world, and using them
> as steps to ascend continually with that absolute beauty as one's
> aim, from one instance of physical beauty to two and from two
> to all, then from physical beauty to moral beauty, and from moral
> beauty to the beauty of knowledge until from the knowledge of
> various kinds one arrives at the supreme knowledge whose sole
> object is that absolute beauty, and knows at last what absolute
> beauty is. (S 94)

In other words, Plato has laid out a model that consists of five successive stages in man's search for Love: (1) the love of physical beauty; (2) the love of the soul, of moral integrity and public action; (3) the love of sciences, scientific knowledge; (4) the love of aesthetic beauty, artistic creativity; (5) the love of absolute beauty, philosophical truth. This succession is an organic movement from Love of the particular to that of the universal, from a small self to an enlarged sense of Self, from a small love, the lowercased love, to the capitalized Love.

In Plato, physical contact with a beautiful object is needed in order to beget noble sentiments when the lover is young. (Fielding dramatizes this idea in *Tom Jones*.) But the lover is expected to grow and improve. "Later he will observe that physical beauty in any person is closely akin to physical beauty in any other, and that beauty exhibited in all bodies is one and the same" (S 92). Once he reaches this stage, "he will relax the intensity of his passion for one particular person, because he will realize that such a passion is beneath him and of small account" (S 92). "The lover will be compelled to contemplate beauty as it exists in activities and institutions," and be led to consider physical beauty "a poor thing" in comparison with the beauty in public life (S 92-93).

The love of public life, so called "moral love" in Plato, is still a lower stage of love. "From morals he [the lover] must be directed to the sciences"—the love of wisdom, which, he believes, "may bring forth in the abundance . . . many beautiful and magnificent sentiments and ideas." Making love with these "beautiful and magnificent sentiments and ideas," he will be "strengthened and increased in stature," until at last, "he catches the sight of one unique science," whose object is the beauty of Truth (S 92-93). That "unique science" is philosophy, and the Love of philosophical truth is the highest stage in Platonic love.

In this ultimate stage of Love, Love is "indifferent." Eliot praises such a state of being in "Four Quartets":

> Love is most nearly itself
> When here and now cease to matter. (Eliot, "East Coker," 129)
>
>   . . . .
>
> Attachment to self and to things and to persons, detachment
> From self and from things and from persons; and growing
> Between them, indifference
>
>   . . .
>
> Though never indifferent. (Eliot, "Little Gidding," 142)

In the novel, Ralph Ellison's *Invisible Man* approaches such a moment of indifference. When the Invisible Man withdraws from the world to write his story in the dark, dark cellar, it is a moment of total obliteration of his former existence:

> I denounce and defend . . . I condemn and I affirm. . . . And I
> defend because in spite of all I find that I love. In order to get
> some of it down I have to love.[23]

With the conviction that to love is to write and to write is to live, Ellison
merges aesthetic love with philosophical love. The philosophical fictionist
writes in the faith of Platonic love.

Stage IX: Alcibiades and Novelistic Love

> Go, go, go, said the bird: human kind
> Cannot bear very much reality. (Eliot, "Burnt Norton," 118)

If Socrates has attained the ultimate reality of Love, it is certainly not the
kind of reality that mortal sense can bear or mortal sight may penetrate. As
Emily Dickinson teaches us through the revelation of poetry:

> Success in Circuit lies
> Too bright for our infirm Delight
> The Truth's superb surprise
> As Lightning to the Children eased
> With explanation kind
> The Truth must dazzle gradually
> Or every man be blind— (Dickinson 1129)

Joseph Conrad, a novelist who also writes in the Platonic tradition, well
understands such a human condition: "The most idealistic conceptions of
love and forbearance must be clothed in flesh as it were before they can be
made understandable."[24] So in the last episode of Plato's *The Symposium*,
Alcibiades' mock panegyric is designed to awaken the audience from the
dreams of the Indian Cave, from the beautiful and the sublime world, back
to the feast of food and wine. Socrates' own account of his renunciation of
the material world has left us with a tragic spirit. Alcibiades' story, in which
he tells how he failed to seduce Socrates when the two of them spent nights
together, provides us with a comic vision, a mortal sight of the ultimate
reality of a philosophical lover. At the same time, it affirms Socrates'
"self-control and courage," the sacrifice he has made to be initiated into the
mystery of Love (S 107).

The affirmation may serve as a defence against the public charges of Socrates' character. Thus the hidden agenda of Plato's *Symposium* comes to light. His political intention, though unsaid, is nevertheless spoken in the "internal persuasive discourse" of Alcibiades' dramatic presentation. It speaks for the sainthood of Socrates, and argues for his innocence in his relationship with young boys who admired him. Whether it is historically true or not is irrelevant, because Plato is proposing a philosophy, a role model, instead of tracing biographical or historical "facts." But historically speaking, one recognizes that novelistic love ever since Plato has always contained political arguments. Plato's composition of these "Greek" love stories is his last "apologia" for the ill fate and ill use of a Philosopher Ruler.

Against the public discourse of his day, only a big farce such as Alcibiades performs may achieve the humorous effect of persuasive power and, more importantly, break the limit of free speech. If Aristophanes had presented his panegyric as a dramatist, Alcibiades in his turn chooses the role of a player. Instead of composing his love panegyric the bird acts it out. "Crowned with a thick wreath of ivy and violets" and "helped in by a flute-girl," the "little Tippler" has come in from the "window"—"Leaning against the—Sun—!" He leans upon the "doorway," that midway position, between the unfathomable depth of God and man's incurable desire for love. He performs his role as the messenger as well as the interpreter of Socrates. The function of such a mediator is identical to the function of novelistic love that I previously discussed. Now, before "the veiled face" of Socrates, "the Sun," Alcibiades "forgoes his very self" by self-parody and self-mockery, pouring out the bitter, sour, "awful truth" from "a liquor never brewed."

Of all the panegyrics presented so far that are either mythical or imaginary, this last and most incredulous account turns out to be a real life story. And more absurdly, while the others all praise Love seriously, Alcibiades mocks it in a parody. He really has little to propose in terms of an ideal, the others having all proposed it as such in one way or another. So his role, more than anybody else's, proves to be a pure instrument of presentation and performance. He plays his role self-consciously. He mocks Socrates: "[Y]ou produce the same effect by mere words without any instrument" (S 101). He serves Socrates as his "instrument," in his own words, "filling in the hollows" of Socrates' theoretical "piping," telling the "untold stories" in Socrates' philosophical discourse. He is Plato's idea and, indeed, Socrates' naked "bodyguard"—his "body" language.

"Agathon, give me some of those ribands to make a wreath for his head too, for a truly wonderful head it is," says Alcibiades, his own head abrim with spirit. With the ribands Agathon gives to him, "Dionysus" crowns the "bearded goat" as poet laureate. At this point, we've already been told that the poet is the maker of human speech. Speech is what makes a villain fall in love with a saint. Alcibiades makes his confession of love, he adores the sound, the "melodies" of Socrates' "piping." His overwhelming admiration of Socrates' eloquence (S 101) creates a kind of sentimental effect, which brings forth the emotional power that Socrates' sainthood bears upon a mortal being. Since Socrates' power of Love lies in his "words," his "philosophical talk," Alcibiades shows that the ultimate power of Love is the power of language and philosophy.

While he is fascinated with the power of his speech, he also feels so sorry for the hollowness inside Socrates' "flute" (S 100). Taking his liberty as a doomed mortal, he comically expresses his ironic sorrow for Socrates' incapacity to be human. There is definitely a chill in his mock-heroic stance and pathos. The implied message is a tragic irony: The top of the ladder is a lonely place. The truth he reveals inspires awe, if not terror. Thus the literary effect of his account is practically tragicomic. It turns out to be Plato's idea—to end his drama by inventing an ingenious ideal mode—the tragicomic mode. Plato reveals his artistic intention before he drops the curtain:

> Aristodemus did not remember most of what passed . . . but the main point was that the man who knew how to write a comedy could also write a tragedy, and that a skillful tragic writer was capable of being also a comic writer. (S 113)

The questions is: Who is that skillful writer? Plato himself turns out to be such a writer, a truly experimental dramatist, a metafictionist. If we may further ask the question of what the form of Plato's drama is, a tragedy or a comedy, we find it is both and neither—a tragicomedy. Love is thoroughly discussed but deferred, never fulfilled in the end. He has developed his drama through various stages and forms finally into a self-parodic mock-epic that dissolves catharsis in a comic relief and fills the comic world with tragic sublimity.

In effect, Alcibiades' "love story" fills up the vacuum of the unspeakable "bodily" truth that Socrates is unable or unfit to articulate in his broken heavenly talk. As a lover and the beloved of Socrates, Alcibiades exemplifies what Diotima has predicted: He is the beholder of "not mere reflected images of goodness but true goodness, because he is in contact not with a reflection but with the truth" (S 94-95). Of course he only fulfills such a role in a comic sense by playing a clown, while he makes Socrates a tragic hero. Even so, his comic performance affirms Socrates' immortality by touching the absolute beauty with a human possibility. His account bridges the gap between the ideality and the reality of Love, the still point of that mystic gaze and the presence of bodily warmth, an abstraction and a representation in the art of storytelling. Alcibiades performs the very function of novelistic love as an agency between idea and reality, art and philosophy, fiction and theory.

Such an ending achieves a healing effect. "One man of healing shall a host outweigh" (S 99). Now if we recall the line Alcibiades quotes from Homer's *Iliad* as a "preface" to his "love story," we realize that the insane condition of the Tippler is probably a fake, since he seems to know his part inside out when he pops in birdlike to play the last scene. However marginal his account appears to be, his power of demystification shall all the myth making "outweigh." Or, we may assume, it is Plato's idea to put in his speech that power once endowed upon Diotima—the maternal instinct of healing man's alienation from God.

In a sense, Alcibiades' farce is another feminine fiction. The difference lies in that Diotima had to remain behind the screen, whereas the "painted bird" hops in, indulgently feasts upon the table. This is because, by appearance, he passes for a "man." In reality, he is half-man, half-bird—a man with a womanhead. The identity of his character blurs the gender distinction. Alcibiades is possessed with both the feminine "truth in wine" and the masculine "wisdom of a woman." This "Pregnant Invert" fertilizes the bed of Socrates' philosophical discourse, and thereupon he begets a beauty of "truth's superb surprise."

Aesthetic love, as I argued before, is still fertile and fruitful, because it produces works of Art for mortal speculation. Philosophical love often suffers from the death instinct. Losing touch with earthly interest, it grows into cynicism. The ideal situation is a balance between the two, that which takes the form of novelistic love.

Novelistic love is by itself the healer and the fertilizer. It accommodates various modes of love and dramatic forms to procreate a mode that becomes pluralistic. In the novel, Nabokov's *Lolita* features such a pluralistic style. The "love story" is a comic tragedy; the style of the confessor/narrator is also self-parodic, a humming bird, "Humbert Humbert" by name. As an immigrant novelist in an immigrant country writing about his immigrant experience, about his love for "Lolita . . . my America," Nabokov begets an American beauty that we behold with such pleasure. In *Lolita*, all exotic modes and models of love converge and diverge—the epic, the courtly, the modernist and the postmodernist, the utopia and the romantic, the aesthetic and the philosophical—a pluralistic mode of novelistic love. Nabokov brings in the Russian, the French, the Irish, the Italian modes of Love to heal the German and fertilize the Emersonian. The pluralist mode is the American model—the product of a "melting pot."

It is Nabokov, it might be said, who revived the Platonic tradition of novelistic love in American postmodern fiction and who recreated in the American novel the style of Pope and Fielding. From Plato to Emerson, Pope to Nabokov, Sterne to Barth, Fielding to Faulkner, Conrad to Vonnegut, literary inheritance, as the Russian formalist Shklovsky contends, passes down not necessarily from father to son, but from uncle to nephew.

Notes

1. Plato, *The Symposium*, trans. with Introduction by Walter Hamilton (London: Penguin, 1987), 9. Subsequent references will be indicated as S. "Symposium" also means "dinner party."
2. *Ralph Waldo Emerson: Representative Selections*, ed. Frederic I. Carpenter (New York: American Book Co., 1934), 231-32.
3. John Barth, *Lost in the Funhouse* (New York: Doubleday, 1988), 72, 73.
4. Laurence Sterne, *Tristram Shandy*, Norton Critical Edition, ed. Howard Anderson (New York: W. W. Norton and Co., 1980) IV, xv, 211.
5. Arthur Christy, "Introduction," *The Orient in American Transcendentalists* (New York: Columbia University Press, 1932), 34-38.
6. Friedrich Nietzsche, "The Will to Power in Art," in *A Modern Book of Esthetics*, 5th ed., ed. Melvin Rader (New York: Holt, Rinehart & Winston, 1979) 103.
7. D. H. Lawrence, *Women in Love* (London: Penguin, 1987), 361.
8. See George Klosko, *The Development of Plato's Political Theory* (New York: Methuen, 1986), 145.
9. Samuel Beckett, *Malone Dies*, in *Molloy, Malone Dies, The Unnameable: Three Novels* (New York: Grove Press, 1965), 181.
10. James Joyce, *A Portrait of the Artist as a Young Man: Text, Criticism, and Notes*, ed. Chester G. Anderson (New York: Penguin, 1986), 208.
11. In Richard Ellmann, *James Joyce* (New York: Oxford University Press, 1959), 74.
12. Desmond Lee, "Introduction" to Plato's *The Republic*, trans. Desmond Lee, 2nd ed. (London: Penguin, 1987), 264.
13. Kathryn Hume, "Science and Imagination in Calvino's *Cosmicomics*,"

Mosaic (5 December 1982): 47-48.

14. "What are the roots that clutch, what branches grow/Out of this stony rubbish? Son of Man" (T. S. Eliot, "The Waste Land," 38).

15. Beckett, *Molloy*, 86.

16. Kurt Vonnegut, *Slaughterhouse-Five* (New York: Dell Publishing Co., 1969, 114.

17. Karsten Harries, "Metaphor and Transcendence," in *On Metaphor*, ed. Sheldon Sacks (Chicago: University of Chicago Press, 1978), 74.

18. Ralph Emerson, "Friendship," in *Selected Writings of Emerson*, ed. Donald McQuade (New York: Random House, 1981), 213.

19. Emily Bronte, *Wuthering Heights*, Norton Critical Edition, 2nd ed., ed. William M. Sale Jr. (New York: W. W. Norton & Co., 1972), 266.

20. Marcel Proust, *Remembrance of Things Past*, vol. 1, trans. S. K. Scott Moncrieff and Terence Kilmartin (New York: Random House, 1982), 4-5.

21. Henry Sussman, *The Hegelian Aftermath: Readings in Hegel, Kierkegaard, Freud, Proust, and James* (Baltimore: Johns Hopkins University Press, 1982), 229.

22. Ibid., 223.

23. Ralph Ellison, *Invisible Man* (New York: Random House, 1952), 566-67.

24. Joseph Conrad, *Under Western Eyes* (London: Penguin, 1987), 136.

Chapter Three

Epic Love and the English Novel

In the next two centuries [after Milton] the Puritan conception of marriage and sexual relations generally became the accepted code of Anglo-Saxon society to a degree unknown elsewhere; in the words of Frieda Lawrence, who must be allowed considerable expertise in the matter, "only the English have this special brand of marriage."

—Ian Watt, *The Rise of the Novel*

While reading Plato's *Symposium*, I identified Phaedrus's love panegyric as the model of epic love. Epic love celebrates individualism and marriage. In this chapter I shall discuss the idea of marriage in the eighteenth-century English novel in relation to history and politics. I argue that epic love is the dominant model in the English novel established by Richardson's *Pamela*, which becomes the capitalist mode of love; the "Pamela syndrome" is a middle-class syndrome. Fielding in *Tom Jones* is writing under the domininat model of epic love; but in a way he deviates from the norm, subverts the model, and demystifies its value system. With a different political agenda, he reappropriates in his novel a different value system.

When I propose epic love as a model, I do not intend to treat it as an equivalent to the epic as a genre or study love stories in the epic form. What I identify as epic love only shares certain features of the epic. First, epic love is also concerned with conserving or restoring the place of the individual within a dynastic consciousness of origins. On the conceptual level, the subject of epic love deals with the distribution or redistribution of social wealth and titles. Legitimacy, accordingly, becomes a central issue.

As I examined the value system of Phaedrus's panegyric in Chapter Two, epic love is materialistic and worldly. The beloved object stands in relation to the lover as a ritual prize or legal property. The beauty of the beloved being identified with a piece of social property, physical possession is a priority. The lover must "earn" the prize, not by playing pipes or singing love songs, but by demonstrating his valor or virtue. Thus love is war if the lover is to capture the object of desire. War is encouraged and justified in the name of love. In other words, the lover must prove to be "worthy" of the ritual prize established by its community. Only by community recognition can he claim the prize, or by public consensus can he own the property.

Epic love must be consummated in the public eye. The legitimacy of the lover's credit or ownership must be authorized in the form of a social contract—a lawful marriage. The settlement of marriage, consequently, comes prior to the fulfillment of passion. The novelistic intention works toward such a settlement to secure the legitimacy of the lover's place in a lawful society. In *The Epic Strain in the English Novel*, E. M. W. Tillyard suggests that "the Epic Spirit must have faith in the system of beliefs or way of life it bears witness to." [1] Indeed the epic hero seldom challenges the established value system of a society. Aggressive as he is, the epic lover is fundamentally a social conformist. He fights in order to defend or enter society. Epic love is a conservative model.

I suggested in Chapter Two that, from a comparative perspective, epic love is an English model, for only in the English novel are love stories preoccupied with marriage, public morals, social recognition, and material possessions. Great English novels—*Pamela, Tom Jones, Pride and Prejudice, David Copperfield, Jane Eyre, Vanity Fair*—all idealize marriage as the end of a love affair. In contrast with masterpiece love stories in Chinese, Russian, French, and German novels, such as *A Dream of Red Chamber, Madame Bovary, Anna Karenina, The Idiot, The Sorrows of Young Werther, Carmen, Camille, Nana,* and the like, it is arguable that the celebration of marriage in love stories, as Ian Watt may agree, as I quoted from him in the beginning of this chapter, is really "a special English brand" (137).

This hypothetical assumption can be further established by a brief speculation upon the literary tradition, national character, religious sentiments, social-economic condition, and historical events that affect the composition of the English novel in the eighteenth-century. Maurice Valency in his *In Praise of Love* has good reason to say that "True Love was never really at home in England." [2] By "True Love," he refers to the Italian mode of courtly love. As we know, the English poets from Shakespeare to Swift have always been cynical in their adaptation of the Italian mode of courtly love. Even the Cavalier poets do not strictly observe the "courtly" motif. Its demand of pure motive and high worship of a female image might be culturally and religiously disagreeable to the English sentiment even in the Renaissance. According to Ian Watt, as early as Chaucer's "Franklin's Tale," there were signs of the reconciliation between courtly love and the institution of marriage; but it is evident that the celebration of marriage is epitomized in Spenser's *Faerie Queene*. Milton's *Paradise Lost*, Watt proudly proclaims, is "the greatest and indeed the only epic of married life." So he asserts: "In the next two centuries, the Puritan conception of marriage and sexual relations generally became the accepted code of Anglo-Saxon society *to a degree unknown elsewhere*."[3]

The reticent and reserved Anglo-Saxon temperament also has a natural distaste for sentimental love, generally associated with French romance, that some critics call "romantic love." Among the English novelists, as Watt declares, "romantic love has certainly had no greater antagonist among the novelists than Defoe" (67). Neither Richardson nor Fielding took to romantic love in its French mode. Such a distaste for the Continental style is even expressed in the rising English patriotism as a defence against the threat of French interference during the period of Jacobite rebellion. To the English commoner, the very idea of adultery conceptually signified either Catholic conspiracy or the fancy luxury of the French court brought home by the Stuarts. Even the English country squires may have identifed adultery with the decadence of the city and the corruption of the court.

The economic and political momentum that impacted the social changes during the late seventeenth and early eighteenth centuries also favored the mode of Epic Love. As I proposed above, epic love deals with the distribution and redistribution of social wealth and titles. Its goal is to establish the legitimacy of the individual's place in a lawful society. The epic scope provides ample space for the "no-name" lover to display his prowess through love and war, thereby claiming his title. Marriage as the end of war promises the resettlement of a social order, or the restoration of a dynastic origin. One must remember, this was the period when England saw the reestablishment of a Protestant regime and significant redistribution of legal and political power between the crown and the parliament, the church and the government, the aristocracy and the individual man of property. Thanks to two royal marriages of the Stuart daughters (Mary in Holland and Sophia in Hanover), the Protestant regime was preserved. But the legitimacy of the English throne remained a source of national anxiety. It was unsettling, under constant threat of Jacobite revolt at home and the Pretenders' war from abroad.

This was also the period when England had accumulated its national wealth through the victory of wars and the development of a capitalist economy. The middle class, the London merchants and Dissenters, under the Bill of Rights (1689), the Tolerance Act, and a long Whig administration, had gained considerable legal rights, religious tolerance, and individual freedom. The moneyed class began to display its power not only with its economic success, but also by supporting the government in international wars and parliamentary elections. When Parliament won its supreme power over the Crown, it recognized the middle class for its proven "virtue." As the middle class earned its recognition in English society and entered national politics to claim its dues, the prospect of a "glorious marriage," in the vein of the Glorious Revolution, symbolized bloodless transformation of power. The compromi-sing nature of epic love held a special appeal to the English commoners.

Richardson's *Pamela* timely speaks of the middle-class dream. I call it the "Pamela syndrome," similar to the "middle-class syndrome" discussed in Chapter One. Even today, in the same spirit, the Pamela syndrome still dominates, by and large, the mode of love stories in popular romance, soap operas, Western movies and in a predominantly middle-class society. The prospect of a self-made and hard-earned marriage through love and war frequently projects "the American Dream" into the image of a winsome millionaire or a sexy blonde. The endeavor is certainly heroic; but the outcome often turns into boredom.

This Pamela Syndrome is a reflection of the middle-class' "self-negating impulse," to borrow Michael McKeon's more precise description, "a will to be assimilated into the aristocracy."[4] McKeon's seminal work, *The Origins of the English Novel 1600-1740*, makes a conscientious effort, as he claims, "to comprehend not only Richardson but also Fielding," thus to develop the theory of Ian Watt. However, Mckeon's class consciousness, reflected in his work, may not transcend the limits of the Pamela syndrome; rather, his comprehension of Fielding is unfortunately impaired by such a syndrome. "Tom, although of gentle lineage, is truly a bastard. Born to be hanged . . . yet basically virtuous . . . a rogue figure," says he; whereas he takes Lovelace as "the real thing": "If Lovelace is for his part a vile aristocrat, he is at least the real thing" (418). Thus McKeon ends up in close alliance with Richardson but fails to comprehend Fielding. His "progressive ideology" only speaks for the position of the middle class, thus it remains a bourgeois ideology.

Watt's theory on the rise of the English novel, widely accepted in the 1960s and 1970s, simply claims the novel to be the product and property of the middle class. He asserts that the novel is a new genre that comes into being under the influence of Locke's philosophical realism, the formation of a capitalist economy, and the rise of Protestantism; and that the novel is invented to address the needs of individualism, and the institution of marriage, as well as the power struggle between the middle class and the aristocracy. As McKeon and other critics have already pointed out, Fielding's novel certainly proposes problems for Watt's theory. I think his theory even fails to account for Defoe for reasons I shall explain shortly. As his theory consciously advocates the mode of epic love, it does speak well for the social-economic ambitions and religious beliefs of the middle class.[5] Ironically enough, Watt takes a Marxist approach to a certain degree; but he uses Marxism only to praise the "virtue" of the middle class and glorify the triumph of capitalism.

As Protestant ethics lays the foundation of the ideology of modern individualism and capitalism, epic love serves as the ideal mode of love under capitalism. In fact, it became a dominant mode when a capitalist economy was fast developing in England. It characterizes the English novel because it is about the same time the English novel popularized. In other countries, for instance, in China or Russia, the novel was popularized long before industrialization. The momentum of capitalism encourages economic competition, individual freedom, social mobility, expansion abroad, and the conquering of nature. The mode of "love and war" and "love is war" challenges the ambition of the modern individual, who struggles to establish himself in a competitive society with the opportunities a bourgeois democracy opens for him.

With *Pamela* as an exemplary model, the celebration of marriage in the English novel is mythologized. Marriage is naively idealized in God's name as the triumph of "puritanical virtue" and puritanism. In his theory on "love and the novel," Watt creates a "religious" myth that Calvinism liberates human sexuality and that legal marriage is advocated by the English Protestants to counteract adultery and celibacy, which "improved" the conditions of low-class women. What Watt fails to tell us is the political implications embedded in the name of religious beliefs. First, Watt must be over-optimistic, if not exaggeratory, in his claim that the appropriation of marriage in the eighteenth-century English novel is the triumph of puritan virtue and puritanism (156-57). To idealize marriage as the "virtue" of puritanism is virtually middle-class propaganda. Its real objective is but to domesticate those below and castrate those above, particularly in this historical period. Practically, in the eighteenth century, marriage was institutionalized by law to transfer more political power from the church to the bench. In other words, the institution of marriage was a political counteract. The Marriage Bill, which had met with strong Tory opposition and eventually passed in 1757, was used as a campaign issue much as the anti-abortion issue is used today. In reality, it didn't really protect the interest of servant girls or improve the condition of low-class women, as Watt extols. Fielding, who was liberal enough to have married his housekeeper after the death of his first wife, had to seriously suffer from the consequence of such a marriage in his later career. The Magistrate maintained a satirical attitude toward "lawful marriage" only because he knew the reality of married life in English society better than someone who served merely as ghostwriter of love letters for servant girls or wrote novels out of marriage fantasy. In *Tom Jones*, for instance, Fielding's handling of the two marriages, those of Harriet to Brian Fitzpatridge, and Nancy Miller to Nightingale is well supported by the document of social history.[6]

The middle class, with its pragmatism and lack of respect for ideology, lacks the intellectual capacity to justify its value system; and it has failed to develop a new ideology that may replace religious belief in modern society. As a result, it is wont to return to medievalism, that is, to control mass consciousness in God's name. The mercantile mind functions not as an innovator, but as a manufacturer of signs. "God's name" is such a rich and resourceful sign that can be utilized and reproduced in the hands of politicians who are "the good servants" of the moneyed class, or good "salesmen" of servant girls. The manufacturer can always make the phallic sign, one way or another, to yield profit for economic and political purpose. Even human sexuality can be utilized and exploited as a natural resource. The Calvinists knew this from the very beginning. Watt explains to us:

Calvinism in particular tended to make its adherents forget the idea that labor was God's punishment for Adam's disobedience, by emphasizing the very different idea that untiring stewardship of the material gifts of God was a paramount religious and ethical obligation.[7]

What a "smart" interpretation of "God's truth"! In other words, Adam's sin can be pardoned by the economic "redemption" of capitalism—"the untiring stewardship of the material gifts." When marriage becomes an "obligation" to accumulate wealth, love is taken as the means and end of production.

> Now love is dwindled to intrigue,
> And marriage grown a money-league.
> . . . .
> That Modern love is no such thing
> As what those ancient poets sing;
> A fire celestial, chaste, refined,
> Conceived and kindled in the mind.[8]

These lines from Swift's "Cadenus and Vanessa" are representative of many satirical verses on the subject of love written during the early eighteenth century. In Swift's poem, a strong sense of historical discontinuity indicates the fundamental change of times and tradition that affects the style of literary love. It probably explains why Pope, Dryden, and Fielding preferred mock-epic to the courtly motif. "Mock-epic," simply put, mocks the mode of epic love. The Tory writers, who still possessed the power of language after their political power was impaired, took literary production as an ideological warfare. So they wrote satirical verse and "love stories" to criticize the system of rising capitalism.

Here the old argument between "the Ancient and the Modern" needs to be reassessed and repositioned. As scholars of the eighteenth century have become increasingly aware in recent years, there is definitely a "retrospective radicalism" in "conservative" writers' critique of capitalist ideology. As William C. Dowling points out:

> Such writers as Pope and Swift and Gay demand to be seen in this light because they were carrying out a proto-Marxian critique of early capitalism, alert as Marx would subsequently be to the terrible consequences of an economic system working blindly to transform human beings into mere interchangeable integers or market units.[9]

Such critical reassessment puts to rest many earlier conceptions of Augustan writing as "conservative." The Ancients, at least in their moral critique of the bourgeoisie, seem to share a united front with the Marxists; and the postmodern fictionists happen to share their position with the eighteenth-century Ancients. Namely, the Ancients proposed a critique exactly as Marx was to declare a hundred years later:

> The bourgeoisie . . . has drowned the most heavenly ecstasies of religious fervor, of chivalrous enthusiasm, of Philistine sentimentalism, in the icy water of egotistical calculation. It has resolved personal worth into exchange value, and in place of the numberless indefeasible chartered freedoms, has set up that single, unconscionable freedom—Free Trade. In one word, for exploitation, veiled by religious and political illusions, it has substituted naked, shameless, direct, brutal exploitation. . . . The bourgeoisie has torn away from the family its sentimental veil, and has reduced the family relation to a mere money relation.[10]

The dominant critical opinion in the United States has always privileged Richardson's "progressive" stance over Fielding's "conservative" or "aristocratic" position. This position needs to be reassessed, too. Remarkably, Fielding played the role of a radical Marxist critic one hundred years before Karl Marx wrote the *Communist Manifesto*. High-church minded as he was, he did not hesitate to tell the public that religious fallacies could be used as a political device, a "state-engine to awe men into obedience." In writing his "Proposal for an Effectual Provision for the Poor for Amending Their Morals and for Rendering Them Useful Members of the Society," with his "blunt irony," Fielding offered a radical criticism that at once shocked and delighted the Oxford historian Basil Williams:

> Heaven and hell, when well rung in the ears of those who have not yet learnt that there are no such places, are by no means words of little significance; . . . Magistrates have always thought themselves concerned to cherish religion, and to maintain in the minds of men the belief of a God and another life, (as acknowledged by atheists who say it was) at first a political device and is still kept up in the world as a state-engine to awe men into obedience.[11]

One can understand why William Empson, in his "larger defence" of Fielding's position, thinks that "the chief reason why recent critics have belittled Fielding is that they find him intimidating."[12] Even so, the twentieth-century Fielding critics in England are more fair-minded than the ones criticized by Empson. As Williams expains:

> The established religion was indeed regarded by most politicians, and many churchmen too, of the eighteenth century, first as a safeguard for the Whig system of government, and especially as a valuable form of police control over the lower classes. Aristocrats like Shaftesbury, Chesterfield, or even Bolingbroke might safely be left to their free-thinking propensities, so long as they abjured extreme Tory doctrines in the state and were careful not to contaminate the poor by too popular a presentment of their heresies.[13]

But Watt, on the contrary, is convinced that marriage was advocated by the English Protestants to counteract not only adultery but also celibacy, "since in Roman Catholicism the highest religious values are connected with celibacy."[14] Paradoxically, celibacy, as Watt has to admit, was not necessarily exclusive to the clergy. It was widespread among the wits and aristocrats, a problem menacing social stability. Moreover, spinsterhood was also serious and widespread at a lower social level, as Watt also admits:

> There is, then, a considerable variety of evidence to support the view that the transition to an individualist social and economic order brought with it a crisis in marriage which bore particularly hard upon the feminine part of the population.[15]

Evidently, the "crisis in marriage" rises from the start of modern individualism. It is inherent in the capitalist economy, a latent contradiction of social relationship in bourgeois society, as Marx criticized. Left or right, few scholars disagree with Marx in this respect. For those who have lived through the 1970s and 1980s in caplitalist America, such a crisis is not only imaginable but familiar. Ironically, divorce rates tend to be the highest in a middle-class society. Neither puritan virtue nor "the God-given unity of marriage" ever builds a happy family in a Protestant society.

Religion, in the hands of the merchants and politicians, is only a tool. To the public, chastity is advertised to preserve the idealism of puritanism. In reality, the Protestant regime cannot tolerate the "highest religious values" connected with celibacy. Such a contradiction only reveals the absence of religious value in a middle-class ideology. The anti-abortion issue today may help us understand the English middle-class ruling strategy since the eighteenth century. In the good name of "human rights" and "religious freedom," anti-abortion, a pre-Enlightenment movement, has come back so well handled under a Protestant ruler, George Bush, that it will surely help counterbalance the population growth of non-whites, meanwhile reducing the surplus of women in the labor force by forced "labor of love." Even Swift's "Modest Proposal" sounds no less modest than the modifications of the anti-abortion legislations in America in 1990s. How strange history reinvents its wheel that has made Swift sound more progressive than the rhetoric of debate over the issue of abortion in modern American society today!

That "the idealization of marriage is distinctively Protestant" is also a myth. It is inaccurate for Watt to say:

> In England the break with the originally adulterous character of courtly love was so complete that George Moore was almost justified in claiming to have "invented adultery, which didn't exist in the English novel till I began writing." [16]

George Moore was a later nineteenth-century novelist. Watt must have completely forgotten the very subject that he is dealing with in his own book—Defoe's and Fielding's novels. Both Defoe and Fielding were unquestionably Protestants, but they wrote extensively on the subject of adultery.[17] Fielding quite generously pardons male adultery in the name of "good nature." Defoe's heroines, both Moll Flanders and Roxana, only make their fortunes out of adultery and step out of wedlock to cast off their misfortunes. The Puritan myth of "the God-given unity of marriage" in Milton, when the middle class first rises, might have been an innocent idealism. In Defoe, it is an honest disillusion, a horror. In Richardson, it is either a sexual fantasy or the imaginary unknown. In Fielding, as A. O. J. Cockshut puts it, "the experience of marriage is left to imagination."[18] The various stages might suggest a historical discontinuity in the testimony of Puritan virtue from the Glorious Revolution to the fall of Walpole.

It is nonetheless true that most of Defoe's and Fielding's novels end up in marriage, too. One can only presume, therefore, that there is indeed one thing common in the works of Defoe, Richardson, and Fielding: marriage does stand as the final reward for the heroic deeds the lovers have performed, or the virtue displayed. It appears that there is a social norm to which the novelists conform and a dominant literary convention they observe: the model of epic love. The novelists adopt the model because it is the available and most popular mode of production within the system, just as the postmodernists also use the popular motif of sex, violence, and mystery in their fictions. Whether the novelists agree or disagree with the ideological implications of such a model is absolutely another matter.[19] It depends on their treatment of such a model. Evidently they have a hot debate going. Richardson is a conformist in exemplifying such a model in his *Pamela*. But Defoe and Fielding are rather satirical and carnivalesque in their treatment of such a popular mode of love. I think it is only fair to ascertain that the model of epic love is a common denominator in their construction of love stories, while those variants above the fraction line stand for the actual weight and wisdom—the true light of value in their argument.

Since the novel is a middle-class genre, it is used as a political instrument fashioning the custom and ideology of a middle-class society. While the Calvinist myth of marriage becomes the popular belief in the nation's public life, the capitalist mode of love is reinforced and transformed into a more popular genre to reach a wide range of middle-class audience. But the voices that participate in the novelistic discourse sound pluralistic rather than univocal, just as the social and political forces behind them are diverse.

The eighteenth-century novel opens a space for the men and women in the modern world to discover new possibilities of achievement. The novelists are self-consciously inventing or redefining a value system for a new society. The task itself is epic-making. One can see that in the process of creating their fictional characters, the novelists are proposing role models for modern men and women. The essential question that preoccupies their common interest is: What kind of hero and heroine deserves the title of the ultimate reward, and by what chance, from whose hand are they awarded their dues? On the conceptual level, epic love pertinently addresses such a question. But within the framework of epic love that formulates the common question, each novelist has a different answer of his own design. For Fielding, virtue is awarded by Providence; for Defoe, it is through expedition.[20] Only in the case of Richardson is virtue awarded through calculating domestic negotiation. So it must be noted that virtue does not mean Puritan virtue alone; it signifies different values in Fielding, Defoe, and Richardson. Although the word stands as the dominant sign, the signified varies significantly from the signifier, cleverly disseminated in the hands of the novelists. Between Richardson and Fielding at least, there is a difference between the middle-class virtue and elite virtue, which defines the difference of their respective role models. Even for Defoe, virtue means "diligence and self-employment," far from "chastity" in the sense Richardson conceives it. If "chastity" and "chivalry" describe the difference between Richardson and Fielding with respect to sexual virtue, Defoe has chosen "chivalry," not to extol kings and knights, but to advocate "women's lib."

Yet the praise of female virtue has its strong political implications that ought not to be underestimated even in feminist criticism. In proposing their role models, Defoe and Richardson advocate female virtue, while Fielding praises male virtue. Considering the historical fact that the Hanoverian line comes from female lineage (secured in 1701) and, the dethroned Stuarts are the male issues, I would argue that gender construction in fiction is less biological than political—it is a representation of party line. In other words, the political sympathies and affiliations of the eighteenth-century writers may determine their portrayal of male and female virtue, their conception of love stories at large, more decisively than their personal attitude toward women.

Defoe, who joined the forces of William of Orange in 1688, has an implicit design for Roxana's marriage. Roxana's legal husband, whom she first married in England and then reencounters in France, means nothing to her but a threat. In spite of the fame and luxury she has enjoyed as the "Fortunate Mistress" in the French court, the dream of her life is to settle down in England, which she cannot accomplish by herself, until she sails for Holland and marries her Dutch husband. Is it only incidental that England, too, ends her political turmoil by that "God-given marriage" from Holland? Roxana's marraige could be metaphorical. Placed in a historical context, the reader may approach the politics of gender on a metaphorical level. Roxana's "murthering" (mothering/murdering) her own issues from a previous marriage, the most disturbing action in regard to female virtue which, may be comical and acceptable to those who read Defoe's novel as political satire, and understood the political implication of Defoe's use of that carnivalesque word "murthering" (mothering/murdering) as double talk and a metaphor. It is said that the earlier Presbyterians had always regarded the Church of England as a Mother; and Defoe was schooled at a good Presbyterian academy. His politics toward the Church of England may be reflected in that ambivalent word. Those who lived through England's historical nightmare in Defoe's time—the haunting horrors of Jacobite revolts, the religious sanctions imposed upon the Dissenters, because of the "issues" left by previous royal marriages who kept pretending the throne by war—and were tired of it, might smile at Roxana's "virtue."

Swift and Pope, on the contrary, often attack female virtue because they bear a grudge against the female monarchs.[21] Especially in Swift's poetry, the satire on "womankind" is frequently associated with the image of the Crown. Pope's *The Rape of the Lock* can be read also as a political satire on the "silly womanhead" that rules the court. Queen Caroline is said to be "remarkably able" as Walpole's "coadjutor," especially in managing the king during 1727-37.[22] Political satire from the Opposition, to which Fielding belonged, was only too ready to conceive the Whig supremacy as a "petticoat" regime. With a ruler such as George II on the throne, who did not speak English and had to rely upon his queen as a "translator," the criticism of petticoat politics was not so seriously a gender issue as it was a question of competency in leadership.

The eighteenth-century writers played a significant role in the nation's political life. Swift, Defoe, and Fielding were political writers in public; their creative writing only provided them extra room, a "teahouse," for political gossip. In fiction and poetry, these writers found themselves more relaxed than in public speech or journalistic writing in expressing their personal opinions of history and politics. The topic of women and sex, therefore, freely circulated with the news of the day. Political gossip created an intertextuality in their "love stories." Thus throughout the eighteenth century, the age of satire, "female virtue" as a target of Tory criticism, holding it responsible for the corruption and deficiency of the Whig administration, almost established as a literary convention. Unfortunately, it is a lyric law in the English language, which dictates that words such as—"Walpole" and "woman," "Whig" and "womankind" or "womanhead," "Wife" and "Widow"—all alliterate that created a linguistic convenience for Tory writers. So when it came to Fielding, sexual identity in political and ideological controversies was even less a personal choice than a public norm.[23] As he tells us in *Tom Jones*, one of the favorite party gossips among the country squires at that time was "the Abuse of Woman and of the Government." In other words, Fielding the novelist is operating within the accepted assumptions and within a system of social linguistic codes. Squire Western's conviction that "all the husbands in London are Cuckolds" is not only a rhetoric hyperbole but also a political gossip, a grievance against the petticoat politics in the Hanoverian court. In the ear of those who share the accepted assumptions (as satire functions on agreed assumptions) such a metaphor is not to be mistaken.

One example might show that political gossip is a thematic concern prior to gender identity in Fielding. In that well-quoted, but often misread, scene when Western calls his sister "the Presbyterian Hanoverian B——," the squire has Fielding's sympathy with good reason. Fielding makes fun of Western's sister, the ex-courtier from the Hanoverian court, for her lack of manner and wisdom in using "a good servant," Mrs. Honor. "A Good servant shall not want a position," retorts Mrs. Honor. Honor is also a

woman, not a lady, but a woman who has a character. Possibly, when
Fielding refers to Pope's line "most women have no characters at all" (TJ
XIV, i), he has little doubt that Pope lays two stresses on the word
"characters" (arbitrarily using the word in its plural), while the word
"women" is not stressed. Fielding's depiction of Mrs. Honor transgresses
gender difference, for he compares her to the Greek Lover Socrates:

> She viewed all handsome Men with that equal Regard and
> Benevolence, which a sober and virtuous Mind bears to all the
> Good. —She might, indeed, be called a Lover of Men, as
> Socrates was a Lover of Mankind, preferring one to anther for
> corporeal, as he for mental Qualifications; but never carrying this
> Preference so far as to cause any Perturbation in the
> Philosophical Serenity of her Temper. (TJ V iv)

"Honor," a chivalric male virtue conceived in a female figure, is
transformed into modern ethics as an asexual "honor code" in public service.
The highlight of Honor's spirit and the repetition of the word "servant" only
opens a higher level of criticism. The term "public servant" used to refer to
administrators in the government assumably strikes a much more familiar
and honorable note in the ear of the English public than the way American
readers might take it. Actually, the treatment of an old servant is an essential
measurement of "worthiness" in the character of a noble. Benevolence,
generosity and understanding are Fielding's touchstones of "nobility," the
test of "elite virtue." Ill-use of an old servant only calls into question the
character of the mistress, in this case, the "mid-wife" in court. The question
raised satirically is, of course, if she is decent, well bred, and competent
enough in handling her power.

In Fielding, the "womanhead," naive or arrant, is often identified
with the incompetency in decision making that, in most episodes, is
evidenced by the outcome of action. For example, in the above-mentioned
scene, Squire Western, for fear of losing his title in his sister's will, pretends
to be persuaded by his daughter to compromise. "'So I must go and ask
pardon for your fault, must I?' and answered Western. 'You have lost the
hare and I must draw every way to find her again?'" (TJ VII, iv, v). Here,
"hare" puns with "heir." Western, the Tory country squire, is gossiping.
"The abuse of woman is the abuse of government." The English throne has
lost its heir, the court has to go all the way out to fetch a "hare" from
Hanover. Such gossip, once revealed, may give us a clue to the critical
controversy over Fielding's politics, namely, whether he is anti-Jacobite or

pro-Hanoverian. I believe he is both and neither, which I will explain later. The point I wish to make here is only that Fielding and Richardson are not simply fighting a war over the issue of "women's liberation."

While Richardson follows the public discourse "to create the uncreated consciousness" of the middle class, Fielding chimes in, in fact, to demystify the middle-class syndrome. In *Pamela*, marriage means the promotion of the *"upper servants* of great families" (the Italics are in the original).[24] As a political gesture, the marriage between the aristocracy and the maid servant is not only conservative, but also corruptive. It is conservative in the sense that the lover preserves herself by preserving the established status quo. It is corruptive because all this "good servant" argues and insinuates to obtain is the promotion of her own status instead of public welfare.

Pamela's virtue is identified in terms of prudence, chastity, and servitude. But her virtue is only used as a means. It is not preserved as the end of being and action. When all is put on for the show, virtue is as good as advertisement. It is ethically meaningless. Once she is married, her virtue is but displayed in a different manner—revenge and governance. She takes little action to improve the condition of her folks or to raise the servants' status in the household; all she does is to manipulate her husband to deal with Lady Davers and subdue Mrs. Jewkes. Such an attitude, not unlike the gesture of Western's sister, is typical of those "upper servants" in a bourgeois government—insinuatingly courting those above and insolently lording over those below, which I consider perfect "bastard behavior." Even so, Pamela's success is rather piteous, insecure, and self-deceptive. Pamela is virtually a poor role model for the working class girl. Rather she is a victim of the middle-class syndrome. She is so anxious to be "a good girl" in the eye of her lord that she loses sight of what is truly good in a lord. What Cockshut says of her might be vicious, but not without truthful insight:

> It does not seem to occur to her that men, and even squires of broad acres, vary; that not all are brutes, and that a man's character is at least as relevant as his social position in assessing a girl's chances of happiness in marriage.[25]

Pamela's problem, or the tragic flaw of the middle-class syndrome, lies in the metaphysical blindness of the middle class, its total disregard of the innate virtue of nobility, that is, "character." After the fall of Walpole, Richardson is to learn his lesson and strike a tragic note in *Clarissa*. Clarissa's unreal desire for a "glorious" marriage turns out to be only an adolescent sexual fantasy, whose blindness might be identified with what McKeon calls "naive empiricism."

The true noble spirit, as Williams points out, is "the consciousness of civic duty." It is this sort of consciousness in the English nobility as "a class of the public spirit and public duty," according to Williams, that has eased the inevitable change in its relations with the lower classes, and "made such a change much easier than was possible in the countries where aristocracies had no purpose in society beyond amusement and military glory."[26] Fielding in *Tom Jones* is offering a well-thought program to ease the social and political changes that have been taking place in English society during his life time. He proposes a radical model of "Elite Virtue" that teaches the "princely lore" to the "foundlings" in modern society and provides an ethical standard for the modern ruler. He not only transforms classic values into a modern context, but also challenges the accepted norm of the day—the divine rights of kings, cardinal virtue, worldly prudence. In every respect, fortunately and unfortunately, he is ahead of his times.

Instead of chastity and prudence, Tom's virtue is defined in terms of benevolence, chivalry, and generosity. Surely such qualities are derived from the heroic virtues in romance and aristocratic norms; but one must recognize that by writing a "modern epic," Fielding has transmitted such values into the kind of public spirit as Williams appreciates in the twentieth century. What Fielding has done is to establish the ethical codes for civic service. He praises "Elite Virtue" as a critique to negate the middle-class virtue; and in so doing he creates a role model for rulers in modern government. "Elite virtue" such as benevolence, generosity, and chivalry exemplifies the highly desirable, but only too rare, qualities of a public servant in modern democratic society: Unconditioned service to the weak and poor, uncalculated love and devotion to a deep-rooted ethical ideal, a compassionate and forgiving nature toward those around and below him. From a contemporary viewpoint, Fielding's model certainly is more valuable than Richardson's Pamela. It virtually has more to offer to both men and women in executive positions.

As I said before, the implied ideology of epic love is the ideology of capitalism. Ideologically, Fielding can be characterized as an anticapitalist and antimaterialist. His novel is a social protest against all the bourgeois ideology that Richardson represents. Technically, he is a deconstructionist in treating the canonic model. By the time Tom eventually gets married, Fielding has already deconstructed the myth of lawful marriage by mocking all sorts of bargains of marriage throughout the whole novel. Tom's marriage is not "gained" through a bargain, courtship, or servitude according to the popular norm, as Richardson has constructed in Pamela's marriage. It is only by incident that Jenny Jones comes back, tells the story, and saves the foundling from desertion. Tom's marriage comes as though by "miracle." It is an "award" from Providence for a character blessed by Heaven and free from Hell. By marrying Sophia, Tom is not selling out but regaining his self-identity. He is the master of a marriage that promises a happy state, a healthy and loving human relationship, plus a better education system (Sophia hires the good Parson Adams to tutor her children). In it, the woman has an equal status in economy and government. Since the lovers were playmates since their childhood, as we are told, the "little Tommy" bird used to "perch upon Sophia's Finger, and lie contended in her Bosom" (TJ IV, iii), that ideal relationship contains the seed of romantic love. Romantic love is a higher stage of Love as I discussed in Chapter Two; and I will demonstrate in Chapter Five that it is ideologically anticapitalistic, an antithesis to epic love. Fielding, ahead of his times, has introduced an infant model of romantic love under the canopy of epic love that, as he foresees at the end of the novel, is only to be nurtured in the spirit of "charming Ages yet to come" (TJ XIII, i). Moreover, Sophia is created not simply as a physical object of desire, but as a pure artifice of symbolic identities—in her name is conceived the Hanoverian throne, philosophy itself, the ultimate reality of truth and beauty (which I shall discuss in the following chapter). Fielding indeed handles the canonical model of epic love in a unique way. He is in it but not of it. He lives with it, but dismantles its ideology with his marvelous critique.

Insightful critiques often come from the marginal position. The margin of a printed page is not composed of the two straight lines so called "the left and the right" alone; the top as well as the bottom are also excluded. In his politics, Fielding actually took side with neither "left" nor "right," which does not mean he's a turncoat or has his "political uncertainty," as some critics suspect. In reality, the world is never made of two parties only. Fielding himself proclaims, especially around 1745, "I am of no Party."[27] It is inadequate, if not malicious, to label a writer with arbitrary oppositions—either Tory or Whig, either anti-Jacobite or pro-Hanoverian, either Christian or atheist, either Stalinist or neo-Marxist, either pro-freedom or antidemocracy, either Republican or Democrat, either feminist or sexist, either postmodern or classic, either deconstructionist or new historian, either white or black, either East or West . . . what about South and North? The best one can say about an author is what s/he is and is not. But what s/he is does not mean what s/he is not. As Fielding reminds us:

It was impossible to discourse philosophically concerning
Words, till their Meaning was first established; that there were
scarce any two Words of a more vague and uncertain
Signification than the two he had mentioned: For that matter
there were almost as many different Opinions concerning Honor
as concerning Religion. (TJ III iii)

During the period of Jacobite revolts, it was a Whig political strategy
to label all the Tories as Jacobites.[28] Later critics who are in favor of
Fielding's work find it a convenient strategy to claim him a strong
pro-Hanoverian, a true patriot, even a Whig.[29]

Yet the word "Hanoverian" itself carries several stages of historical
discontinuity. "Patriotism" doesn't necessarily signify "anti- Jacobite" either.
It also implies anti-Hanoverian, if "Hanoverian" stands for George II. The
patriots in Fielding's time were critical of the Hanoverian kings because of
their interest in Hanover that was often opposed to the interest of England.
Fielding was devoted to a group of nonpartisan "Boy Patriots" from the top
of the aristocracy, his old friends—Lyttleton, the Granvilles, Cornet
Pitt—"A Galaxy of Political Stars" surrounding the Prince of Wales (sire
of George III). The prince, also a Hanoverian descendent, had a bitter
relationship with his parents, both the king and the queen. Encouraged by
the "Patriots," he quarreled openly with his parents. In 1738, he made the
breach irreparable by carrying off his wife, in the pains of labor, from the
parental roof.[30] In politics, he aligned with the Opposition against Walpole.
Thus the Hanoverian prince was honestly "anti-Hanoverian," which,
however, does not indicate that the group of people who surrounded him
were "anti-Hanoverian," if "Hanoverian" signified a future ruler.

Rather, this group consisted of those called the "Broad-Bottoms,"
who had a far-reaching influence and strong support from the bottom of the
Parliament as well. It actually included both Tories and Whigs, both
Chesterfield "patriots" and old henchmen of Walpole—almost everyone,
who was considered to be sufficiently talented or influential to be
formidable. In 1744, the Broad-Bottom Administration was constituted as
a "Coalition Cabinet," sort of a united front. "Every interest was consulted
and satisfied," but the King was never in favor of it, especially because of his
displeasure with Pitt, and pronounced them "pitiful fellows."[31] Fielding is
said to be the most formidable and faithful servant of the Broad-Bottoms. In
Tom Jones, which is dedicated to Lyttleton, he quietly puts across his
admiration for the Broad-Bottoms. In one place, Partridge says: "But if the
Top of the Hill be properest to produce melancholy Thoughts, I suppose the

Bottom is the likeliest to produce merry ones, and these I take to be much the better of the two" (TJ VIII, x). In another place, Fielding writes, "The deepest Politicians, who see to the Bottom, discover often a very different Aspect of Affairs, from what swims on the Surface" (TJ XV, vi).

If contemporary critics can "see to the Bottom" of Fielding's politics and get hold of Tom's "Broad-sword" (TJ VIII, x), I am sure we will discover "a very different Aspect of Affairs from what swims on the Surface." But first and foremost, the conventional critique of left and right, Tory and Whig, Progressive and Conservative, aristocratic and middle-class, even feminist and patriarchal in regard to the Richardson and Fielding controversy must be revised. Now, as we look back at history, we realize that in the long run, Majority is not a divine right, and Minority not a permanent status. The middle class certainly had its "glorious" day; but it is long over.

Fielding proves to be a radical critic of a bourgeois government, which is ruled by the moneyed and for the moneyed. No one is more prescient and perceptive than he is in observing the middle-class follies and demystifying the appearance of virtue and prudence. Before I proceed to investigate the love stories in Fielding's *Tom Jones*, let me quote a "Top" opinion that levels my "Bottom" line:

> Richardson was not a gentleman, and he could not transcend the bourgeois milieu to which he properly belonged. Fielding, though he lived most of his life in bourgeois surroundings and among bourgeois people, was never absorbed by them. He was above them, not of them.[32]

That Richardson is more conservative and less noble than Fielding can be testified by their own remarks on the issue of birthright that I will quote as epigraph in the following chapter.

Notes

1. E. M. W. Tillyard, *The Epic Strain in the English Novel* (London: Chatto & Windus, 1963), 17.

2. Maurice Valency, *In Praise of Love: An Introduction to the Love-Poetry of the Renaissance* (New York: Schocken Books, 1982).

3. Ian Watt, *The Rise of the Novel: Studies in Defoe, Richardson, and*

Fielding (Berkeley: University of California Press, 1957), 137; emphasis added.

4. Michael McKeon, *The Origins of the English Novel, 1600-1740* (Baltimore: Johns Hopkins University Press, 1987), 3.

5. See Watt, "Love and the Novel: Pamela," in *The Rise of the Novel,* 135-73.

6. See Basil Williams, "Prisons and Fleet Marriages," in *The Whig Supremacy* (Oxford: Clarendon Press, 1939), 131-32.

7. Watt, *The Rise of the Novel,* 73.

8. Jonathan Swift, "Cadenus and Vanessa," in *The Complete Poems,* ed. Pat Rogers (New Haven, CT: Yale University Press, 1983), 13-14, 130-31.

9. William C. Dowling, *The Epistolary Movement: The Poetics of the Eighteenth-Century Verse Epistle* (Princeton, New Jersey: Princeton University Press, 1991), 15.

10. Karl Marx and Frederick Engels, *The Communist Manifesto,* 28th printing (New York: International Publishers, 1989), 11.

11. Williams, *The Whig Supremacy,* 74.

12. William Empson, "Tom Jones," *Kenyon Review* 20 (1958): 249.

13. Williams, *The Whig Supremacy,* 73.

14. Watt, *The Rise of the Novel,* 155.

15. Ibid., 148.

16. Ibid., 137; George Moore (1852-1933) wrote *A Mummer's Wife* in 1885 and *Esther Waters* in 1894.

17. Defoe published *Conjugal Lewdness* in 1727.

18. A. O. J. Cockshut, *Man and Woman: A Study of Love and the Novel (1740-1940)* (London: Collins, 1977).

19. I don't quite agree with Michael McKeon's theory that the romance is authorized by the aristocratic ideology; the novel advocates progressive ideology.

20. Even though expedition is profitable, still conjugal love in Defoe is not virtue but horror. Moll Flanders has a nightmare of a marriage in the Puritan society of North America. Roxana's legal husband is always a disaster, a threat to her life.

21. Swift had wanted the deanery of Derry but was disappointed in 1699 under Queen Mary. Again, in 1707, Swift was commissioned by Archbishop King to solicit the queen's bounty for a remission of the First Fruits for the Church of Ireland, but the mission failed. Though he succeeded in this mission later in 1710 with Queen Ann, the queen's displeasure with Swift is well known. It originated with the publication of *A Tale of a Tub* and was compounded by the antipathy of the queen's favorite, the duchess of Somerset, who never forgave Swift for publishing a part of Temple's memoir, in which there are reflections on the character of her uncle, Lord Essex. As a result, Swift never fulfilled his ambition of obtaining the preferment in England; instead, he took the deanery of St. Patrick's as a gift from the duke of Ormond. After the queen died in 1714 and the Whig power became entrenched, Swift's ambition was doomed for good.

22. See Dudden, *Henry Fielding* (Hamden, CT: Archon Books, 1966), 193-96.

23. Whenever he speaks on the literal level free of political allusions, Fielding is very sensitive and sympathetic with women's status in society and their relationship with men in love or marriage. As Cross says of him: "Women, it is everywhere clear . . . for all their whims he never lost respect for them; they were the best part of God's creation. . . and it was a gentleman's duty to shield them from insult" (Wilbur L. Cross, *The History of Henry Fielding* [New York: Russell & Russell, 1963], vol. 3, 267).

24. Samuel Richardson, *Pamela* (New York: Norton, 1958), 531.

25. Cockshut, *Men and Women*, 32.

26. Williams, *The Whig Supremacy*, 143.

27. M. A. Locke, "Henry Fielding and the Historical Background of the 'Forty-Five,'" Introduction to Fielding's *The True Patriot: The History of Our Own Times* (Binghampton: University of Alabama Press, 1964), 1-11.

28. According to Locke, Sir Robert Walpole for years had played up the dangers of a Jacobite rebellion as a means of weakening the position of the Tories, whom he readily sought to identify with Jacobites. Ibid., 3.

29. Brian McCrea claims Fielding to be a Whig in his *Henry Fielding and Politics of Mid-Eighteenth-Century England* (Athens: University of Georgia Press, 1981). Peter J. Carlton claims that Tom and Sophia's marriage signifies Fielding's reconciliation of England's Stuart past with its Whig-Hanoverian present. See Carlton, "Tom Jones and the 45's Once Again," in *Studies in the Novel* 20 (Winter 1988): 361-73.

30. Williams, *The Whig Supremacy*, 194.

31. See Dudden, *Henry Fielding*, 510, 525. For Fielding's affiliation with the Broad-Bottoms, also see Thomas R. Cleary, *Henry Fielding: Political Writer* (Waterloo, Ont. Canada: Wilfrid Laurier University Press), 1984.

32. Duddon, *Henry Fielding*, 1084.

Chapter Four

The Legitimate Lover of "Sophia" and the Rightful Ruler: Fielding's *History of Tom Jones, a Foundling*

What Reason has he to make his Tom illegitimate, in an Age where Keeping is become a Fashion? Why did he make him a common—What shall I call it?

—Samuel Richardson, Letter [1]

The Words "dishonorable Birth" are Nonsense, . . . unless the Word "Dishonorable" be applied to the Parents; for the Children can derive no real Dishonor from an Act of which—they are entirely innocent.

—Henry Fielding, *Tom Jones* [2]

We learn incidentally Fielding presumed men ought to be promoted to the ruling class, as a regular thing; the point is

89

merely that the system of promotion should be adequate to save it from contempt. . . . But it seems mere fact that Fielding's society needed a governing class, however things may work out under universal education; so it is reasonable of him to take a reformist view, as the Communists would say, and merely recommend a better selection.

—William Empson, "Tom Jones" [3]

A Sleeping Beauty: The Argument of Legitimacy

In epic love, legitimacy is the center of plot and actions. It is the essential argument the novelist conceives in the design of "love stories." The more provocative the arguments are, the more likely it is that they are embedded in most sensational scenes of pleasure. In Fielding's *Tom Jones*, the argument of legitimacy is evoked at the very outset: The night Allworthy returns from London and retires to his bed, he beholds an "Infant wrapt up in some coarse Linen, in a sweet and profound Sleep between his sheets" (TJ I, iii).[4] Where does the infant come from? The appearance of this "sleeping beauty" has been one of the most intriguing scenes in the history of the novel. Its idea is as provocative as it is sensational, for it evokes the question of Tom's parentage, the question of the legitimacy of a male issue to be adopted by a magistrate in Paradise Hall. The subsequent plot, Allworthy's adoption of the foundling, is immediately unfolded over the argument of Tom's legitimacy in Paradise Hall. The argument not only complicates the whole plot, but also functions as the motivating source of all actions. The novel ends with Tom's restoration to Paradise Hall through a rightful marriage to Sophia, but not until the initial question of legitimacy, his birthright, is solved can his marriage come to pass. Thus the structure of epic love parallels the structure of the argument over legitimacy: The legitimate lover ends as the legitimate ruler of Paradise Hall.

The argument of legitimacy makes Tom's identity a crucial issue, especially in regard to his lineage. The recovery of Tom's lineage as the son of Bridget, sister of Allworthy, thus establishing Tom's birthright in Paradise Hall, is a historically controversial critical issue. Because of such novelistic design, Fielding has been exposed to criticism left and right. On the right, moralists have attacked him with Richardson's "bastard" fallacy—"What

Reason has he to make his Tom illegitimate, in an Age where Keeping is become a Fashion? Why did he make him a common—What shall I call it?" (see epigraph). And on the left, restoring Tom's lineage to an aristocratic origin has been unacceptable to modern critics in the age of democracy. In the middle of the two opposed positions, the goodness of Fielding's design, which contains his own political agenda, remains a critical ambiguity. To understand Fielding's argument over legitimacy, Tom's true parentage, his title to Allworthy's estate, and even his allegorical identity need to be reexamined. In this chapter, by way of reexamining Tom's identity, I shall demonstrate how the study of novelistic love may serve as an effective approach to reach the heart of the matter in the novel.

So far, I have proposed that "love stories" are the heart of the matter in a novel. The construction of "love stories" in the Platonic tradition is often a dramatization of the novelist's historical vision, political ideology, philosophical speculations, or cultural criticism. The economy of "love stories," with its sensational elements, seductive programming, and entertaining mechanism, produces a power of free speech that enables the novelist to speak the unspeakable and include the excluded subjects under hard historical circumstances. Novelistic love functions, as I suggested in Chapter One, as an effective "internal persuasive discourse" dialogizing against the public discourse of history. Fielding's novel *The History of Tom Jones, a Foundling* provides an exemplary and interesting model to illustrate such a theory. Fielding's argument of legitimacy is well conceived and concealed in a number of intriguing "love stories"—Bridget's "sexual comedy," Mrs. Waters's highway rape scene, the Upton seduction scene, the incest charge, and the beauty of Sophia. These "love stories" are the most sensational elements in the novel. A study of these sensational "love stories" shall reveal Fielding's idea in constructing Tom's legitimacy; thus Fielding's historical vision and political ideology around 1745 may come to light.

The reader will see that Fielding's projection of a political ideal—the ideal of the rightful ruler—is well plotted and constructed in the "love story" of Tom Jones and Sophia Western. In the name of "Sophia," Fielding creates a cubist construction, a "Picasso" of his Platonic ideal: first, the absolute truth/beauty that only goodness may behold; second, philosophy itself; and third, the English throne. Working within the structure of epic love, he sets up the marriage to Sophia as the highest award for the legitimate lover. The consummation of Sophia's marriage involves the process of redistributing Western's estate and the re-establishment of Paradise Hall. That process is allegorical to the historical experience England is going through: the resettlement of England's land and political power around midcentury. Fielding creates Tom and Blifil as rivals by way of presenting two different role models of the future ruler. In terms of lineage, the two are actually real brothers of the same parenthood, except that Tom is born out of a love affair and Blifil into a marriage of convenience. Although for two centuries literary critics have taken Fielding's "word" for word that Summer is Tom's father, testified by Jenny Jones in the end, my reading will argue that Summer is not Tom's father. Fielding is playing a practical joke on his reader, for Bridget actually had the two sons from one lover—Dr. Blifil.

Tom's true legitimacy lies not in the family name, but in the name of love, for Tom is the child of love and Blifil is the fruit of prudence—worldly wisdom. Based upon the difference in nature, Fielding suggests that legitimacy, which is finally awarded to the one born out of wedlock, is not a birthright. It is the gift of a good character, bred by experience, and blessed by Providence through the testimony of ultimate goodness. His argument has its logic: The legitimate lover of Sophia is the lover of philosophy and absolute beauty. Since Sophia's legitimate lover shall be the rightful ruler of both Paradise Hall and Western's estate, it is not impossible, as Plato recommends, that the Philosopher Ruler ought to be the rightful ruler of England's future state. This is what the "story" of Tom's lineage and legitimacy is all about. But not until the legitimacy of the "love stories" are fully recognized will "the naked Charms" (Dedication) of Fielding's Platonic wisdom come into view.

The word "bastard" in the ear of an eighteenth-century English commoner is certainly not the same thing as "a child of a single parent" to us in the late twentieth century. The legitimacy of the English throne from Cromwell to George III had been a source of national anxiety. We have a good picture of the popular mentality in *Tom Jones*. In the Quack's public house, as soon as Tom is identified as a "Parish Bastard," "all the Compassion" the landlord had lavished upon him immediately vanishes, "and the honest, plain Man went home fired with no less indignation than Duke would have felt at receiving an affront from such a person" (TJ VII, x). Such a reaction shows the "common sense" of "an honest plain Man" in eighteenth-century England.

Imaginably, the charge that Richardson makes against Fielding is a serious one: "What Reason has he to make his Tom illegitimate, in an Age where Keeping is become a Fashion? Why did he make him a common—What shall I call it?" Ten years after he had painstakingly established the legitimacy of Pamela's "ladyship" through a socially illegitimate marriage, Richardson found himself in a good position to question the obscurity of Tom's birthright. The "trace" of his "progressive" mind-set seems to betray the most conventional, dull, and conservative idea: A bastard is always a bastard, and a "common" is unfit for the hand of Sophia. Isn't that what he had to say? One wonders what he would have said about the legitimacy of Pamela's marriage in his own theory. Indeed, Richardson failed to tell us what happened to his Pamela after the marriage, how long conjugal love lasted, and if Pamela survived the fate of Anne Boleyn—abandoned for failing to produce a male issue, and soon executed under the charge of incest.

The aftermath of a "royal marriage" is unfortunately not very "democratic." The Richardson/Fielding argument in 1749 discernibly takes a different twist from that when it started.[5] The fall of Walpole in 1742 and the Young Pretender's war in 1745 marked a historical discontinuity. Instead of the legitimacy of love and marriage, the issue is now pinged upon the legitimacy of lineage. History had staged a new landscape for Fielding's novel, his "New Province of Writing."

Fielding's argument over the issue of legitimacy is probably too serious and profound for Richardson to comprehend. As William Empson suggests, "what nobody will recognize, I feel, is that Fielding set out to preach a doctrine in *Tom Jones* (1749), and said so, a high-minded though perhaps abstruse one."[6] His doctrine, as Empson has observed, is "a theory of ethics" illuminated in his design of irony and plot. Fielding's "theory of ethics" is based on his earnest study of contemporary historical events as well as classics. He is proposing an anti-Machiavellian political philosophy to deal with the real problems accrued in a corrupted state power. "Men, who in all other Instances want common Sense," as Herriet teaches Sophia, "are very Machiavels in the art of Loving" (TJ XI, iv). In *Tom Jones*, the selection of a lover parallels the selection of a ruler. Fielding's adaptation of chivalric love challenges the dominant mode of epic love. Chivalry, removed from its medieval origin, turns into the sign of the honor code in modern government. If Machiavelli's *The Prince* (1532) is a theory of prudence for rulers in a modern state, Fielding's *Tom Jones* invents a postmodern neo-Platonic theory of goodness for "all worthy" statesmen (and women).

The essence of Fielding's philosophy is stated in his Dedication: "It is much easier to make good Men wise than to make bad Men good." "Goodness" in Fielding is identical to the Platonic concepts of wisdom and truth. It is conceived as the source of Enlightenment and identified with the Sun (Son) itself. Fielding proposes goodness not as a moral judgment, but as a political necessity in endowing judicial and legislative power. Fielding, like Plato, did not consider bourgeois democracy an ideal model for a happy state. Rather, his ideal is inspired by his knowledge of Greek philosophy on the one hand, and deeply rooted in the political reality of his time on the other. He is convinced that a good character in a powerful ruler is the guarantee of peace for the state; whereas a bad character is always a source of trouble. Power in the hands of such a ruler shall bring nothing but war and violence. Most of the plot and characters, primary as well as secondary, are created to dramatize such a conviction. If Richardson's novels were conduct books for servant girls, Fielding's fictions were conduct books for rulers. His characterology is less concerned with the ethical behavior of Everyman than that of a future ruler. *Tom Jones*, dedicated to George Lyttleton, whom some critics have identified with Allworthy, is Fielding's earnest recommendation to all those "worthy" of their power to select the rightful ruler. "I declare," as he states, "that to recommend Goodness and Innocence hath been my sincere Endeavor in this History."

The concept of "goodness," which becomes Fielding's absolute criteria for legitimacy, recalls Plato's praise of the Philosopher Ruler. Fielding's use of Plato as source material in his writing is not an infrequent practice. He has used Plato's "The Myth of Er" as a subtext in his earlier writings.[7] In *Tom Jones*, there are numerous references to Plato, some of which I shall discuss in this chapter. The Platonic subtext in his fiction, once revealed, may hopefully redress the balance of critical opinions that used to place Fielding's ethics either in a Christian humanistic context or "conservative ideology."

Chapter three of Book III can be read as Fielding's "Modest Proposal" over the argument of legitimacy. Writing a satire on "The Character of Mr. Square the Philosopher, and of Mr. Thwackum the Divine; with a Dispute concerning—," as the chapter is entitled, Fielding exposes the follies of the two dominant theories in his time concerning the legitimacy of the Crown—the rule of right on the right, and the authority of Protestant religion on the left. To the right, there is Mr. Square. Square is a classicist, "profest Master of all the Works of Plato and Aristotle." Fielding makes fun of him by deconstructing his "classicism":

> In Morals he was a profest Platonist, and in Religion he inclined to be an Aristotelian. But tho' he had, as we have said, formed his Morals on the Platonic Model, yet he perfectly agreed with the Opinion of Aristotle in considering that great Man rather in the Quality of a Philosopher, or a Speculatist, than as a Legislator. (TJ III, iii)

Square holds "Virtue and Honor as synonymous Terms"; but he believes "they are both founded on the unalterable Rule of Right, and the eternal Fitness of Things." Thus his classic learning is used to defend a Royalist position, a conservative stand.

To refute Square's theory, Fielding tells a "love story." Tom's discovery of Square's "naked truth" in Molly Seagrim's bedroom—another "Sleeping Beauty"—is the most comic and sensational "love story" in the novel. When "Philosopher Square" is exposed behind Molly Seagrim's bed "among other female Utensils in a Posture," what is comically but crudely mocked, on the conceptual level, is the "Posture" of his moral superiority. Fielding's use of pleasure in this comic scene demystifies the philosophical posture of the rule of right, "so that when the Idea of Philosophy was added to the Figure now discovered, it would have been very difficult for any Spectator to have refrained from immoderate Laughter" (TJ V, v).

Also being laughed at is Thwackum, the parson, who is politically on the left, in defence of the Protestant religion and the power of the Church of England. The parson argues that "Honor must be antecedent to Religion" and that "honor" is manifold, "because there are various Sects and Heresies in the World," which he cannot tolerate. "Nor is Religion manifold," says he,

> When I mention Religion, I mean the Christian Religion; and not only the Christian Religion, but the Protestant Religion; and not only the Protestant Religion, but the Church of England. (TJ III, iii)

By exposing the parson's narrow-minded and very limited view of religion, Fielding makes him ridiculous and his theory absurd. Fielding's satirical touches upon Thawckum imply that Fielding's view of religion might be more liberal and tolerant than the posture adopted by the present Church of England.

Fielding's own position, which belongs to neither of these two dominant schools of thought, is quietly expressed in Allworthy's sentence of both Square and Thwackum's opinions: "Mr. Allworthy interposed, telling them very coldly, they had both mistaken his Meaning." Versed in Greek philosophy as he is, Fielding is not the kind of conservative, muddle-headed, dogmatic classicist as is the pair of pedants he satirizes. He distrusts both the Tory doctrine of "the Rule of Right" and the Whig Supremacy of Parliament, which leaves him neither a Tory nor a Whig. Yet unfortunately, his own belief, which transcends the limit of both, has no place in the binary religious, political, and philosophical debates of his day.

As the two dominant theories are diametrically opposed to each other, the center is obscured, excluded. The truth of Plato's philosophy is virtually lost. The issue of goodness is excluded as well: "In one Point only they agreed, which was, in all their Discourses on Morality never to mention the Word Goodness." Goodness, which for the Greeks is the essence and ethics of great wisdom, is absent in the "orthodoxy" of their theoretical debate. Goodness, in Plato's philosophy, signifies the attainment of excellence. The Philosopher Ruler would have to go through a rigorous education program to achieve his legitimacy. Yet Mr. Square, with his favorite phrase "the natural Beauty of Virtue" innate in the divine right of kings, could have denounced education as necessary. Thwackum, asserting the authority of the Protestant religion, would have called Plato's philosophy "heathen heresy." Unfortunately, it is the mind of these blockheads that dominates the ideology of the day.

Fielding's depiction of Molly's bedroom projects a metaphorical paradigm of such an ideological hierarchy in the English court:

> The room, or rather Garret, in which Molly lay, being up one
> Pair of stairs, that is to say, at the Top of the House, was of a
> sloping Figure, resembling the great Delta of the Greeks. The
> English reader may, perhaps, stand upright anywhere but in the
> Middle. (TJ V, v)

The superstructure of the English court is biased like a "sloping Figure," where the Square preoccupies a piteous place—"the Place would not near admit his standing upright." "The great Delta of the Greeks" satirically reflects upon the Square's misuse of Plato's model for his "morals." The metaphor contains a double irony. In Molly's lopsided bedroom, an Englishman may find shelter under the petticoat of politics, but will have great difficulty to "stand upright" in the "Middle" of binary partisanship. Thus Fielding's central belief in Plato's philosophy of government has no place in Molly's bedroom.

Nevertheless, Fielding is far-sighted in his judgment. Living in a world whose social and economic structure was undergoing fundamental changes, he was looking forward rather than backward. His "upright middle position" is not to stop "the Man of Progress" from advancement, but from corruption. Even McKeon, who criticizes Fielding for his "conservative ideology," recognizes that Fielding stands in a "middle way": "Fielding's Anglicanism is not Swifts's," and Fielding's ethics "resists the customary restriction of 'absolutism' to the sphere of princely 'authority.'"[8] Fielding argues, instead, that the legitimacy of the future ruler should *not* be determined by his birthright, but by his competency and character. His argument, being difficult and unpopular, is therefore "abstrusely" constructed.

Writing against the popular belief and the majority opinion feminizes the voice of even such a hearty and staunch writer as Fielding. The literary strategies that he invents to deliver his voice—for instance, double ironies and multiple ambiguities—are not sheerly stylistic innovations, but political tactics. Though he recognizes that human understanding functions on various levels depending upon the diversity of taste, literacy, interest, and values, he believes that goodness, which signifies the proper appreciation of truth/beauty/wisdom, is virtue itself in reaching good understanding. Therefore, he has increased the chances of indeterminacy in his text including his practical jokes, only to challenge the understanding of his true lovers. His text comically resists empirical interpretations, as it mercilessly makes fun of logocentrism. While the indeterminacy of his meaning is deliberated for his enemies, his "wondrous light," the transparency of his language, is to be shared with his friends in a "Text of Bliss." However abstruse and indeterminate truth might be, in Fielding as in Plato, the attainment of truth/beauty is never impossible, provided the lover is good enough. With such an understanding, I shall proceed to reveal Tom's lineage.

"Squire Hamlet":
The Forgetting of a Failed Fatherhood

He [Tom Jones] once ventured to make a Jest of the Rule of Right; and at another Time said, He believed there was no Rule in the World capable of making such a Man as his Father, (for so Mr. Allworthy suffered himself to be called). (TJ III, v)

"I know it is but a Play: And if it was really a Ghost, it could do one no Harm at such a Distance, and in so much Company . . . . Nay, perhaps, it is the Devil—for they say he can put on what Likeness he pleases.—Oh! here he is again.—No Farther! No, you have gone far enough already; farther than I'd have gone for all the King's Dominions." (TJ XVI, v)

Now, as this was a Discovery of great Consequence, it may be
necessary to trace it from the Fountain-head. We shall therefore
very minutely lay open those previous Matters by which it was
produced; and for that Purpose, we shall be obliged to reveal all
the Secrets of a little Family, with which my Reader is at present
entirely unacquainted; and of which the Economy was so rare
and extraordinary, that I fear it will shock the utmost Credulity
of many married Persons. (TJ II, ii)

The incidental emergence of an unknown, dead character, Summer,
toward the end of the novel has been criticized as a "flaw" in Fielding's plot.
Summer's ghost, recalled to be the "father" of Tom Jones, seems to be too
important a figure to be left out completely in the novel until the end, and
treated in such a casual and hasty manner. Yet neither R. S. Crane's plot
study nor Sheridan Baker's "case history" of Bridget thoroughly questioned
the probability of Tom's fatherhood.[9] Is Summer really Tom's father?
      To trace Tom's fatherhood from the "Fountain Head" of Tom's
motherhood, we must reread what Baker calls "Bridget's sexual comedy."
The first love story of our "First Lady" betrays a different story of Tom's
fatherhood: Bridget had the two sons from one lover—Dr. Blifil, who was
driven away from Paradise Hall shortly after Bridget married his brother. He
died in London where, intriguingly, his ghost returns on stage when his son
Tom comes to see a play, *Hamlet*. Tom comes to the playhouse accompanied
by Partridge, his living "ghost father." When the ghost of Hamlet's father
appears on stage, Partridge calls him "Squire Hamlet," instead of "the King."
The novelistic design in which Partridge the Jacobite reduces the sovereign
status of the ghost king to the status of a "squire" suggests that Fielding, the
"True Patriot," wishes his hero a forgetting of a failed fatherhood. Secretly
and silently, he protects his Tom from repeating the tragedy of Prince
Hamlet, so that "Tom Summer," innocent of his parenthood, shall return to
Paradise Hall in a happy state of mind to rule with peace and harmony, free
of guilt and revenge. Fielding subverts Shakespeare's tragedy in a surprising
way.
      His subversive writing strategies are designed with deep historical
implications and political necessity, and they deliver his ideological
argument over legitimacy. The "naked Charms" of "Bridget's sexual
comedy" quietly deny the rule of right on the right, and defy the criticism of
"aristocratic ideology" on the left. To the right, the very fact that Fielding
"makes his Tom an illegitimate . . . a common" indicates a radical challenge

to the privilege of birthright. To the left, the fact that Tom and Blifil were born from the same family, same class, same lineage, yet one proves to be good, the other evil, problematizes the deterministic theory that class origin determines class consciousness. Fielding, in spite of his belief in so called good-breeding, believes that good-breeding comes from the spirit of Love, from education and experience, rather than class privilege.

Fielding contends that legitimacy, either in exercise of political power or in claim of philosophical truth, largely depends upon literacy and that it must be gained, as Plato recommends for the Philosopher Ruler, through a well-designed education program, which involves rigorous training in abstract reasoning, as well as practical experience. Therefore, his text itself is programmed as an exercise of intelligence. His "love stories" are truly "adult" books—for those who have good knowledge and experience only. A good understanding depends on good judgment—to detect and decipher what cannot be seen and cannot be said—"you can't always know the Inside by the Outside" (TJ VII, xiii). Fielding is tempted to play off the kind of reader who take words at face value, and truth from God. He despises Parson Thwackum because "the latter decided all Matters by Authority; but in doing this, he always used the Scriptures and their Commentators, as the Lawyer doth his Coke upon Littleton, where the Comment is of equal Authority with the Text" (TJ III, iii). He'd rather undermine his own "authority of the author" to invite metaphysical speculations from the reader. His "love stories" are composed in a way that tests the reader's "Sagacity" in taking the pleasure of his text:

> Reader . . . thou are highly mistaken if thou dost imagine that we intended, when we began this great Work, to leave thy Sagacity nothing to do; or that, without sometimes exercising this Talent, thou wilt be able to travel through our Pages with any Pleasure or Profit to thyself. (TJ XI, ix)

Those who were fooled by Fielding in the beginning into believing that Partridge and Jenny Jones are Tom's parents could very well be fooled again by Jenny in the end. His "ghost story" is and is not a practical joke.

Carl R. Kropf's study "Judgment and Character, Evidence and the Law in *Tom Jones*" proposes a sagacious approach to the novel.[10] Kropf suggests that *Tom Jones* may be read as a virtual handbook on the abuse and misuse of evidence, Fielding's satire on the legalistic point of view that does not admit evidence related to motive and credibility of the witness. The eighteenth-century law and trial reports show that anything a witness said under oath was to be taken as true unless directly contradicted. Kropf reports, "virtually anyone without an unpardoned conviction *pro crimine falsi* could swear to virtually anything, and unless his testimony was directly contradicted by other evidence, his word stood as legal proof of the fact in question."[11] Fielding was well aware of the liabilities inherent in the fact-oriented, legalistic point of view. He composed *Tom Jones* in the midst of a lively legal debate over the proper use of evidence—"its validity or invalidity, its admissibility or inadmissibility, and its interpretation." In writing the novel the Magistrate judges his characters, as Empson puts it, "as though when he was on the bench." The reader is the juror whose function is to decide the merits of the case based on the admissible facts. "Facts, Fielding demonstrates, do not speak for themselves." Though the narrative is open to multiple interpretations because of the deliberate misinterpretations and misuse of evidence, "the result is that . . . the narrator by his silence or by his misinterpretation of events calls attention to the only interpretation that common sense could approve and that is made conspicuous by its very absence."

Kropf's suggestion can be well applied to a reinvestigation of Tom's parentage. There is nothing more "conspicuous by its very absence" than Tom's father in Fielding's "lawyerlike design." The story of Summer's ghost is a black hole, a conspicuous gap, a question mark in the text, that "common sense" cannot approve as "the only interpretation." More questionable is the motive and "credibility" of witness used in the novel. In the study of the novel, "common sense" lies in the judgment of the probability of character, action, and motive, of which *Tom Jones* has been widely acknowledged as an exemplary model. A proper investigation of these elements only reveals many problems in determining the "validity or invalidity," the "admissibility or inadmissibility," of the witnesses involved. There is evidently a prominent misuse of evidence. If one construes the promiscuous character and problematic motives of Mrs. Waters/Jenny Jones, whose "twice-told tales" have twice been taken as testimony of Tom's fatherhood, there is no guarantee of truth in such evidence.

The "fact" we have in hand is Jenny Jones' second confession based on a "confession" Bridget "honestly" made to her. It is also a complete withdrawal of her first account made "honestly" to the same Magistrate, Allworthy, in the same manner of a "court confession." Allworthy, as Kropf judges him, is a character who "meticulously accumulates facts but refuses to look beyond them." In fact, the "fact" he has is a story three times removed from its original account. Judging from the character of the two confessors, we must recognize, Bridget is superprudent, and Jenny Jones overeducated. When they tell their respective "stories," their motives are nevertheless clear: Bridget is employing Jenny Jones to cover up her scandal; and Jenny Jones, who now has no need to cover up the scandal of the dead, is only too anxious to clear herself from what could be an incest charge. Fielding the Magistrate knew that from the legal point of view there's no legitimacy in their accounts. In other words, he properly undermines and even cancels the probability of what appears to be only a novelistic expediency. Bridget is the plotter of all plots, an utterly "unreliable narrator." There is no conceivable motive for being true to Jenny Jones either. Fielding himself is an even better plotter; he throws out a red herring to cancel the legitimacy of Mrs. Waters's (Jenny Jones's) story: Allworthy recalls that Bridget had disdainfully declined his offer to help her marry Summer. By character Bridget is not the kind of woman who doesn't know what to do with such an offer, given she was indeed in love with Summer. On the other hand, it is not improbable that she might have named a dead person to satisfy Jenny's curiosity. Suppose she's still carrying on her affair with Tom's father at that time; if so, she would not want to reveal his identity. If there is any chance that she should speak truth, the truth could only have been in her will. Fielding mentions several times that her will is intercepted by Young Blifil; but he never lays it open. Fielding keeps silent about the will, about the possible truth. As Kropf suggests, "the narrator by his silence. . . calls attention to the only interpretation . . . that is made conspicuous by its very absence."

The scandal over Bridget's will, which ultimately exposes the evil character of Blifil, may entail a very dangerous historical reference that Fielding would never have been able to articulate in a public discourse and that accounts for his narrative silence. George I had drawn his will in 1716 that after his death, whenever any of his successors had two sons, the elder should retain the Crown but hand over the electorate (of Hanover) to his next brother. George II, on coming to the throne (1727), did his best to suppress the will. He obtained the copies of the will lodged by his father in duke of Wolfrebuttel's keeping and sent them with his own copy to be lodged in the arcana of the Hanoverian Records. Moreover, George II had always had the intention to exclude his elder son, Frederick, from the English throne and have his second son, William, succeed as king.[12] Frederick was patron to the Opposition and the Broad-Bottoms, to which Fielding was attached. But after the Battle of Culloden, William ("Billy the Butcher") had a better chance as a rival. It is very likely that Fielding's implicit contrivance of the rivalry between the two future rulers of Paradise Hall, Tom and Blifil, and the two lovers, the elder Blifil as well, contains the fiction of a contemporary history.

I am not tempted to believe that Fielding would take Frederick, the prince of Wales, as an ideal role model for a future ruler, knowing his reported ill character. By character, Fielding was apparently in favor of his "little Tommy," his fictional projection of "the Young Chevalier," a detailed picture of whom I will present in a later section of this chapter. The projection of a third possibility is always Fielding's "wonderful idea"—a literary strategy to break through the "diametrically opposed" dead end. He has invented the idea, as a political alternative, to adopt the "foundling," a prince in exile, educate him properly, and make him a patriotic king. Accordingly, Partridge's argument that "Prince Charles was as good a Protestant as any in England" may not be read as a fallacy, but at least as "a wonderful Idea." His idea may not be altogether infeasible; in fact, the English lords had a history of adopting infant foundlings anyway, for instance, the Protestant adoption of James I. As I mentioned before, Fielding's fundamental belief in selecting a rightful ruler, as he states in his Dedication to Lyttleton, is that "it is much easier to make good Men wise, than to make bad Men good." So his argument over legitimacy places character over birthright. His argument is all the more convincing once we face the reality that Tom and Blifil, like the Blifil brothers, are not half brothers, but are born of the same parentage. With such a historical subtext in view, Bridget's identity stands larger than a country prude. Her "sexual comedy" symbolically sets the stage for a long nightmare in English history: the curse of incestuous adultery.

Bridget's sexual comedy contains a logical progression of a feminine fiction, a counternarrative that holds the reader's attention to the author's silence. The knowing reader really does not need Jenny Jones to discover Tom's parenthood. One only needs the common sense of adult love, or "adultery." Fielding, the founder of Scotland Yard, has actually written a detective story in Bridget's sexual comedy. Read as a detective story, the reader can easily come up with what Kropf views as "the only interpretation that common sense could approve" of Tom's fatherhood.

Book I "preconceives" the idea of legitimacy and lineage. If we follow the idea, as soon as the argument is evoked with the discovery of the "Sleeping Beauty" in the bachelor's bed, Fielding's narrative quickly directs our attention to the character of Bridget, her marriage, and her sexuality. It is an alarming fact that Bridget marries the younger Blifil only because the elder Blifil, in spite of his love for her, cannot marry her. The elder Blifil is a married man, spiritual and religious, a Catholic. Fielding speaks of him in a solemn tone:

As Sympathy of all Kinds are apt to beget Love; so Experience teaches us that none have a more direct Tendency this Way than those of a religious Kind between Persons of Different Sexes. The Doctor found himself so agreeable to Miss Bridget, that he now began to lament an unfortunate Accident which had happened to him about ten Years before; namely, his marriage with another Woman, who was not only still alive, but what was worse, known to be so by Mr. Allworthy. This was a fatal Bar to Happiness which he otherwise saw sufficient probability of obtaining happiness with this young Lady; for as to criminal Indulgences, he certainly never thought of them. This was owing either to his Religion, as is most probable, or to the Purity of his Passion, which was fixed on those Things, which Matrimony only, and not criminal Correspondence, could put him in Possession of, or could give him any Title to. He had not long ruminated on these Matters, before it occurred to his Memory that he had a Brother who was under no such unhappy Incapacity. This brother, he made no doubt would succeed; for he discerned, as he thought, an Inclination to Marriage in the Lady. (TJ I, x)

The character of elder Blifil, as we are told, is capable of committing romantic folly to protect his lady's interest as she desires it—not unbecoming the character of Tom's progenitor. There might be true love in his case; if so, it well explains the affection Bridget later lavishes upon *his* son, Tom. If Tom is Summer's son, however, there is no stated reason why she should love him more than young Blifil.

Even so, Fielding still raises sufficient doubt for the reader to think twice about the motive of the doctor's extraordinarily "generous" deed:

But why the Doctor, who certainly had no great Friendship for his Brother, should for his Sake think of making so ill a Return to the Hospitality of Allworthy, is a Matter not so easy to be accounted for. (TJ I, x)

The "First Lady" must be pregnant again. We are immediately told that Captain Blifil's courtship takes "less than a month, during which the Captain preserved great distance of Behavior to his Lady in the Presence of the Brother." But the lady "had not been many Times in the Captain's Company before she was seized with this Passion" (TJ I, ii). Then "the Captain and the Lady were Man and Wife" without the knowledge of Allworthy. What occasion is it that causes this "prudent" lady to sell herself out in such a hurry? Fielding explains it with a humorous pun on the capitalized word "Issue": "Little previous Ceremony is required, to bring the Matter to *an Issue*, when both Parties are really in earnest" (TJ I, xii). Comically enough, when the elder Blifil breaks the matter to Allworthy, "it cost him some pains to prevent now and then a small Discomposure of his Muscles" (TJ I, xiii). The sort of Pains it costs him will have its real consequence after Bridget's marriage. Fielding's capitalized words are highly suggestive. "Eight Months after the Celebration of the Nuptials between Captain Blifil and Miss Bridget Allworthy," Fielding ironically calls the married Bridget, now a mother-to-be, by her maiden name with an emphatic tone—"a young Lady of great Beauty, Merit, and Fortune, was Miss Bridget, by reason of a Fright, delivered of a fine Boy." And we are explicitly told: "The Child was indeed, to all Appearance, perfect; but the Midwife discovered, it was born a Month before its full time" (TJ II, ii). Why does Fielding call the reader's attention to the time gap?

The premature birth of her second child might account for the failure of her marriage. There must be a reason why Captain Blifil treats her "with that Haughtiness and Insolence, which none but those who deserve some Contempt themselves can bestow, and those only who deserve no Contempt can bear" (TJ II, vii). Since Bridget cannot bear what had she done to deserve such contempt? That the captain must have some knowledge regarding the progeny of the two children can be a possible explanation of his behavior toward both his wife and his brother after his marriage. Otherwise, how could the Captain be so brutal and ungrateful toward his brother that he must drive him away from Paradise Hall? The elder Blifil "once intended to acquaint Allworthy with the whole; but he could not bring himself to submit to the Confession, by which he must take to his Share so great a portion of Guilt" (TJ I, xiii). The capitalized words—"Confession," "Share," and "Guilt"—are indicative of Fielding's emphatic "double-talk."

He went directly to London where he died soon after of a broken Heart" (TJ I, xiii). Here ends Book I, when Tom's parentage, the essential question in this chapter, had properly been illuminated. "The narrator by his silence or by his misinterpretation of events" has sufficiently called our attention to "the only interpretation that common sense could approve": The doctor had sired both Tom and Blifil. He couldn't accomplish his love affair with Bridget partly because of his Roman Catholic religion, and partly because of "the Purity of his passion." In order to comply with her interest in marriage and the secular law, he arranged for his brother to marry his lady. This way, at least his second son could have the name of his family. As it worked out, the young Blifil was saved from the name of "bastard," being born timely into a wedlock, but Bridget committed incest and started the curse in the family. The captain, having found out "the Fruits of Sin" (TJ II, ii) (note Fielding's use of the plural) planted by his brother and his wife, showed no paternal affection toward the young Blifil, resented his brother, and illused his wife when he strangely died of a stroke. Thus Bridget is left free to lament her doomed love by lavishing her affection upon Tom—the child of a loving memory, the first born, but born out of wedlock, and without the legacy of a name. Her widowhood must be haunted by not one but a pair of ghosts, with whom she had committed incest.

Fielding has thus shown the absurdity of legitimacy and lineage. Between the two children who grow up to be rivals as heir to Allworthy, there is little difference in their "planned parenthood." The difference between a legal heir and a deprived child is only instituted by the marriage law, while the law is blind to the truth of legitimacy. For in truth, Tom is the first born by birthright. Blifil is a real bastard, because he was born in a bed of incest and adultery, and he shall have no means to identify whose son he is and is not. If there is a difference between the two, it is the mystery of Love at work: Tom has a good character because he is born out of the spirit of love. With that gift, he wins the heart of Allworthy and the love of Sophia naturally. Blifil lacks character because he lacks the spirit of love. With a calculating mind, selfish interest, and jealous temperament, he ruins his own legitimacy as the rightful heir. While the difference of legitimacy is inscribed in the illegitimate beginning, in the "fountain-head" of a noble family, the conventional notion of legacy is thoroughly and ironically subverted through Fielding's "love stories."

The theme of Tom's fatherhood and lineage is further resumed and reinforced in Chapter Five of Book XVI when Tom comes to London and goes to a playhouse, accompanied by Patridge, his known "father" unknown to him. Notably, Fielding enacts two scenes from *Hamlet*: the ghost scene and the grave-digging scene. In Fielding's fictional theater, the graveyard becomes the metaphor of a dynasty that owes the lives of an amazing "Number of Skulls thrown upon the Stage." "It was one of the most famous Burial-Places about Town," says Tom. Partridge replies: "No wonder the Place is haunted." Partridge complains loudly that the grave-digger is not efficient and fast enough, and that the action Hamlet takes drawing his sword in the bedroom scene is nothing but "any good Man that had such a Mother, would have done exactly the same." He even claims that only the ghost has played his right part to prompt an action in his son. The historical implication and political satire are but grave and penetrating. Offstage and in history, that was the time Billy the Butcher's slaughter in 1746 and all the subsequent executions of lords and Jacobites had made London a bloody hell, a graveyard. Fielding undermines the reality of presentation by creating a gap, a fake, and this time a "farce" in an illusory theater. His literary strategy blurs the distinction among history, drama, and fiction.

In the playhouse, the center of attention is Partridge—Tom's living "ghost father." Partridge makes a great farce at seeing the Ghost appearing onstage, as though the ghost were his own mirror image. At first, he refuses to take the ghost as a ghost. "No, no, Sir, Ghosts don't appear in such Dresses as that, neither." But the ghost evokes a deep sympathy in him, almost a self-pity. Tenderly, he calls the ghost "Squire Hamlet" instead of "the King." Partridge's misarticulation, comic and full of dramatic irony, as I read it, entails a significant reference to Partridge's politics. What it indicates is that Fielding stages Partridge as the type of Jacobite who has rationally accepted the abdication of the "Old Pretender." He is interested in the son because he is dissatisfied with the present regime. He swears that he himself, now also in the position of a "ghost father," will not put up with such a condition: "I would not be in so bad a Condition as what's his Name, Squire Hamlet, is there, for all the World." So he takes over the part of the ghost father in a more radical fashion than Hamlet's father. In Shakespeare, the king orders Hamlet not to do any harm to the queen; Partridge, in his radical subversion, instructs Tom what a son should do to a "vile wicked" mother:

> Ay, no Wonder you are in such a Passion; shake the vile wicked Wretch to Pieces. If she was my own Mother I should serve her so. To be sure, all Duty to a Mother is forfeited by such wicked Doings. —Ay, go about your Business; I hate the Sight of you. (TJ xvi,v)

While the dramatic irony is intended for the reader, Tom, unlike Hamlet, is kept ignorant of the "ghost talk." Fielding has never wanted Allworthy's foundling to know his real father and assume his blood lineage in his father's name because, as we have learned, Dr. Blifil is a strict Roman Catholic and failed his responsibility as the legitimate lover. Before "Squire Hamlet" appears onstage, enlightened by the candles lit onstage, Partridge had a momentary recollection of the Gunpowder Treason (1605). Secret Jacobite that he is, he shows no interest in a popish plot, for he knows that gunpowder and violence cost too much for the national well-being: "That here were Candles enough burnt in one Night, to keep an honest poor Family for a whole Twelvemonth." It is tactful of Fielding not to expose the identity of Tom's fatherhood to public knowledge, and more importantly, to the knowledge of his son. Tactically, if Tom ever knew who his real father was, and learned his father's "ghost story," he would not be able to escape the Hamlet complex. Burdened with guilt and filial duty, he might alienate himself, seek revenge, and possibly start another family feud or court tragedy, which, predictably, might bring nothing but another dynastic catastrophe. Fielding may have had sympathy for the persecuted rebels and Jacobite lords after 1746, but he had no intention to justifying the Rule of Right.

Peace and mercy are the dominant tones in the novel. Fielding loathed the bloody persecution of the rebels that was going on in London, so that he wrote the novel in a sense just as Ralph Ellison realizes what the novel is capable of when he speaks of Mark Twain's novels—"a comic antidote to the ailments of politics."[13] With benevolence and sagacity, the Magistrate demonstrates his political tactics in settling the criminal cases of lords and commons. According to a classic lore in government, if a prince commits a crime, he should be punished by the law that applies to a common; but corporal punishment is not applied in the trial of distinguished government officials. For such personages, the punishment of humiliation is by itself sufficient. Fielding functions under such a philosophy, which presupposes that a prince ought to be properly punished because his duty is to learn proper behavior. This is the reason why he exposes young Blifil's evil doings and deprives his title. Even Tom is always punished for his follies. The treatment of a head of the state must be different, not because of his social privilege, but because his public punishment will only endanger social stability. It may not sound "democratic" in a superficial sense, but in reality, it works with its own ethics and prudence. Destructive action leads nowhere unless a revolution is well guided by wise directors and with clearly defined, constructive objectives. Fielding is reluctant to publicize the scandal of "Squire Hamlet," but he quietly removes him from the throne.

His reason is well stated and well explained also in the telling of an interesting "love story." This time, the reader's attention is evoked with an exotic beauty (TJ XII, xii). In the court of the Egyptian king, Partridge, inflamed with wine and desire, is involved with a "Female Gypsy" and caught by her husband. The case is brought to court before the king. Tom offers the husband a guinea as compensation; but the man wants five, and the deal is settled for two. Tom is about to pay the money when his "Egyptian Majesty" stops him and addresses himself to the husband as follows:

"Me be sorry to see any Gypsy dat have no more Honor dan to
sell de Honor of his Wife for Money. If you had de love for your
Wife, you would have prevented dis Matter, and not endeavor to
make her de Whore dat you might discover her. Me do order dat
you have no Money given you; for you deserve Punishment, not
Reward; me do order derefore, dat you be de infamous Gypsy,
and do wear Pair of Horns upon your Forehead for one Month,
and dat your Wife be called de Whore, and pointed at all dat
Time: For you be de infamous Gypsy, but she be no less the
infamous Whore." (TJ XII, xii)

The king's verdict can be read as Fielding's "apology" for being silent in
delivering the very truth of "Bridget's sexual comedy."

Fielding's ideal projection of Tom Jones as the promising heir is
future-oriented. It proposes a precondition of forgetting the cause of the Old
Pretender. That Tom be raised as a foundling and a Protestant is Fielding's
wishful design. His proposition is that in spite of his lineage, the Young
Chevalier must forget his Roman Catholic origin, which has been a major
obstacle in his father's cause. There is a moment of revelation in Partridge's
big farce that Restoration of another Stuart dynasty is impractical: "—Oh!
here he is again.—No Farther! No, you have gone far enough already; farther
than I'd have gone for all the King's Dominions" (see epigraph). Once a
political regime is exiled over half a century from its mainland, "the King's
Dominions," and becomes a parasite in the a foreign court, it is practically
hopeless to redeem its lost cause together with its political ideology, because
its principles have already lost momentum in the popular mind. "And if it
was really a Ghost," says Partridge, "it could do one no Harm at such a
Distance, and in so much Company." Fielding must have been convinced
around 1748 that Jacobitism had lost its course and offered no more
substantial threat to the Hanoverian regime.

On the other hand, the domestic situation was a bloody mess; it took
radical measure to make a fundamental change. A new settlement of the
throne with a rightful ruler was a way out. Yet the choice is so limited that
it must be made among the princelings. He chooses the Young Chevalier,
not because of his birthright, but because of his legendary character
displayed during the war. He expects him to be a better monarch than both
the "Blifil brothers." Like Partridge, he secretly hopes that the prince may
settle the score with his "Mother"—petticoat politics and "witchcraft" in
court. Partridge's loud cry at Tom, "To be sure, all Duty to a Mother is
forfeited by such wicked Doings," frees the heir also from his maternal

lineage. If the Stuart lineage stands for a patriarchy of a dead past, the Hanoverian court is conceived as a matriarchy of the present. Fielding creates his "Prince" for a future regime. He wants him to forget his failed fatherhood of a French patriarchy and, by radical reform, to redeem the curse of his mother's incestuous adultery with Germany. It doesn't matter whatever birthright he has. It works all the better that he has not. As Berit R. Lindboe observes, "Fielding's propensity for alluding to Shakespeare's tragedies or to the darker moments of the comedies and the histories even allows him to suggest alternatives to the action which we see unfolding in his novel."[14] In suggesting alternatives to theatrical as well as political action, Fielding is more sagacious than Shakespeare. He shows a great statesman's craft in performing his fictional art—he is able to reduce the ancient score of kingly revenge and resolve the tragic irony of princely duty.

He is more progressive than Plato by naming his hero a no-name commoner. Fielding knows that in modern society and after the collapse of the feudal system, social and economic mobility is increasingly high; class consciousness can hardly remain a constant with its original identity of a family economy. To judge a man or a woman by his or her birth certificate is as reactionary as claiming the origin of an inviolable birthright. Class consciousness is doubtlessly conditioned by economic status, but it changes when the economic status undergoes substantial change. Fielding argues that children are not guilty for their parents' ill doings. He argues most forcefully in the speech of the good widow Mrs. Miller. As she says:

> The Words "dishonorable Birth" are Nonsense . . . unless the Word "Dishonorable" be applied to the Parents; for the Children can derive no real Dishonor from an Act of which they are entirely innocent. (TJ XIV, v)

Mrs. Miller, Allworthy's best lady friend, is a foster mother figure to Tom Jones. When Tom watches *Hamlet* in the playhouse, also present is Mrs. Miller, as though protecting the child from his bitch of a birth mother. At any rate, a new family, a new regime, is what Fielding had in mind.

Like Plato, Fielding believes in the value of education in developing the competency of the future ruler. The Egyptian king's foreign theory is part of Tom's education, which teaches him a great deal of "Gypsy Civilization."[15] The broken English spoken by the gypsy king is apparently carnivalesque, disruptive of the king's English, the official language. It is Fielding's invention of a paradoxically truthful language, an alternative speech system—"Huckspeech," as Neil Schmitz has humorously coined the term for Mark Twain's fictive language.[16] Outside the language of Christian doctrine on the right, and capitalist legacy on the left, Fielding offers the future ruler a precious chance to observe an alternative model outside the system of the existing hierarchy. The model is derived from "the enlightened absolutism of old Egypt" under the rule of its "Philosopher Kings":

> "About a thousand or two thousand Year ago, me cannot tell to a Year or two, as can neider write nor read, there was a great what you call, —a Volution among de gypsy; for dere was de Lord gypsy in dose Days; and dese Lord did quarrel vid one anoder about de Place; but de King of de gypsy did demolish dem all, and made all his Subject equal vid each oder; and since dat time dey have agree very well: For dey no tink of being King, and may be it be better for dem as dey be, for me assure you it be ver troublesome ting to be King, and always to do Justice; me have often wish to be de private gypsy when me have been forced to punish my dear Friend and Relation; for dough we never put to Death, our Punishments be ver severe. Dey make de gypsy ashamed of demselves, and dat be ver terrible Punishment; me ave scarce ever known de gypsy so punish do Harm any more." (TJ XII, xii)

The political ideal Fielding suggestively introduced in this "Huckspeech"— the idea of a "revolution" that makes all subjects equal with one another, that demolishes the court of gypsy lords who quarrel with one anther, and that proposes a benevolent king who does not want to be a king but a private civilian—is shockingly progressive and radical. In educating his princes Fielding is future-oriented, idealistic, and prophetic of enlightened rulers such as Thomas Jefferson in America a century later.

William R. Taylor in *Cavalier and Yankee*, an interesting character study, discusses the difference between Jefferson and Adams over the issue of ruling class. After the American Revolution, both of them were deeply concerned with the kind of social mobility republican institutions were producing in America. What class of men would replace the ruling aristocracies of Europe? The moneyed or the talented? The choice is limited indeed. After the overthrow of a feudal system, "rule by talent" or "rule by wealth" seems to be the only choice for a modern society. Yet it is that choice that makes all the difference between a bourgeois democracy and a true democracy. Jefferson was most concerned with eliminating the vestiges of colonial aristocracy. He observed a cultural difference, that is, in New England, members of certain families had probably once possessed qualities which won them deserved respect, and this respect had been passed along to their sons and grandsons, more or less independently of their individual worth. Whereas, in Virginia, the sons of certain families which had accumulated wealth for generations might not win popular votes or attain political power merely by the magic of their family names, but by their personal qualities. He wrote to Adams:

> From what I have seen of Massachusetts and Connecticut, there seems to be in those two states a traditional reverence for certain families. . . . In Virginia, we have nothing of this. . . . A Randolph, a Carter, or a Burwell must have great personal superiority over a common competitor to be elected by the people, even at this day.[17]

Adams, on the contrary, told Jefferson that he would expect to find a "White Rose and a Red Rose" in "every Village in the World" (30). He expected that the families that remained prominent—"Our Winthrops, Winslows, Bradfords, Saltonstalls, Quincys, Chandlers, Leonards, Hutchinsons, Olivers, Sewalls etc.—would continue to monopolize political power" (30). Taylor considers Adams's anticipated new social world to differ "very little from the old" (30). Adams was a Calvinist, Taylor explains. Jefferson, very much like Fielding, was not a religious fanatic. His personal ideal would have agreed with the statement of Fielding's gypsy king quoted above.

    Both Jefferson and Fielding were nurtured in the spirit of Enlightenment thinking. Fielding wrote *Tom Jones* only twenty-five years before the Declaration of Independence. Jefferson presented his educational proposals to the Virginia Assembly in 1779, precisely thirty years after the publication of *Tom Jones*. The Jeffersonian ideal of "natural aristocracy" is based on "a great personal superiority" cultivated through a well-designed education program. The result would be the establishment of what we call an "elite" leadership. But that elite class is not the old aristocracy, but a new class of rightful rulers trained for the operation of a new system. As Taylor points out, Jefferson hoped that "by removing the top layer of society, he might be able to eliminate both the half breeds and the pretenders from the scene as well. He anticipates a world in which aristocratic aspirations would play little or no part" (33). Jefferson used the word "pretenders" to refer to those "who from vanity, or the impulse of growing wealth . . . sought to detach themselves from the plebeian ranks" (33). Jefferson was attached to the yeomanry because "it possessed no aristocratic yearnings of any kind" (33).

From the viewpoint of Jeffersonian democracy, Fielding's class consciousness can be better understood. In theory, Fielding's criteria in selecting the rightful ruler of England are removed from the Royalist position of Toryism, but opposed to the practice of Whiggery. His well-balanced and well-measured "Midway position" does not fit into the opposition of a two-party system, nor does his Platonic wisdom enjoy the popularity in a materialistic society. As a result, his political ideal is easily excluded by the mainstream of a political discourse, which functions on a blind binary party line. In fiction, he discovers his own space to project his political ideal—"a New Province of Writing."

Within the specific context of *Tom Jones* and dressed up in the form of "Huckspeech," Fielding is projecting a utopia as Swift and Thomas More had both done before him and as Faulkner is to follow in his wake. What Fielding envisions is possibly what in the West we call a modern "authoritarian" state. But this is not to say that Fielding knew not the problems involved in establishing the legitimacy of a centralized power. In reality, Fielding knew the difficulty in securing a rightful ruler:

> In reality, I know but of one solid Objection to absolute Monarchy. The only Defect in which excellent Constitution seems to be the Difficulty of finding any Man adequate to the Office of an absolute Monarch: For this indispensably requires three Qualities very difficult, as it appears from History, to be found in princely Natures: First, a sufficient Quantity of Moderation in the Prince, to be contented with all the Power which is possible for him to have. 2ndly, Enough of Wisdom to know his own Happiness. And, 3dly, Goodness sufficient to support the Happiness of others, when not only compatible with, but instrumental to his own. (TJ XII, xii)

The three qualities that he desires in the rightful ruler—self-control, wisdom, and altruism—can be cultivated only through practical training and classic education. He proposes these personal qualities not as Christian "virtue," but as political science. Kenneth Rexroth believes that Tom Jones could be a non-Christian, a "typical Chinese hero":

> Tom is the Good-Nature Man, but by this Fielding means more than his contemporaries meant by the eighteenth century catch phrase—something very like the "human-heartedness" of Confucius. Several times Fielding interpolates little lectures on good nature that sound exactly like translations from the Chinese.

Tom is very much the typical Chinese hero, and the novel could easily be restated in Chinese terms and setting. Not least of its Chinese characteristics is its decorum. Fielding wrote *Tom Jones* against the lachrymose soul-probing of Richardson's heroines, as a protest against bad manners.[18]

I would not assume Fielding was knowledgeable of Chinese classics; only it happens that the model of Plato's Philosopher Ruler turns out to be not impossible or a "miracle," but a traditional practice in Chinese government, with its system of imperial examinations, its intellectual elitism, its respect for Confucius the Philosopher, its emphasis on literacy and wisdom, and its belief in ethics, benevolence, and good nature as a guarantee for a happy state. This is, after all, what Fielding argues as a political necessity in selecting the rightful ruler:

> Now if an absolute Monarch, with all these great and rare Qualifications, should be allowed capable of conferring the greatest Good on Society; it must be surely granted, on the contrary, that absolute Power vested in the Hands of one who is deficient in them all, is likely to be attended with no less a Degree of Evil. (TJ XII, xii)

In other words, Fielding knew the the difference between Stalin and Hitler, Mao and Madame Mao.

Even though Fielding's projection appeared to be a utopia in 1748, it was somewhat worked out a decade after his death when George III came to the throne in 1760. The German princeling raised in England became the first "Patriotic King." The king revolted against his Hanoverian forefathers, took the exclusive council of his tutor Bute, and recalled Pitt back to power. Pitt was Fielding's friend, also, the head of the Broad-Bottoms. As Fielding would like it, George III was educated to believe that he was born to cleanse the corruption of the government.[19] More than Fielding could have wished, the king was advised not to marry an English woman so as to protect himself from petticoat politics. He married Princess Charlotte Sophia, a "Miranda" from the dukedom of Meklenburg Strelitz. With a "wondrous light," novelistic love not only provides the possibility and freedom of speech for Fielding to advocate his political ideology, but also makes "the improbable the inevitable" ahead of history and time. In writing *Tom Jones*, Fielding had long prepared his future ruler for the hand of his Sophia. Now let's take a close look at the "naked charms" of Fielding's Sophia.

Sophia: "The Emblematic Redaction of
the Platonic Metaphor"

> If thou has seen all these without knowing what Beauty is, thou
> hast no Eyes; if without feeling its Power, thou hast no Heart. (TJ
> IV, ii)

> Here Nature appears in her richest Attire, and Art dressed with
> the modestest Simplicity, attends her benignant Mistress. Here
> Nature indeed pours forth the choicest Treasures which she hath
> lavished on this World; and here human Nature presents you with
> an Object which can be exceeded only in the other. (TJ XI, ix)

More in the vein of Plato than Cicero, Fielding's object of beauty is
not a mere "Object of Sight," but a subject of metaphor that, as he describes,
"strikes us with an Idea of that Loveliness, which Plato asserts there is in her
naked Charms" (Dedication). In order to hear Fielding's argument embedded
in the text of pleasure, the reader must, at the author's demand, be able to
envision naked charms beyond the feast of the visible World, which Plato
distinguishes from the intelligible world. Fielding, in his fictional universe,
actually draws Plato's "dividing line" between the two worlds—the world
of sight and the world of Reality. That is also the line between the world of
signs and the world of truth, the world that is full of "sound and fury
signifying nothing" and the world that moves in "the mute eloquence of
love." We will visit these worlds in the following pages.

The primary object of desire is Sophia. Martin C. Battestin has
nicely named Sophia "the emblematic redaction of the Platonic metaphor."
Battestin's interpretation of Sophia is very instructive:

> The apprehension of *Sophia* was the goal of Plato's philosopher;
> the acquisition of *Prudentia*—which begins with the intimation
> that the Good, the True, and the Beautiful are one—is the quest
> of the *vir honestus*. Fielding's intention in *Tom Jones* is to
> demonstrate the nature, function, and relationship of these
> correlative ethical concepts.[20]

The character of Sophia by name is created as that Platonic ideal. In Plato, the ultimate goal of the Philosopher Ruler is to attain the absolute truth/beauty in an ideal world, but the belief in ideal beauty and the acquisition of worldly experience are not separate, but complement rather than conflict with each other. Platonic love is accomplished through a sequence of five progressive steps, as I analyzed in Chapter Two: the love of physical beauty; of moral integrity and public action; of science and philosophy; of aesthetic creativity; and of absolute beauty. The legitimate lover must climb these steps with a constant vision of the ideal in view. Therefore, Fielding puts Tom through these steps before he qualifies him to marry Sophia. Tom's love affair with Molly Seagrim is the love of physical beauty. When he volunteers to serve in the king's army, he is motivated by the love of moral integrity and public action. His respect for the Man on the Hill shows his love for science and philosophy. His theatergoing in London cultivates his love for aesthetic activities. Finally, the consummation of his love with Sophia is the attainment of absolute beauty.

Sophia is not the kind of embodiment of middle-class virtue as Richardson's readers may expect (rather, her behavior might impose a question mark upon the "sainthood" of Clarissa). She is not a "role model" for ladies or maidens in terms of virtue either in court or in "attic." As a real character, she has black hair, lies to her father, runs away from home, keeps secret correspondence with her lover, gets lost on the road, ignores Herriet's good advice. She makes herself a victim of a London Rake, only to be rescued, ironically, by her daddy's timely arrival on the point of a rape—"Here's a good girl, my Sophy." In short, Fielding creates Sophia not as a model of female virtue, but as an artifice, an adequate idea, but self-insufficient (TJ IV, ii).

In his presentation of Sophia, Fielding's literary strategy is similar to Socrates' method in *The Symposium*—a fake, a drama, a gap. His obsessive "Elevation of Stile" is a fake—a bombastic overture followed by a comic pastoral invocation, which lasts as long as two chapters (TJ IV, i-ii). He fakes because he "thought it proper to prepare the Mind of the Reader for her Reception, by filling it with every pleasing Image." In a mock-heroic manner, the image of Sophia is identified with everyone from a Greek goddess to "the basket-woman" onstage. With piles upon piles of epic similes, courtly conceits, singsong lyric, superficial euphemism, and "other kinds of poetical Embellishments," Fielding practically ruins all the cliches of female beauty, and thereby he exhausts the possibility of identifying Sophia with any existing sight of beauty.

His staging of Sophia is so elaborate and sensational that as a rule of the game, one must look deep into his intent. "With a Flourish of Drums and Trumpets . . . to rouse a Martial Spirit in the Audience, and to accommodate their Ears to Bombast and Fustian," he stages a world of "sound and fury signifying nothing," meanwhile inventing a provocative ideological discourse that disrupts his theatrical discourse. The novelist questions the competency of "the Politician's good nose," "the Priest's vision of 'Deity'," and "the ear of Locke's blind Man if he mightn't have grossly erred" in missing the voice by the sound (TJ IV, i). In effect, his elevated rhetoric undermines the realism of his drama. It violates the surface of language and reveals the gap between the world of senses and the world of substance.

Fielding cautions the reader not to approach the subject of Sophia at face value; there are touches beyond what is skin-deep. The lover of her "absolute beauty," if he's "good" enough, may kiss her "lips," feel her "blood" pulse, and communicate with her "body" language, which is suggested in the two quotes from Suckling and Donne (TJ IV, ii). There, the good lover discovers, her lips themselves recall the name of Plato—"Some Bee had stung it newly." Her blood "pure and eloquent," running like a speech—"Spoke in her Cheeks, and so distinctly wrought,/ That one might almost say her Body thought." Her "Body" stood, as it were, a vessel of a philosophical discourse.

Bees are said to have fed the infant Plato with honey. While introducing Sophia, Fielding, the prompter offstage, is ushering in Plato with "his eloquent thought and speech." The idealization of a woman in a monumental statue of a great philosopher is rare in Christian tradition, although it exists in Greek civilization and other "heathen" cultures, such as Socrates' Diotima in *The Symposium*. In Christian society, feminine intelligence has been suppressed, and the Platonic tradition survives on a marginal position. Fielding belongs to the margin. Writing in the Platonic tradition, he also identifies Platonic love with the feminine:

> That refined Degree of Platonic Affection which is absolutely detached from the Flesh, and is indeed entirely and purely spiritual, is a Gift confined to the female Part of the creation. (TJ XVI, v)

That "female Part of the creation"—Platonic love—is the "bottom part" of the story, the tail of the tale enveloped in Fielding's feminine fiction. The Platonic tradition being "heathen" in the public discourse of a Christian society, the novelist has to cover his feminine part with theatrical costumes and stage rhetoric. Its naked beauty lies offstage in a decent intelligible world," not exposed to the visual world. Thus in Fielding, visual appearance turns out to be a theater of illusions. The surface of a story, heavy with "facts and details," is only a dress, a drama, a tool, or an instrument of the idea. While the tale of his "history" is staged in a drama, the "tail" of history coils underneath the surface of a love story. He seems to take delight in what I call the "non-Western and non-Christian femininity." "Those who object to the Heathen Theology," says he, "may, if they please, change our Goddess into the above mentioned Basket-woman" (TJ IV, i). With such a warning, Fielding challenges his Christian readers to make a choice between a heresy and a mockery.

Sophia's identity with the philosopher, if it is delicate in the beginning, becomes more and more explicit once she leaves home running on the road:

> When they had gone about Two hundred Paces from the Inn, on the London Road, Sophia rode up to the Guide, and, with the Voice much fuller of Honey than was ever that of Plato, though his Mouth is supposed to have been a Bee-hive, begged him to take the first Turning which led toward Bristol. (TJ X, ix)

The risks and haphazard she runs into during her journey to London and her ill use by Lady Balleston and Lord Fellamar happen to be symbolic representations of a drama Plato has enacted in the chapter on "The Philosopher Ruler" in his *Republic*:

> So Philosophy is abandoned by those who should be her true lovers, who leave her deserted and unwed to pursue a life that does not really suit them, while she, like an abandoned orphan, suffers at the hands of second-rate interlopers all the shame and abuse which you have said her detractors accuse her of, when they say that half her companions are worthless and the other half downright wicked. (*The Republic* 291)

Plato is describing metaphorically the misfortune of a society in which there is no right or wrong. Wisdom/truth/beauty, the goal of philosophical love, is not pursued as a principle and value in government, but raped, ransacked, abused, in the hands of mediocre and malicious critics and politicians, who in turn become the rulers of that rapacious society.

Corresponding to Plato's metaphor, in his presentation of the "love stories" of Sophia Western, Fielding is literally dramatizing Plato's conviction that, in government, sagacious judgment with ethical commitment is a necessity. Sophia's experience shows that without the competency to identify the directions down the road, distinguish truth from rumor (the rumor about her lover Tom), nor character to maintain independence (as Defoe's heroines do), nor power to resist wicked advices and rude advances, "pretty girls" are lost in the hands of conspirators and rapists. History is full of such tragedies as honorable revolutionary courses run into chaotic violence. Putting the lovely Sophia through all kinds of distress and dangers in the chaotic state of courts and inns, Fielding stages such chaotic violence in a democracy.

Fielding's political ideal might be subject to the criticism of "patriarchy"; but on the other hand, to assume bourgeois democracy without patriarchy is a pure fallacy. Patriarchy or a privileged class so far exists in every model of human society, either under the system of bourgeois democracy or proletariat democracy. The difference lies in the selection criteria and system of promotion. It depends on how privilege is established. Whether it is established on the basis of wealth or wisdom, with or without the excellence of human decency, is the real issue. Under a feudal system privilege is first established by military valor and then it can be inherited by birthright. Under a capitalist system, privilege can be established by economic power, yet it still can be inherited by family money. For instance, prep schools and private colleges are a privilege for the moneyed to be better prepared for promotion. If privilege has to be awarded by proof of good nature and true wisdom, Fielding might think of such a system as a more civilized model in establishing even a "privileged" ruling class. This is, as Empson argues, what Fielding proposes in *Tom Jones*:

> We learn incidentally Fielding presumed men ought to be promoted to the ruling class, as a regular thing; the point is merely that the system of promotion should be adequate to save it from contempt. . . . But it seems mere fact that Fielding's society needed a governing class, however things may work out under universal education; so it is reasonable of him to take a reformist view, as the Communists would say, and merely recommend a better selection.[21]

As to whether the model of Plato's Philosopher Ruler is possible in a capitalist economy, that is a different issue. One fundamental problem with the moneyed class in government, which Fielding witnessed in his lifetime, is ruling inefficiency and bureaucratic corruption. In a society where money becomes the measure of success and prestige, there is no material base for honor and virtue as the goals of human excellence. They become empty words, have little strength or sustenance to resist the temptation of money and bribery. Fielding's depiction of Sophia's guide is a dramatic presentation of such a problem, which I will discuss shortly. When ethical codes in government or business gradually lose their meaning, honor and virtue become painful restraint instead of a source of self-respect and self-satisfaction. The devil fears nothing except for the punishment of law. Yet by and by, legal practice relies on trained sophistry, and law becomes only a language.

Plato's idea of the Philosopher Ruler is significant in Fielding's time, a premodern period when the modern state power began to develop, and in our times too, postmodern times, when the problems Fielding philosophically speculated become the sight of public. First, it addresses the problem of bureaucratic corruption and inefficiency that the modern state power has exposed to the world for a while. Second, it proposes an educational program to prepare the rulers, which addresses the deficiencies caused by a bourgeois educational system, namely, cultural and ideological illiteracy. Third, Plato not only argues for the necessity of authority, but also sets up a role model for such an authority, that challenges the criteria and privilege of the ruling class present.

Fielding's theory is not pure abstraction from Plato, but based on his years of practical experience in office and the political reality of his time. Chaos and mob rebellion were the historical situation England was going through during the time he wrote *Tom Jones*. In his creation of Sophia as "the emblematic redaction of the Platonic metaphor," Fielding blends in also the metaphor of England's historical condition in 1745 and the emblem of the House of Hanovor. The drama of "Sophia lost on road and abused in London" is a metaphorical presentation of England lost in chaos and stagnation, suffering from rapacious violence and court conspiracies (TJ X, ix).

Fielding's rhetoric is highly suggestive. He links Sophia's voice to Plato—the voice of truth/beauty—even the horse "on which the Guide rode, is reported to have been so charmed by Sophia's voice, that he made a full Stop." However, the guide, less than a horse, is not inspired to follow Sophia's voice. So Sophia has to withdraw her "voice," but fulfil her "Word" (both capitalized) with "two guineas," which immediately sets the mercenary guide going and forgetting his original duty to his "Measter" (TJ X, ix). The guide is a typical character of the hired officer, a prototype of the modern employee, who functions under the pressure of money and power; nothing can motivate him but material incentives. The proficiency of his service so motivated turns out to be very poor. He leads Sophia in the wrong direction. Had he been self-motivated, the effect would have been totally different. Since he knew where Jones went, he could well have told Sophia to save her trip thither.

In this episode, Fielding demonstrates that linguistic materialism results from cultural materialism. People who are money-minded and hold their votes for a "promise" easily grow used to taking language or "Words" not for worth, but for cash value. The "Voice" of truth and wisdom, being less "indefinite" than a lump sum, will have no bearing upon "human behavior." The ruler, who has to resort to mercenary means or troops, is an unhappy ruler. As in the case of Sophia, she's easily misled and lost in her pursuit. In contrast, her father, Western, who's self-motivated, is apt to catch his "fox" on the right spot. Western speaks a language less determinate, his is a "Fox-hunter's language" that tells the "trace" by the scent. Even though his daughter is not within his sight,

> he doubted not in the least but Sophia travelled, or, as he phrased it, ran the same Way. He used indeed a very coarse Expression, which need not be here inserted; as Fox-hunters, who alone would understand it, will easily suggest it to themselves. (TJ IV, ii)

Fielding relies upon the "Fox-hunter's language" to send his message to his knowing reader. The reader who can "smell" can also sense that during this episode Sophia's symbolic identity is undergoing a metamorphosis. Her sweet voice of truth, which has inspired everyone's love at home, is now lost. She is seen in the position of a ruler who cannot function well with those who surround her. Her distress is identical with the chaotic state of the Hanoverian regime around 1745.

As we know, the Hanoverian throne came in the name of Sophia, the Electress of Hanovor. The image of Sophia Stuart Augustus of Hanover was cherished as "a clever, witty and lively old woman" in the memory of her English admirers, who used to call her "Queen Sophy." She was known to have broad interests in learning and a cosmopolitan outlook, a friend of the philosopher Leibniz. As heir apparent, she was more popular than her German princelings for being "abler in playing off English politicians against each other" and "less parochial than her son George." The Tories had expectations of her when she died three months before Queen Anne's decease in 1714. This miniature of a "memoir," however inadequate, may help us to envisage "the portrait of a lady" that Fielding expects to recall from the national memory of his contemporaries without too much difficulty. In his "Reception" aforementioned, he suggestively identifies Sophia with the "Galaxy" of England's historical portraits, "the Gallery of Beauties at Hampton-Court":

> Thou may'st remember each bright Churchill of the Galaxy, and all the Toasts of the Kit-cat. Or if their Reign was before thy Times, at least though hast seen their Daughters, the no less dazzling Beauties of the present Age; whose Names, should we here insert, we apprehend they would fill the whole Volume. (TJ IV, ii)

His fox-hunter's language becomes increasingly suggestive, directing the reader's attention not to the presence of the living character but to an absence of a spirit:

> Yet is it possible, my Friend, that thou mayest have seen all these without being able to form an exact Idea of Sophia: For she did not exactly resemble any of them. She was most like the Picture of Lady Ranelagh; and I have heard still to the famous Duchess of Mazarine; but most of all, she resembled one of whose Image never can depart from my Breast, and whom if thou dost remember, thou hast then, my Friend, an adequate Idea of Sophia. (TJ IV, ii)

Thus "the adequate Idea of Sophia" is associated with a public image that Fielding expects to exist in the public memory. The time Fielding tries to recall is probably the period before the distinguished members of the Kit-Cat Club, Walpole in particular, gained the royal favor to rule, when "Queen Sophy," as she's called, was expected to ascend the English throne. Those who had seen her recognized her as one of the brightest "Daughters" of the Stuarts. Therefore, her fond memory seems to be another source of persuasive power that Fielding draws from history. It strikes a nostalgic longing of England's good old days. It is against such a historical background and in a symbolic relationship with her that Tom Jones gains his chivalric appeal as "the Preserver of Sophia" (TJ V, xii) and "the Redeemer of the Lady" on the road (Mrs. Waters, not Sophia in person).

It has to be noted, however, that Fielding's recollection of an ideal past is imaginarily projected into the future as a hopeful attainment for the rightful ruler. Partridge, who is convinced that Tom is the "Heir Apparent," follows Tom, and transforms that nostalgic longing for England's good old days into a "Great Expectation." He urges Tom to behold the "spirit" of Sophia who's now in the moon, and live up to her excellence as his mirror image:

> Heaven be praised, she's gone; and if I believed she was in the Moon, according to a Book I once read, which teaches that to be the Receptacle of departed Spirits, I would never look at it for fear of seeing her: But I wish, Sir, that the Moon was a Looking-glass for your Sake, and that Miss Sophia Western was now placed before it. (TJ VIII, ix)

In the following chapter, Fielding tells us Tom "at length yielded to the earnest Supplications of Partridge and both together made directly towards the Place whence the Light issue" (TJ VIII, x). There, Tom is first initiated by the Man of the Hill to the intricacies of English politics and European history. That episode is a significant part of Tom's education program. Though he is not self-conscious of his role until later, after he gains such knowledge, he does grow up to accept his mission. The "Book" that teaches "the Receptacle of departed Spirits" mentioned in the above passage might be comically rendered identical to Sophia's lost "pocket-book," which, also through the design of a sensational incident, happens to be in Tom's possession. As if taking his oath, with his right hand on the book, Tom swears to restore the lost values to the right "Owner" of England:

> "Lookee, Friend," cries Jones, "the right Owner shall certainly have again all that she lost; and as for any further Gratuity, I really cannot give it you at present." (TJ XII, iv)

The evocation of beauty, excellence, and order from the national history and memory, nostalgic as it may appear, recalls the original ideal of the Glorious Revolution. The lost ideal of the past imposes upon the devastating present a fictional, but forceful, critique. As Cockshut writes:

> The history of general statements above the tone and standards of any given time and place is a history of unsupported and often wild panegyrics and diatribes. And there is a strong tendency to contrast the present state of affairs with an imaginary ideal future or with an ideal (and perhaps equally imaginary) past.[22]

Fielding's history is indeed a discourse of "wild panegyrics and diatribes." In composing *Tom Jones*, he is probably more constructive than ever. He is in earnest search for an ideal state much needed by "the present state of affairs" in England. His creation of "Sophia" both as the ideal of wisdom and an adorable monarch is embraced by a historical necessity when the Hanoverian regime, having gone through a period of social and political turbulence, looks forward for changes and a new order. Meanwhile, it also looks backward for historical lessons drawn from an immediate past.

The Young Chevalier: Fielding's Platonic Self of the Rightful Ruler

She has indeed changed the Name of Sophia into that of the Pretender, and had reported, that drinking his Health was the Cause for which Jones was knocked down. (TJ VIII, ix)

From speaking in Behalf of his Religion, he assured me, the Catholicks did not expect to be any Gainers by the Change; for that Prince Charles was as good a Protestant as any in England; and that nothing but Regard to Right made him and the rest of the popish Party to be Jacobites. (Ibid.)

If the "naked charms" of Sophia lie hidden in her "lips" and "blood," those of Tom Jones are exposed to the public eye in the name of chivalry. Chivalry is Tom's "cardinal virtue" in the story, a token of his identity. Since "the Young Chevalier" is a popular nickname of Bonnie Prince Charlie, the chivalric character of Tom Jones reveals his birthmark. During his journey to London, Tom performs several chivalric actions in a mock-heroic fashion. He fights several "battles" in the name of "Love and War." He challenges a king's soldier to defend Sophia's name. He rescues Mrs. Waters from rape and robbery, which leads to the "amorous battle" at Upton, a climax. At Upton, Sophia Western is misidentified as "Jenny Cameron," whereas it is "Tom French," as the gossip goes among the king's soldiers, who brings "Sophia Western" (instead of Jenny Cameron) "at any Tavern in Bridges-street." Even in rumor and gossip, the mixed identities are suggestive enough. They blur the distinction between truth and truism. They are made impressive when a female subject and sensational elements are involved. The art of novelistic love effectively directs the reader's attention to the concealed identity of a warrior, a lover, and a potential ruler—the Pretender of the English throne.

The presence of Charles Edward during Tom's journey to London is first generated by rumors and gossip—deliberate misinterpretation and misinformation, gradually transmitted into the realm of the imaginary—in the reader's mind's fancy, and eventually in a fictitious and mock-heroic manner, cast in the chivalric character of Tom Jones with a symbolic identity. The landlady's fabrication of Jones's "battle" in the public house exemplifies such a process. While gossiping with Partridge, "She has indeed changed the Name of Sophia into that of the Pretender, and had reported, that drinking his Health was the Cause for which Jones was knocked down" (TJ VIII, ix). In the narrative consciousness, her wistful misinterpretation of Tom's "wound in the head" marks a moment of Tom's "metamorphosis"— Tom becomes a Jacobite, at least in the mind of Partridge who listens to her. Her fantasy literally casts Partridge under its "wondrous" spell and turns him on. The fellow takes her fancy as truth, holds it as wisdom, and lives with it as his ideal. Inspired, he faithfully guides Tom—"the Son, the Heir" as he calls him—following the Young Pretender toward London. Partridge's actions are motivated by a pure idea, yet surprisingly, it works for him. It eventually brings him home, restores him with a new life and a happy marriage. His "romantic" action does attain a romantic reward: Allworthy entitles him to marry Molly Seagrim, so that he becomes the rightful owner of "the object of desire" at the second rank.

Such pleasurable details, being exceedingly comic, contains provocative messages. Fielding demonstrates that the power of language can produce "miracles" if properly used to serve a revolutionary ideal. But in the same way, ill-controlled "mass media," which spread malicious rumors and political gossip, can easily cause violence, chaos, massacre or tragedy, so as to ruin a revolutionary movement. Therefore, principles, idealism, and pure motive are absolutely a political necessity in the exercise of that power. Beyond that, literacy must be taken into account in popular vote, because reading skill counts for the intelligence to distinguish truth from rumor in receiving information from public media. In Fielding's presentation of that chaotic world Tom is fallen into, Partridge is singled out to stand above the "Divided Line" in Plato's cave simile, who directly sees the sun above the cave. The barber, whose job is to polish the image in the mirror, turns out to be the only one who lives in the light of an absolute truth—Tom is the "Sun/Son." Such a position suites him, as a victim of rumor, the exiled schoolteacher, and the philosopher.

When "Mr. Jones" sets out on his journey heading towards the

Bristol Channel, Charles Edward has crossed the channel marching toward London. Within the fictive geometrix, the channel builds up a "bridge" of identity between the two. Fielding's stage setting is removed from a "domestic government" to the battlefield of the Jacobite rebellion. The director intentionally involves Tom in the actual happenings of historical events. Staging Tom against the background of "the late Rebellion," the Young Pretender's war becomes Tom's war.

Although Tom initially considered serving the king's army as a volunteer, the device is a fake. As it turns out, he practically fights all his battles with Cumberland's troops. At the Quack's house, he is provoked to challenge a king's soldier, a lieutenant, in defence of "Sophia's name." He is beaten up, but in the next battle, he wins a big victory redeeming "the lady" from rape and robbery by an officer, this time of a higher rank, a sergeant. After he meets Partridge, who dresses up his wound in the head, Tom is metaphorically "baptized" by the "barber" of his knowing "father" (though unknown to him), and he immediately changes his destination following the direction of the Jacobite war toward the capital. As we know, Partridge is an avowed Jacobite. He escorts Tom as a volunteer only because he is convinced that Tom is "the Son" and "the Heir."

Discernibly, there is a chain of events in Tom's adventure that metaphorically parallels the military ups and downs of the prince. As Tom suddenly changes his destination, Charles Edward also has an abrupt change of route. While Cumberland waited to intercept him at Stone, near Stafford, he took "the longest march that had ever heard under the cover of darkness" and surprisingly landed at Derby, where he achieved a legendary success in English military history. Tom and Partridge also take a night trip under the "Moon," "a Stars," and "an Angel," while the "Sun/Son" is lost in the dark, until they reach the noble's "house" "halfway" up the hill. There enlightened by the knowledge of the Man of the Hill, Tom is initiated into the secrets of European history and English politics. He comes out of the house with the wisdom of "the Man of the Hill" just in time to fight his most brilliant battle with "the Man of War" (TJ IX, iv). As we know, the Young Pretender succeeded as far as Derby, but failed to capture London. Tom's chivalry also sees its day before he reaches London. At Upton, Fielding tells us that the gossip of a kitchen maid costs him the precious chance of meeting Sophia. That incident, being so intricately wrought and climactically presented, must not be neglected. The nature of Tom's misfortune is similar to that of the Young Chevalier, whose amorous affairs did much harm to his reputation during the war. Similarly, after his "amorous battle" at Upton, Tom's luck is all the way downhill until he ends up in prison in London, never able to make his way up by himself. Yet just as Prince Charles was assisted by his highland mistress who furnished him with a passport to go back to France, Tom is released from the charge of murder at the mercy of Mrs. Waters, the lady he once rescued on the road.[23]

So far I have related the allegory of Tom's identity as a warrior. Fielding's contrivance of "love stories" will further reveal the identity of a legendary Lover. Before I proceed, it has to be noted that while allegory is normally two-dimensional, Fielding is a cubist in his construction of fictive identities. The feature of the real aesthetic object is only discernible in an abstract form from a multiple facade. For Fielding, disclosure and concealment are equally necessary in delivering the disguise of Tom's fictive identity. Therefore, he is least inclined to "put the two and two together." Most often, it takes three, instead of two, to make an equation with the "real thing." Only in love's triangular geometrix one may catch a glimpse of the ideal truth.

At Upton, Sophia is misidentified as Jenny Cameron, thus by logical inference, her presumed lover is indirectly identified to be the Young Chevalier. This kind of logic may be characteristic in the Platonic tradition, as Joyce formulates it—where the possible was the improbable and the improbable the inevitable. Fielding reasons the same way. At the same time upon the same spot, "Jenny Cameron's lover" is in bed with Mrs. Waters. Fielding never treats Sophia seriously as the "real thing" in love and war, he presents Mrs. Waters, also "Jenny" by first name, as "the Queen of the Amazons" (TJ IX, v), more closely identifiable in person with Lady Cameron, who's alleged to be over forty, a matron figure, Prince Charles's mother's age, and who followed him during the war. Mrs. Waters turns out to be "Jenny Jones" in disguise. Since Jenny once claimed herself to be Tom's mother, she must be Jenny Cameron's age, more closely identifiable with the prince's mistress. If so, then her young lover is also indirectly identified with the Young Chevalier. I have drawn a full circle to reach the same point of implication.

Mrs. Waters, who is actually in Tom's company, has two concealed identities as both "Jenny Jones" and "Jenny Waters." Yet her first name made "conspicuously absent" at Upton only indicates the presence of a real possibility: that she is "the real thing," the "object of desire" that Fielding stages to attract the reader's attention. Before Tom and Mrs. Waters reach Upton together, the reader must have been properly alarmed by the rape scene. It is a formal chivalric performance, through which Tom earns his name as "the Redeemer of the Lady" (TJ IX, ii.), and then becomes the lover of the redeemed.

The scene is followed by the most shocking exposure of Mrs. Waters's naked top, a temptation to Tom all the while he carries her to Upton. However, in Fielding, what can be seen is not the real thing: The lady's naked bosom is exposed to show the "naked charms" of her transparent identities. The stage director makes frequent references to the "disappearance" of her torn dress, which is a theatrical device used to indicate a disguised identity under disclosure (he has already displayed such a device before when he described the coarse and curious robe of the Man of the Hill to indicate a royal personage in disguise). The sensational effect is only an "appetizer" Fielding serves to prepare his reader for "the Act of eating" (TJ IX, v). After the reader's appetite is properly stimulated by the "appetizer," there comes the main course, a "sizzling steak"—the Upton seduction scene. The reader might be expecting the "real thing" when the novelist presents "The Whole Artillery of Love" with nothing real, or material. The whole chapter is written in a mock-heroic fashion mixed with pastoral romance. His style appears as artificial and theatrical as in the scene when he first stages Sophia, which I discussed before. It is tilted with an elevated tone, lavished with chivalric tropes, courtly conceits, and epic similes, and carried off in a voice of stage chorus. "After presenting Human Nature to the keen Appetite of his reader in a simple and plain country manner," as Fielding promises in the beginning, now he chooses to "hash and ragoo it with French and Italian Seasoning of Affectations" (TJ. I, i). The art of his novelistic love reaches its climax.

This is the scene that Fielding declares to be "a Description hitherto unessayed either in Prose or Verse" (TJ IX, v), and it must be discussed in detail for it is an exemplary design of novelistic love.

> But here, as we are about to attempt a Description hitherto unessayed either in Prose or Verse, we think proper to invoke the Assistance of certain Aerial Beings, who will, we doubt not, come kindly to our Aid on this Occasion. (TJ IX, v).

His evocation brings into association the trace of a feminine fiction, the presence of Ariel from *The Tempest*, which recalls another tale of a prince in exile. This subtext stands in the background of the stage setting, a "magic lantern" over the "dinner table" projecting a romantic ideal. This time Fielding himself plays the part of Prospero. He assigns the spirit of novelistic love, which heals the gap between the ideal and the real, to Ariel: "Spirits, which by mine art/I have from their confines called to enact/My present fancies" (*The Tempest*, IV.i, 120-22). While he follows his own "fancies" to design a happy ending for the "foundling," he calls in Ariel to enchant such an overture:

> "Say then, ye Graces, you that inhabit the heavenly Mansions of Seraphina's Countenance; for you are truly Divine, are always in her Presence, and well know all the arts of charming; say, what were the Weapons now used to captivate the Heart of Mr. Jones." (TJ IX, v)

The whole "love story" is related briefly within a set of quotation marks. What it suggests is that the narrative is only "a play within a play." It is staged as a masquerade on Prospero's no-men island, with Shakespeare's musical comedy, its pastoral mood, marvelous visions lingering somewhere in the air, while the heir becomes "apparent" on the foreground of the stage.

With a transformation of style, Tom's identity as the common fellow instantly loses its reality. His princely visage emerges in the realm of the imaginary. Almost halfway through the novel, Fielding for the first time cares to offer his reader a close-up of Tom's face. He invites the reader to look the hero in the eye:

> Mr. Jones, of whose personal Accomplishments we have hitherto said very little, was in reality, one of the handsomest young Fellows in the world. His Face, besides being the Picture of health, had in it the most apparent Marks of Sweetness and Good-Nature. These Qualities were indeed so characteristical in his Countenance, that while the Spirit and Sensibility in his Eyes, tho' they must have been perceived by an accurate Observer, might have escaped the Notice of the less discerning, so strongly was this Good-nature painted in his look, that it was remarked by almost every one who saw him. (Ibid.)

The solemn tone and suggestive touches reveal the "bonnie" features of a princely visage. "I might call him/A thing divine; for nothing natural/ I ever saw so noble" (*The Tempest*, I, ii)—we hear an echo offstage, and we share the "wondrous light" of Miranda's innocent eye. Once the image of "Mr. Jones" is juxtaposed with a princely visage, Fielding blends in a touch of historical reality. He adds to the burlesque of romance an epic landscape of love and war. With a finished touch, the lover emerges from the dinner table a warrior on a contemporary historical stage:

He then began to see the Designs of the enemy, and indeed to feel their Success. A Parley now was set on Foot between the Parties; . . . . Mr. Jones maintained a Kind of Dutch Defense, and treacherously delivered up the Garrison, without duly weighing his Allegiance to the fair Sophia. In short, no sooner had the amorous Parley ended, and the Lady had unmasked the Royal Battery . . . and the fair Conqueror enjoyed the usual Fruits of her Victory. (Ibid.)

Since the climactic scene of lovemaking is conducted in such chivalric tropes, the "love story" itself is as thin as the "tablecloth" of language—the surface of meaning. The reader, chewing the steak on the table, is still able to have a vague idea of what's going on underneath, while in his plate there is nothing but the picture of a battlefield. The tablecloth of language actually draws the divided Line between the "shadows" of reality under the table and the "stage lighting" aboveboard. Novelistic love is the forbidden fruit, or the steak upon the table, that serves the reader with a good stomach to feel the textuality of a story and taste the flavor of an idea.

If we further ask the question whether the chivalric cliches are used to tell the love story, or whether the love story is dressed up to stage a historical event, we must note that in this key passage, Fielding employs no epic simile or legendary war. His reference to war is fairly recent, such as the "Dutch Defense" in 1745 and its failure "in weighing its Allegiance to the Fair Sophia" (the House of Hanover), which led to the defeat of the Royal Army by its French enemy. "A Parley between the two Parties" implies that the party that had a parley with the Dutch speaks French. Fielding's diction of military tactic is apparently drawn from modern warfare rather than archaic heraldry. The warrior is neither "Tom," nor "Ulysses," but "Mr. Jones." What is the goodness of a doubtful surname for a foundling once exiled from Paradise Hall? The nothingness of a no-name commoner totally obliterates the presence of his identity. Behind his emptied identity, a prince who has lost his battle "yesternight" looms at large. Fielding has rebuilt "the Whole Artillery of Love" with a modern "epic machinery." The engine of his "love story" runs busy with the noise of political messages. His play within a play is an ingenious design of a "Sunroof," which lets in the "air/heir," so that the reader may review a familiar scene upon the contemporary historical stage. This is what he proudly calls a "New Province of Writing and . . . hitherto unessayed either in Prose or Verse." His "Comic Prose Epic" deals with a contemporary history in a comic fashion. The construction of an artifice enables him to expose the identity of a royal personage and address a current issue in national politics.

The issue, as I projected from the beginning of this chapter, is in regard to the judgment of the character of a prince. The chapter is entitled "An Apology for all Heroes who have good Stomachs, with a Description of a Battle of the Amorous Kind" (TJ IX, v). An "apology" in the Greek sense (*apologia*) signifies a "defence." Fielding's thesis, as he states, is to defend the "Act of Eating" in the Greek heroic tradition. "Heroes, notwithstanding the high ideas . . . have certainly more of Mortal than divine about them." Such a statement is apparently opposed to the Christian virtue of chastity. He immediately stages his subject in the high status of "the greatest prince, hero, or Philosopher upon Earth." Then he historicizes his subject by mentioning his hero's folly having a "seasonal" occasion. "The immoderate Ardor with which he laid about him at this Season" brings his subject back to reality and contemporary history.

His theory of "Love ethics" is a dramatization of his theory of government ethics, and his defense of "the Act of Eating" a defense of honor code. Fielding knew that when material incentive becomes the only incentive of man's labor, "ethical values" can only operate either with cash value or by appeal to the unliberated religious sentiment. Chivalry, on the other hand, transformed as heroism in modern society, provides the public servant with an altruist spirit, a desirable motive above the economic incentive. It sets a higher goal in man's labor. If the public servant labors in the name of Love, motivated by sense of honor, he will accept the honor code voluntarily as ethics, instead of a harsh restraint and enforcement of law. He will gain more self-satisfaction and self-respect in his work. This is the value of chivalry renewed from its medieval idealism.

To dramatize his theory, Fielding enacts these pleasurable scenes of "love stories." He explores the motives in lovemaking, or the "Act of Eating." He shows us that when Tom commits the act, he is offering a service to his redeemed lady at her request. Since he has saved her life, as a gentleman he might as well take care of her needs and fulfill her desire, which is "chivalric." He means well; he is not motivated to take advantage of a single woman, as Butcher's soldier does on a country road. On the part of Mrs. Waters, he argues that since love is most likely inspired by the feeling of gratitude, an innocent eye for beauty, and admiration for goodness, Mrs. Waters is also appropriately motivated in her action: "Mrs. Waters had, in Truth, not only a Good Opinion of our Hero, but a very great Affection for him. To speak out boldly at once, she was in Love" (TJ IX, v). As far as motive is concerned, she is innocent, too. Thus Fielding shows that it is the difference in motive that distinguishes chivalry from rape, and liberty from prostitution. Fielding's theory of love ethics is healthy to the soul as well as to the body—an ideal model of modern love. In fact he has challenged and reversed the biblical myth of Adam and Eve: When man and woman are left free, it is not the act of "eating" but the motive in being that determines the ethics of virtue and sin.

In his allegorical construction of Tom Jones as the "foundling" of the English royal house, Fielding has his own wishful ideas and even a political agenda. His model is less a precise portrayal of the character of a real historical figure, Bonnie Prince Charlie, than his own idea of a rightful ruler. Tom's character is developed through several stages that parallel Plato's curriculum requirements for the Philosopher Ruler. For the Philosopher Ruler, Plato proposes a program of moral education until the age of eighteen, followed by two years of military service, five years of mathematical training, and another five years of dialectics. But before he is qualified to rule, the ruler must gain fifteen years of practical experience in subordinate offices. Tom's moral character is shaped in Paradise Hall before he sets out on his journey. His virtue is proven by several accidents, jumping into water to save Sophia, and selling his colt to help the gamekeeper's family. His adventures abroad involve the experience of war, equivalent to a military service. He receives a dialectic education from the Man of the Hill, which includes the knowledge of history, politics, and philosophy. He also has a chance to study "Comparative Government"—observing an alternative model of jurisdiction in an Egyptian court. By performing a little office to help settle the marriage of Mrs. Miller's daughter to Nightingale, he accomplishes an internship in legal office. He survives court seductions and "street fighting" before he is cleared of charges from prison. In a comical fashion, he has fulfilled the requirements for the rightful ruler through these trials.

Tom's "love story" also parallels Plato's model of the legitimate lover, the lover of philosophy. Platonic love, as I discussed in Chapter Two, is developed through "an orderly succession to the altar built upon the solid steps of all previous efforts in search for Love." Such efforts begin with the love of physical beauty in this world, and

> using them as steps to ascend continually with that absolute beauty as one's aim, from one instance of physical beauty to two and from two to all, then from physical beauty to moral beauty, from moral beauty to the beauty of knowledge until from the knowledge of various kinds one arrives at the supreme knowledge whose sole object is the absolute beauty, and knows

at last what absolute beauty is. (S 94)

Tom's "love story" is designed with such an organic movement. His first love is not Sophia, but Molly Seagrim—physical love:

> Her Beauty was still the Object of Desire, though greater Beauty, or a fresher Object, might have been more so; but the little Abatement which Fruition had occasioned to this, was highly overbalanced by the Considerations of the Affection which she visibly bore him, and of the Situation into which he had brought her. The former of these created Gratitude, the latter Compassion; and both together, with his Desire for her person, raised in him a Passion, which might without any great Violence to the Word, be called Love; though, perhaps, it was at first not very judiciously placed. (TJ IV, vi)

Fielding makes a discreet distinction between the love of physical beauty and that of moral beauty. But notably, he treats the two as a sequence instead of opposites. He describes Tom's untutored love of physical beauty not as a sin or lust, but as love of a youthful kind prior to serious commitment—love "judiciously placed." Tom's later involvement with Mrs. Waters and Lady Balleston also serves as part of an experience necessary for the acquisition of "knowledge of various kinds." But it is important that Tom sustains an ideal love in view. Otherwise, he would have lost his soul. All the while, his love for the absolute beauty personified in Sophia remains his sole object and aim. Possessed with an ideal, he is able to ascend the throne. The knowledge he gains from each of his "amorous battles" serves as ascending steps toward his supreme knowledge of himself as a lover and his duty toward Sophia. His legitimacy is hard earned through education, experience, and proven virtue, the least by incident, money or birthright.

In conclusion, Tom's chivalric performances constitute Fielding's subversion of the epic mode of love. Chivalric love traditionally does not end in marriage. Fielding, I must emphasize, handles tradition freely to "make it new." Since the celebration of marriage is a dominant model in the English novel, he writes under the canopy of such a model. But he quietly subverts it and appropriates a different value system. He deconstructs and reconstructs such a model. First, in epic love chastity is virtue until a marriage contract is sanctioned in public as an award to the lover. The final award of Tom's marriage, however, deconstructs such a norm. Chivalry, instead of chastity, bears proof to the goodness of Tom's character and becomes virtue itself. Sophia marries Tom without the proof, not even a promise, of conjugal chastity—fidelity hereafter. Their wedding takes place in a quiet private ceremony. Fielding marries Tom and Sophia to consummate a romantic love—natural, innocent love grown since childhood. Thus the Magistrate projects a radical revolutionary model by doing justice to the deprived legitimacy of a foundling, a "Heathcliff." Second, epic love, as defined before, is motivated by the desire for individual success and social recognition; it aims at possession. Chivalric love, on the contrary, is motivated by the sense of honor to set the beloved object free. The gallant lover has no intention of possessing the object that he rescues. His motive is pure. In Fielding, the motive of action overrules Carroll the performance of the action itself. Not all Tom's chivalric performances are successful, some even foolish. Nevertheless, these actions inspire love, they bring forth the quality of Tom's good nature. The point of Fielding's design, again, contains the argument of his political philosophy: With pure motive, action an be improved, and Tom's performance does improve. Without good intention, "smart" actions such as Blifil's courtship to Sophia will not achieve a good end. Thus the presentation of Tom's chivalric actions is Fielding's repeated premonition to the rulers and lovers "on the human stage": "It is much easier to make good Men wise than to make bad Men good."

Notes

1. Carrol, *Selected Letters of Samuel Richardson* (Oxford: Clarendon Press, 1964), 127-28.

2. Henry Fielding, *The History of Tom Jones, A Foundling.* Both the Wesleyan Edition (ed. Fredson Bowers [Oxford: Clarendon Press, 1974]) and the Norton Critical Edition (ed. Sheridan Baker [New York: W. W. Norton, 1973]) are used in writing this chapter, so in the subsequent quotations cite chapter numbers without page numbers. Fielding's chapters are very short, easy to find the passages within each chapter. The quotation here is from book XIV, chapter v.

3. William Empson, "Tom Jones," *Kenyon Review* 20 (1958): 249.

4. Fielding's capitalized words invite speculation, like today's bold print or other forms of emphasis.

5. As McKeon notes: "Friendly contact seems still to have been possible even after the success of *Tom Jones* and *Amelia.* But the tenor of Richardson's extent allusions to Fielding after 1748 is bitter and narrowly critical" (Michael

McKeon, The Origins of the English Novel, 1600-1740 [Baltimore: Johns Hopkins University Press, 1987], 410). Also see his note 1 in "Conclusion," 506.

6. Empson, "Tom Jones," 250.

7. See Bertrand A. Goldgar, "Myth and History in Fielding's Journey from this World to the Next," Modern Language Quarterly (1990): 235-52.

8. McKeon, The Origins of the Novel, 398.

9. R. S. Crane's essay "The Plot of Tom Jones" and Sheridan Baker's "Bridget Allworthy: The Creative Pressures of Fielding's Plot" are both reprinted in the Norton Critical Edition of Tom Jones.

10. Carl R. Kropf, "Judgment and Character, Evidence and the Law in Tom Jones," Studies in the Novel 21 (Winter 1989): 357-66.

11. Ibid., 358.

12. Basil Williams, The Whig Supremacy, ed. G. N. Clark (Oxford: Clarendon Press, 1939), 20.

13. Ralph Ellison, Introduction to Invisible Man (New York: Vintage Books, 1981), xx-xxi.

14. B. R. Lindboe, "'O Shakespeare, Had I Thy Pen!': Fielding's Use of Shakespeare in Tom Jones," Studies in the Novel 14 (Winter 1982): 303-15.

15. Martin Battestin equates the Egyptian despotism to the doctrines of Toryism in his "Tom Jones and 'His Egyptian Majesty': Fielding's Parable of Government," PMLA 82 (1967): 68-77. I suspect Fielding might have something different in mind. Toryism was an accepted orthodoxy, a public discourse; Fielding wouldn't need to speak of it in such a carnivalesque fashion. Here the ambiguity of his language draws attention to a hidden agenda that must be more provocative than the accepted orthodoxy of Toryism.

16. See Neil Schmitz's use of "Huckspeech" in Chapter 4 of Huck and Alice (Minneapolis: University of Minnesota Press, 1983).

17. Lester J. Cappon, ed., The Adams-Jefferson Letters (Chapel Hill, 1959), Vol. II, 456. Quoted from William R. Taylor, "Prologue: Two Aristocracies: A Dialogue," in Cavalier and Yankee: The Old South and American National Character (New York: George Braziller, Inc. 1961), 23-33,29.

18. Kenneth Rexroth, "Tom Jones," Saturday Review, 1 July 1967, 13.

19. See J. Steven Watson, The Reign of George III, 1760-1815 (Oxford: Clarendon Press, 1960).

20. Battestin, "Fielding's Definition of Wisdom: Some Functions of Ambiguity and Emblem in Tom Jones," ELH, 35 (1968): 188-217; reprinted in the Norton edition of TJ, 833, 819.

21. Empson, "Tom Jones," 219.

22. A. O. J. Cockshut, Man and Woman: A Study of Love and the Novel (1740-1940) (London: Collins, 1977), 11.

23. As Baker notes in the Norton edition (440), it was not Jenny Cameron but Flora Macdonald who obtained Charles Edward a passport and helped him escape the British, disguised as a woman.

Chapter Five

Romantic Love as an Antithesis to the Epic: Faulkner's *Go Down, Moses*

As Stesichorus said the heroes fought at Troy about a mere phantom of Helen because they were ignorant of the truth.

—Plato, "Imperfect Societies"[1]

I would like to plead on behalf of a theory of the novel that could be tested against all manner of texts (including those which our culture calls "great"), without forgetting all its credibility, a "soft" theory (as technology can be "soft") that would allow for a more discriminating approach, one less pre-determined, less arrogantly sure of finding everywhere what it is looking for, mindful of the ways in which ideological threads are woven into fictional textures, without excluding a priori, by decree, the possibility of challenging ideology in the writing process. No such theory is available; it has yet to be invented, and sweeping generalizations are probably not the best way to start. Not that

I believe in a purely empirical and inductive approach, but
against arbitrary theorizing there is no better safeguard than close
examination of individual works in their full complexity. Works
like those of Faulkner . . . will perhaps allow us to formulate
more clearly some of the questions arising from the relationship
of fiction and ideology, and to point out, for working purposes,
some of the directions which future research might profitably
take.

Andre Blekasten, "For/Against an Ideological Reading"[2]

She Cannot Fade, Though Thou Hast Not Thy Bliss: The Urn in "The Bear"

In the last chapter, I discussed Fielding's political philosophy as
intricately conceived and constructed through the plotting and dramatic
presentation of several "love stories" in *Tom Jones*. Fielding's political
ideology is anti-Machiavellian, neo-Platonic, and pre-Jeffersonian. Fielding
proposes that "Goodness" must count as an essential criterion in selecting
the rightful ruler, or the legitimate lover of "Sophia." It is important to note
that Fielding proposes such a criterion not for mere moral reasons, but for
the sake of national security. For Fielding believes that "Goodness," which,
in the Platonic sense of the word, stands for love of beauty/truth/wisdom, is
the guarantee of peace and order, the promise of a happy state, whereas, evil
character in a ruler, such as envy, greed, hypocrisy, ignorance, and low wit,
is a source of trouble in state affairs. Power in the hands of an evil ruler
brings about nothing but war and violence, as that in the hands of King
George, who wouldn't give up his military involvements abroad, and Billy
the Butcher, who displays his militant triumph by slaughtering thousands of
innocents abroad, while calling it "a little blood-letting England needed."[3]
    I argued that Fielding's philosophy is not merely "a theory of
ethics," but more importantly, it is based on a strong conviction of a political
necessity in endowing judicial, legislative, or presidential power. Before I
proceed, I still wish to make the point that although Fielding and Faulkner
are often misread as moralists, I am not moralizing here. Government
corruption, the increase of the crime rate, the decline of spiritual civilization,
social violence, and mass illiteracy—these problems that characterize a
bourgeois democracy in Fielding's fiction are clearly a reality in late

capitalist society, and in socialist countries as well that begin introducing free trade. Faulkner receives worldwide acclaim not only because he won the Nobel Prize, but also because his work addresses a fundamental and universal problem with which the modern world is faced: the rule of the moneyed class, its culture, government, and value system. The profundity of Faulkner's writing questions the value of modern thought and modern government by exposing its destructive and self-destructive tendencies, as well as its doomed destiny.

As Carolyn Porter rightly assesses, Faulkner holds a superior historical vision over his contemporaries, the Agrarians of the 1930s and 1940s. Faulkner did not view the Old South as a world uncontaminated by the spirit of capitalism. Faulkner's vision of the antebellum South also differs decisively from the myth created by the historians in the 1960s and 1970s that the antebellum South is a paternalistic society, "which rightly thought of itself as fundamentally distinct from, and opposed to, the North's competitive capitalist system."[4] Faulkner in fact treats the antebellum South as an oligarchy in which the moneyed class rules the land, but it has lost the spirit of a "benevolent" republic. Thus in *Go Down, Moses*, Faulkner is essentially concerned with the legitimacy of the ruler (the ruling class) and his competency in exercising his power in a modern democratic state. The heart of the matter that thematically and metaphorically unifies all the seven stories in the book as a novel, probably more crucial than freedom and bondage, wildness and land, slavery and injustice to the Negro, as traditionally defined in canonical Faulkner criticism, I will argue, is the question of power—how supreme power is handled or abused, with or without benevolence and self-control, in the hands of "illegitimate lovers and incompetent rulers." The misuse of power gradually leads to the degeneration and decay of "a house divided."

This controlling idea in the novel is abstrusely constructed in the form of a metafiction. Not unlike Fielding, who sets out to preach a doctrine in *Tom Jones*, as Empson points out, and said so, a high-minded though perhaps abstruse one, Faulkner by 1940 also has a high-minded doctrine to preach: Power possessed without the grace of Love is self-destructive. As John Muste rightly points out in his article "The Failure of Love in *Go Down, Moses*," Faulkner believes that a peaceful relation between the black and white must be based upon "an amused mutual tolerance"; but the failure of love between the black and the white results from the fact that "the white man has not known or felt anything about love" for a long time.[5] Muste considers *Go Down, Moses* Faulkner's most bitter commentary on the relationship between whites and blacks. Faulkner's historical vision of the

Reconstruction of the South, the land, and race relations, as his critics generally agree, grows dark, but integral and profound in this novel. He is writing a history with a philosophy that agrees with neither the conservative ideology of white supremacy, nor the "radical" slogans of capitalist democracy. According to Walter F. Taylor, "Faulkner flung himself squarely into the center of the current segregation controversy as a spokesman for the more liberal group of white Southerners."[6] But in the binary partisanship of American politics, he is caught in "the tragic middle," neither left nor right. Unfortunately, he has been attacked by liberals and conservatives alike. As Charles D. Peavy puts it:

> He has been seen as a radical reactionary and a sentimental
> traditionalist; he has been blamed for making the Negro a
> scapegoat for the destruction of the legendary Old South; and he
> has been called a bigot and a "nigger lover." [7]

Such controversial critical opinions sometimes result from the technical difficulties in reading Faulkner, I think, and sometimes from the difference that exists between his public speeches and his private discourse in his novels. Those who deem Faulkner a "radical reactionary" are offended by some public speeches he made in defence of the South against the North. As I suggested before, in public speech, a writer has limits in arguing with popular opinions; only in writing fiction does the writer have the freedom of speech to advocate personal convictions and individual opinions in politics. Known to be a very private man, Faulkner knew his limit in criticizing his own culture, and not until his later years was he free to speak up about what now Toni Morrison speaks as the "unspeakable things unspoken." However, in his fiction, what he cannot state explicitly he tactfully expresses through many textual strategies—gaps, silences, ambivalence; and the most difficult and provocative ideas he conceives are conveyed in his Socratic "love stories" of sorts, as we will see in *Go Down, Moses.*

In a sense, Faulkner had reached in the 1930s a postmodern historical consciousness, as I defined in Chapter One. The postmodern condition for the modernist avant-garde novelist, as Joyce exemplifies in *Finnegans Wake* (1939), is a return to the native ground in search for history and origin. The postmodern metafictionist is one with his native land, takes up his role as the historian of his race, rewriting history through fiction. Joyce discovers the role of "Ollave," the poet and divine historian in the ancient Irish royal family. Faulkner sees himself as "the Sylvan historian" Keats wrought in his "Ode on a Grecian Urn." Like *Finnegans Wake, Go*

Down, Moses is also a creationist text. In it, Faulkner is also creating "the uncreated conscience" of his race: the white man's conscience.

Like Joyce, turning from the avant-garde Parisian artistry to a native heroic tradition, Faulkner, too, locates the phallic sign of legitimacy in the Scottish romance tradition and the honor code of chivalry. Like Fielding, he entertains his "princes" with the best stories he has ever written of hunting, chasing, and lovemaking, while he illustrates his Platonic political ideal and neo-Jeffersonian doctrine with comic elements and double ironies. In his way, he is less amused and optimistic than Fielding. With a kind of stoic tragic mood, however, he finds in the mute eloquence of Love the mythical power of language, which allows him to express the inexpressible and address an impossible political ideal in a world where romantic love exists as light as a feather, the trace of a doe, a squirrel, a Delta woodpecker on a cheap-printed Christmas card.

In dealing with race relations, his treatment of love as a subject ceases to be sentimental (as he sometimes is in his earlier works), but turns out to be philosophical. In *Go Down, Moses*, the spirit of love serves as the measurement of human capacity and human accomplishment. Love stands for the original ideal state in human relationships as well as the ultimate desire in human experience. Love remains the essence of life after God is dead. Therefore, it is projected as the ideal relation of the power structure in human society. In Faulkner's fictional world, it is the need for love and the lack of it that opens the space for his cultural criticism.

The subject of love used as an interrogative rhetorical force to question the power of money and the values of capitalism has its native ground in Southern literature. It finds its finest expression in Sidney Lanier's long poem "The Symphony."[8] In this poem, the subject of romantic love is projected as a strong antithesis to Trade—capitalism personified:

> O Trade! O Trade! would thou wert dead!
> The Time needs heart—t'is tired of head:
> We're all for love,' the violins said.
> Of what avail the rigorous tale
> Of bill for coin and box for bale?
> Grant thee, O Trade! thine uttermost hope:
> Level red gold with blue sky-slope,
> And base it deep as devils grope:
> When all's done, what hast thou won
> Of the only sweet that's under the sun?

True love serves as a rhetoric of challenge to the ultimate futility of a capitalist economy:

> Ay, canst thou buy a single sigh
> Of true love's least, least ecstasy?
> Then, with a bridegroom's heart-beats trembling,
> All the mightier strings assembling
> Ranged them on the violins' side
> As when the bridegroom leads the bride,
> And, heart in voice, together cried:
> "Yea, what avail the endless tale
> Of gain by cunning and plus by sale?"
> Look up the land, look down the land,
> The poor, the poor, the poor, they stand
> Wedged by the pressing of Trade's hand
> Against an inward-opening door
> That pressure tightens evermore.

In Lanier's poem, apparently, there isn't any realistic love story. The "bridegroom and bride" are not individual characters. Instead, they "together cried" for "the poor, the poor." A social, political, and economic concern is dramatized in the voice of love. The poet celebrates love in order to challenge the power of money; and he argues that the ultimate happiness in human life money cannot buy. Presented in the melody of a love poem expressive of the chevalier's true love for his lady, his argument turns out to be powerful and strong; and Lanier's captive utterance, with its soft tones and often feminine rhymes, yields an eloquent persuasive discourse of cultural criticism.

The "Fair Lady" in his poem is also an impersonal subject, whom the chevalier poet defends in the name of ideal love. His weapon is a hunting "horn." The idea of chivalry in the poet's imagination—"that lies upon his head"—is also linked with the metaphor of the horn.

> There thrust the bold straightforward horn
> To battle for that lady lorn,
>
>   . . .
>
> Fair Lady.
> Where's he that craftily hath said,
> The day of chivalry is dead?
> I'll prove that lie upon his head,
> Or I will die instead,
> Fair Lady.

In his discussion of "Faulkner and the Fugitive-Agrarians," Cleanth Brooks reminds us that even in the twentieth century, the Southern poet, the "fugitive-agrarians," such as John Crowe Ransom, still conceives himself as the knight and "the South as the Proud Lady, a kind of patron goddess."[9] Faulkner writes in the Southern chivalric tradition in *Go Down, Moses*. Remarkably, Faulkner's muse, his "Proud Lady," happens to be a black woman. In "The Fire and the Hearth," the "Proud Lady" is Mollie Beauchamp, the "only mother" Roth Edmonds ever knew, "who had given him, the motherless, without stint or expectation of reward that constant and abiding devotion and love which existed nowhere else in this world for him" (*GD, M* 117); Roth defends her honorably. But Roth eventually fails her in "Go Down, Moses," the last story, after he loses his honor and Ike's horn in "Delta Autumn." In "Delta Autumn," Roth's mistress becomes the "Proud Lady," passionate, vulnerable, and dignified. She, too, is a Negro woman. She looks "almost white," but as Ike discovers, she descends from the dark side of the McCaslin family. Placing the ceremonial horn, a cultural legacy, in the hands of a "nigger" woman is more than a liberal gesture on Faulkner's part; it is romantic and revolutionary. As Willie Morris recalls in "Growing Up in Mississippi," in the 1940s, to address a Negro woman as "lady" or "ma'am" was a taboo.[10] This is the lyric subject in Faulkner's text, "the unspeakable things unspoken" in Toni Morrison's words. As cultural reality imposes its limit upon the composition of artistic reality, even poetic justice must be done subtly and silently.

Lanier's poem provides a historical reference for Faulkner's idea of honor and chivalry. Its anticapitalist lyric trope underlines Faulkner's theme and his cultural criticism. Faulkner employs the same rhetorical strategy in *Go Down, Moses* Lanier deploys in his poem. The battle between the romantic vision of selfhood and man's "slavery in the Mammon's cave," the conflict between personal liberty and the possession of wealth and property, one's choice between love and money are all dramatized in the form of "love stories" of sorts, or the love relation between "the knight and his lady." Honor and chivalry are but literary tropes used to construct lyric arguments against history in times of adversity. The "love stories" themselves form an interrogative discourse to question the kind of social injustice otherwise unquestioned, and scarcely addressed either in court or in media and newspapers even nowadays.

Thus in *Go Down, Moses*, novelistic love functions as a medium to raise questions about the exercise of power in race relations. The questions Faulkner raises are very sensitive questions. Again, exactly as Fielding does in *Tom Jones*, the most provocative questions are delivered in bedroom

scenes, dressed up and dramatized in most intriguing "love stories" such as
Sophonsiba's seduction in "Was," Lucas's divorce case in "The Fire and the
Hearth," Rider's mourning of his wife in "Pantaloon in Black," Doom's
adultery in "The Old People," and Ike's discovery of Old McCaslin's
miscegenation and incest in "The Bear," as well as his struggle with his wife
in the bedroom and his emotional encountering with Roth's mistress in
"Delta Autumn." A speculative analysis of these "love stories" and their
metaphorical meaning in the following pages shall reveal that Faulkner's
critique of racial injustice is never sentimental, but profound. Its depth can
only be touched when one touches the heart's truth of his brilliant Love's
interrogations.

One of such moments occurs in the middle of the book, midway
through the fourth chapter of "The Bear," when Ike is studying the family
ledger, discovering the truth or "curse" of his family: incest and
miscegenation that his grandfather committed. Wanting to know the old
man's conscience, his heart's truth, Ike raised the question in the name of
love. He wanted to know the old man's motive. He imagined that there must
have been love, some sort of love between the old man and Eunice. Whether
the love was purely sexual, sexual love, natural love, or manly love, he
would have called it love more than what the beast would do in the jungle.
Since the two lived together there must have been some kind of love more
than just an afternoon's or a night's spittoon (*GD, M* 270).

Ike's question is more touching, profound, and to the point than the
charge of a rape. It innocently and romantically questions the white man's
conscience on the heartstrings, beyond the realm of the law, beyond the
question of social justice and economic equality in race relations. It
questions the white man's manhood, personal integrity, and self-respect. The
question is seldom raised in Faulkner criticism: Between the white old man
and the black slave woman might there be love? Some sort of love? Perhaps
the question itself is a social and critical taboo; perhaps it is beyond the
imagination of most of his critics; and perhaps the question simply has no
place in the binary politics of race relations and in the rational discourse of
social criticism.[11]

But the reader of a "love story" may respond to the question
innocently, irrationally, differently, and with a possibility. If there is love
between old McCaslin and his slave Eunice, which we don't know—but
later in the case of Roth and his mulatto mistress, we do know—then by
denying that love, the white man is not true to himself. If there is no love,
then the white man's lust is not only a social crime, but also a moral crime,
a personal stigma. That crime, judged in the court of justice, can be

redeemed in legal terms and by payment. Judged in the name of love, the white man's failure of his manhood is unredeemable. Faulkner puts the white man's honor and humanity on trial before a social taboo. Faulkner's pen asks for more than legal justice. With the key of love, he opens the door to an individual's private life beyond the public realm, so that we may see through the cultural values and social injustice that poison man's capacity for love. In effect, the power of romantic love serves as a radical critique of racism "at heart."

Another moment of love's interrogation is entailed in the most comic line from Lucas; after he gets back his wife from Zack Edmonds, he asks himself:

> "How to God," he said, "can a black man ask a white man to
> please not lay down with his black wife? And even if he could ask
> it, how to God can the white man promise he wont?" (*GD, M* 59)

The question is tragicomic, and it contains a double irony: Tragically, he is protesting against the white man. Comically, he is pitying the white man. Lucas knows the value of his wife, a black woman, and he also knows Zack, the white man, with whom he grew up like half a brother, so that, from his point of view, he can understand why Zack cannot live without Molly—she is the center of "the fire and the hearth." As it happens years later, Roth, son of Zack the white man, is indeed doomed to fall in love with a black woman again. Tragically, this is a repeated curse, but comically, a resounding echo—"how to God can the white man promise he wont?"

From a romantic point of view, Faulkner conceives love between the black and the white as a natural bondage. In romantic love, as I proposed in Chapter Two, usually the lovers grow up together, share a sense of self. Since the black and the white characters in this novel grow up together and live together, the denial of that kindred love is an unhappy self-denial—a cultural suicide. As Faulkner says in a public speech, "no nation can endure with seventeen million second-class citizens in it nowadays."[12] He sees clearly, later in the case of Roth Edmonds, that the sin of miscegenation or incest lies not in the fault of the white man's sexual fantasy, if such fantasy is but natural. Since Roth was raised by a black mammy, whose love was the only love that he had ever known, it is only natural that he would fall in love with a black woman. So his fault, rather, lies in his self-denial and self-destruction, in his slavish acceptance and defence of the establishment of law, a law of injustice. Roth, the white man, misuses his power, fails his responsibility, in Faulkner's words, as Man.

The question of power, metaphorically projected in the actions of chasing, gaming, racing, hunting, and killing, is simple but mythical: Why does not a worthy and skillful woodsman want to shoot the bear? On the other hand, what is the price Boon Hogganbeck has to pay for having killed the bear? And after all, what is the fundamental difference between Ike's killing a deer and Roth Edmonds's killing a doe? The answer comes in one of those most intense and lyrical moments of romantic love: She cannot fade, though thou hast not thy bliss,/ Forever wilt thou love, and she be fair!

In Chapter 4 of "The Bear," Ike recollects McCaslin's Socratic wisdom in reciting to him Keats's "Ode on a Grecian Urn." The lyric enchantment of the "Grecian Urn" is a recurring theme, an enduring sonata, the "emblematic redaction" of Faulkner's Platonic metaphor. That Greek beauty stands, in the immortal name of romantic love, as a powerful challenge, an antithesis to the epic. "She" is the ultimate test of the endurance and legitimacy of the phallic, the ruling power.

It is a very curious passage (see *GD,M* 296-97) that reveals a great deal of Faulkner's idea of telling "love stories" when the subtext of Keats's poem is revealed behind his text. The lines from Keats's poem: "Ye soft pipes, play on;/Not to the sensual ear" just play in tune with Faulkner's narrative intertextually. Faulkner's method turns out to be surprisingly similar to Socrates' "piping"—a fake, a drama, and a gap, which characterize Socrates' "proper method" in praise of Love, as I discussed in Chapter Two. At the same time, the textual power in Faulkner's narrative is engendered by the lyricism of romantic love. Wondrously, novelistic love in *Go Down, Moses* reaches the summit of Platonic love—romantic love, aesthetic love, and philosophical love dramatized in a still moment of Keats's "Ode on a Grecian Urn." The Urn is the Bear, and the Bear the Urn.

Ike has just told McCaslin (Cass) about his close encounter with the Bear when the typography shifts to italics, which indicates that the narrative shifts to another level of human consciousness. From there on, we enter the narrative consciousness of Ike's childhood memory, as Ike recalls that critical moment when McCaslin asks him the seemingly nonsensical but significant and philosophical question: Why he didn't shoot the bear when he had the gun; why.

McCaslin raises the question emphatically and repeatedly, but he does not wait for the boy to answer the question; therefore, it is a rhetorical question. The scene is dramatic, unreal—Cass is acting as though on stage. Rising and crossing the room, across the pelt of the bear Ike had killed two years ago, McCaslin reaches for the bookcase, and he takes a book, from which he reads Ike a poem. The poem consists of five stanzas. He reads the five stanzas aloud once, then closes the book on his finger. Ike must be fascinated with the poem, so McCaslin reads to him once more, but the second time, he only reads one stanza, then closes the book. From that one stanza, Ike only recalls two lines to share with the reader.

The boy assumes that the poet is talking about a girl, telling a love story about a girl and a boy. From the lyric moment of poetry back to prose language, Faulkner turns the narrative into a "love story." This scene, with its dramatic irony, is a typical example of Socratic "love stories," as I call it, a Socratic "fake." Cass, in this scene, is given the legitimate name of "McCaslin," and legitimately plays the role of Ike's guardian. He is teaching Ike Socratic wisdom in the Socratic manner. After he reads the boy a classic poem, he assumes the role of a teacher and philosopher. He explains to the boy that the poet *has to talk about something* in order to speak truth; and that the truth of love, as simple as a boy's love for a girl, is the same as the truth that may account for the boy's action of not shooting the bear when he had the gun. Although it is Sam Fathers who has taught the boy in the woods how to hunt, when to kill and when not to kill the bear, Sam Fathers might not have had the language or have given the boy a language to speak of the wisdom of woodsmanship, the wisdom of action as a philosophy. So Cass helps the boy to think through his actions, think through language, and tease thoughts out of his good conscience.

The boy can understand Cass's application of the poetic metaphor, relating the "love story" to his relinquishment of the gun before the bear, because he knows by heart that it is true, because he himself has chosen to do so. In his subconsciousness, he can naturally link the lyric moment of Keats's poetry to the moment in the woods when he relinquishes his gun before Old Ben; at the same time, he identifies the voice, the words that come from Cass, book in hand, as quiet as the twilight itself, as truth, the words and philosophy of woodsmanship, that in Faulkner's language consists of first, courage and honor and pride; second, pity and compassion for mankind; and third, love of justice and of liberty. To Ike, Cass's words sound as poetic and as true as the truth of his action itself. What Cass teaches the boy—pride and pity and justice and courage and love—happens to be the same as what Molly teaches Roth in *The Fire and the Hearth*. These words are not mere rules of conduct for boys, but the truth of princely lore, the wisdom of supreme power, the principle of ruling, which teaches the ruler how to rule by peace and maintain peace with others and with oneself. For misused power, as we will see in the case of Boon, is destructive and self-destructive.

Unlike Fielding or Joyce, Faulkner seldom uses direct quotations from books; except for the titles of his novels, his biblical and Shakespearean allusions are implicit rather than explicit, contextual rather than referential. This direct quotation from Keats's "Ode on a Grecian Urn," therefore, is not a casual reference. It has a distinctive place in the text. It is a Proustian "magic lantern" standing "high above," illuminating the symbolic meaning raised by the question. The poetic metaphor provides a moment of revelation for the reader, not for the boy, for the boy obviously does not need an answer for his chosen action; he already has the truth in his heart, though not in his tongue. What is simpler than knowledge, simpler than words and language, simpler than the drama of a "love story," for the boy, is the romantic understanding of heart's truth, a vision of naked beauty attained through the knowledge of love. So the emphatically repeated question about seeing the truth is intended for the reader more than for the boy. It serves as a refrain to call the reader's attention.

The author's deliberate failure to provide an immediate answer to that question is as much a fake as the question. The rhetorical strategy Faulkner employs here is a postmodern development of free association; instead of appealing to an instinctual response through sensory experience, a metaphorical and metaphysical speculation links the poem to the raised question, and the poetic presence of another text supplies the answer to that question.[13] The disruption of narrative action makes the reader pause and ponder as it opens a gap between the rational discourse and "the heart's truth." Such a textual disruption cancels the surface meaning of the question only to yield its self-reflective meaning. If the reader may see through the "bottom part" of the text, a feminine fiction lays bare.

In this case, the feminine fiction is identified with the poetic metaphor of the Urn itself, as we know from Keats:

> Thou, silent form, dost tease us out of thought
> As doth eternity: Cold Pastoral!

The narrative status of the feminine fiction has earned a name and a place in Faulkner's conception of this scene. The "heart's truth," which is apparently repressed in the rational discourse, shines through "silent form." Furthermore, the silent form is identified by the form of "Cold Pastoral"—a form that is opposed to the heroic, the epic, and the dominant masculine force of a public discourse. It opens unto the wildness a space for a feminine discourse: the unheard, sweeter melodies, the enchantment of rustic sounds and romantic love.

As the conversation is broken, neither the boy nor Cass can address the profound, mythical question in ordinary language. How can the author deliver his heart's truth? As Cass suggests to the boy, as well as to the reader, the poet had to talk about something in order to speak about truth; and truth is one, one with the heart. It dawns upon the reader that in such a self-reflective moment, the narrative status of the "love story" becomes transparent: Talking about a girl or about a young man and a girl is simply talking about truth. If truth is one, then the motive of a man's action might be the same in hunting as in loving.

The "love story" is used as a medium, a dramatic presentation to illustrate a profound, philosophical, recurring idea in the novel: Why does a good woodsman not kill the Bear when he has the gun? In order to enlarge the meaning of that question and open its answer as wide as possible, Faulkner has to talk about something, turning to the realm of another discourse for symbolic expression. Then, of course, in order to talk about something, there is probably nothing more appealing, persuasive, and powerful to Faulkner's immediate audience than Keats's well-read Urn, the ideality of that poetic metaphor being possessed with phallic power in the literary imagination of more than one generation of white Southerners.

But the drama has to be erased in order for the reader to see through the idea behind. The veil has to be lifted for the bridegroom to see the beauty, which is also the truth, of that "still unravished bride of quietness," as though it were a ritual ceremony at a traditional Chinese wedding. When Cass repeatedly asks the boy if he sees his point, it is the author's voice that intrudes, and that points to the idea gradually emerging from behind the stage of these dramatic actions. What we see in our mind's eye is a subtext, the feminine fiction of Keats's poem. In Faulkner's text, we do not hear nor see the five stanzas Cass reads aloud to the boy, and repeats by memory. But their sweet absence is the "unheard melodies," which are "sweeter" to the reader who may recalls Keats's poem from memory, especially stanza 2:

> Heard melodies are sweet, but those unheard
> Are sweeter; therefore, ye soft pipes, play on;
> Not to the sensual ear, but, more endeared,
> Pipe to the spirit ditties of no tone:
> Fair youth, beneath the trees, thou canst not leave
> Thy song, nor ever can those trees be bare;
> Bold Lover, never, never canst thou kiss,
> Though winning near the goal—yet, do not grieve;
> (She cannot fade, though thou hast not thy bliss,
> Forever wilt thou love, and she be fair!)[14]

The reader either finds himself in the spirit of a romantic lover when he views the text, or he is barred at the door to the bedroom of his bride. He must be a bold lover, but "never, never canst thou kiss," which suggests he can never exhaust the symbolic meaning of the beloved aesthetic object. He must maintain some aesthetic distance to the true meaning of the text, to that "still unravished bride of quietness," listening to the "unheard melodies sweeter," because the author's lute is piping "not to the sensual ear, but more endeared/to the spirit ditties of no tone: . . . " These lines ideally describe Faulkner's art of novelistic love.

The two lines that come after the colon contain the symbolic message, the piping of his "song":

> Fair youth, beneath the trees, thou canst not leave
> Thy song, nor ever can those trees be bare.

It is the poetic metaphor staged in these two lines in the heart of stanza 2 that, in truth, supplies the missing link between the question and the answer. That idea of a fair youth beneath the trees is transformed into the crucified image of Boon at the end of "The Bear." When Ike reencounters the killer of the bear, he finds Boon perfectly deranged in a state of existential anguish and madness. Boon is sitting against the trunk of a tree, his head bent, hammering furiously his dismembered gun, with the frantic abandon of a madman. His barrel is disjointed, the rest of his gun, scattered. Nevertheless, his heart awakens; his spirit suffers from being alive under the tree, just as the tree is alive with mad leaves and frantic squirrels. The scene is overwhelming, as Faulkner describes it—there are forty or fifty squirrels leaping and darting from branch to branch until the whole tree has become one green maelstrom of mad leaves (*GD, M* 330-31). Boon is panting with guilt and a new revelation of life itself. He does not, possibly cannot, face the boy who is approaching him. But he still has his voice. Strangled in great anguish he shouts that he would not let anyone touch the squirrels, not one of them; and he claims that the squirrels are his, his creatures.

This scene has been regarded as most puzzling in critical interpretations of "The Bear." Even Faulkner's editors had suggested to him that this last paragraph of "The Bear" should be clarified to help the reader.[15] "In a number of ways this scene is extremely ambiguous," Morris Beja suggests, "and whether it reveals anything to Ike is not clear, but for the reader it does at least serve as a symbolic manifestation of the theme of greed and possessiveness that pervades 'The Bear,' and in fact all of *Go Down,*

Moses."[16] The "symbolic manifestation" Faulkner stages in this final scene is an image of abused power. In its "silent form" is cast Faulkner's well-wrought premonition: If such a state of being is the end of a killer, Faulkner is warning the killers that that they may think twice before they shoot. The problem in killing the bear, as dramatized in the case of Boon, is not merely destruction, but self-destruction. As a result, his left ear is shredded, his left arm completely gone, and his right leg deeply wounded; he is deformed, a physically disabled man for the rest of his life even though he survives.

If we consider the consequence of Boon's action on Boon's behalf, the depth of its tragic irony is unthinkable. In his blind killing of the bear, Boon has lost his "better half," Lion, the creature he sleeps with; and even worse, he has to use his own hand to put an end to the life of the man he loves most, Sam Fathers, and subsequently face the cruel mockery from McCaslin, who asks him if he had to kill Sam Fathers and demands that Boon speak the truth. How can Boon bring himself to speak the truth, the tragic truth that he had to kill the man whom he loved most ? He cannot. He said no, but we know that it cannot possibly be true, because McCaslin forces him again to speak the truth when Ike comes between them to protect Boon from the "sentence" of truth. In God's name, he asks Cass to leave him alone *(GD, M* 254). What can be more ironic and piteous for a fierce killer than to be left under the protection of a child! Deprived of peace, joy, truth, beauty, and love, Boon is in the state of an unutterable misery.

The truth that emerges in the last picture, as we see now, is a natural truth, a simple truth, the romantic truth that life will go on, the trees will never be bare, and squirrels will be alive forever; but man, who has to live the rest of his life after the killing, can never, never be happy if he cannot answer for the consequences of his own action in using his manly power. Thus the picture of the fair youth, the bold lover—Boon, crucified under the tree with his borrowed gun, dismembered, scattered, broken into a half-dozen pieces, his self-esteem lost forever, his conscience guilt-ridden and unsettled, filled with grief and remorse, hopeless and loveless—offers a final reflection upon the question why Ike didn't shoot the bear when he had the gun.

In the silent form of "Cold Pastoral" is cast a double image of Ike and Boon. While Boon is apparently the scapegoat, Ike, who has been castrated just in the previous scene, now looms within a short distance like Christ, like the bear, bigger, dimensionless against the dappled obscurity, looking at him. The destruction of Boon, which proves to be a negation of the metallic, machine-like, masculine power he stands for, serves in a dialectic relation as a symbolic affirmation of Ike's action. As Ike reflects on the spot, he knows that he will *never need to grieve* as he will not suffer from the conseqences of his own actions that he has chosen in his own life.

Ike's relinquishments of the gun, the McCaslin estate, and his wife's body are three symbolic actions, which form a thematic chain and which reinforce one another. Metaphorically, the gun is a phallic symbol. Shooting, possessing, and lovemaking all involve the test and control of the phallic power. They are practically identical in spirit: The boy, who is educated in the woods well enough to relinquish the gun, the compass, and the watch when approaching the bear, is consistent in character and action when he grows into manhood, both in repudiating his inheritance and in rejecting his wife's seduction. He is possessed with exactly the same indomitable spirit expected of him—the courage and honor and pride, and pity, and love of justice and of liberty.

Though contemporary critics tend to view Ike's action as futile, irresponsible, and unrealistic, the virtue of Ike's action, as Ike sees himself, lies in the idea of never needing to grieve, which means having permanent peace. Boon, in contrast, is doomed to grieve over what he kills and what he loves. Grief is opposed to the state of happiness, the ultimate goal of human life. This is the idea behind the dramatic presentation of the end of Boon. This idea should well explain why Faulkner ends the story with this scene immediately following Ike's frustration in the bedroom scene. The reader is left with an ultimate vision of the long-range goodness of Ike's self-control in sharp contrast with Boon's self-destruction. The phrase is perceivably inscribed as truth itself in the feminine fiction. Its unheard melodies are written in its silent form, in a lover's discourse:

> Bold Lover, never, never canst thou kiss,
> Though winning near the goal—yet, do not grieve.

The phrase has also appeared, earlier at the end of Chapter 2 of "The Bear," as a prediction of Ike's readiness to face a fatality that befalls the land, the doom brought by a new group of hunters who are not good enough to smell the trace of the killer, and whose misjudgment leads to the killing of the bear instead of Lion. Ike senses that it is the beginning of the end of something, he cannot name it, but he knows that *he would not grieve* (*GD, M* 226). Ike need not grieve because he is wise enough to know the truth before the killing takes place. He knows that the bear did not kill the colt; and he wishes that the hunters ought to have known better as Sam Fathers does. He only makes a philosophical observation that this is neither the first nor the last time men rationalize from and even act upon their misconceptions (*GD, M* 215). Since he knows, he would not grieve.

The phrase appears once more when Cass's reading of the love poem reminds him of his own love story. He is content enough to think that he would never need to grieve over because he could never approach any nearer and would never have to get any further away. This time, the female subject of his reference in public discourse, however ambiguous, presumably is his wife, whom he still loves but has given up his legal right to and power over her body. Yet by self-control he preserves a long-range goal, that is, peace. This is because he has to live with himself for the rest of his life and he wants peace in his life. Peace apparently is what Boon cannot have. [17] Ike, who is capable of restraining himself from a possible rape, never needs to grieve, because he maintains peace with his self, and with the other, too, his wife, his love. Ike, good woodsman that he is, seems to understand that true heroism lies in the ultimate attainment of peace, instead of the glory of war.

In the private discourse of a feminine fiction, the subject of his reference also involves the Urn, the subject of immortal love, his own idealism. Ike seems to identify his own sacrifice with that of the Bold Lover, whose burning forehead, and a parching tongue reminds him of his own suffering in the bedroom. Such an identification is likely, as the bedroom scene is staged shortly after. The bold lover who "canst kiss" yet "never need to grieve" is in fact immortalized through the unheard melodies from Keats's poem in silent form. So is the Lover's sacrifice. Thus Ike's unconsummated love is immortalized through poetic justice. His sacrifice stands still, identical to the Urn, timeless and valueless. In other words, it does not matter that his renunciation does not redeem the curse in the family; his action is but meant to project a gesture of Enlightenment idealism against the Establishment—the family; and the futility of his action only enriches its tragic irony.

What is unheard still and sweeter is the melodies of these lines at the end of Keats's poem:

> When old age shall this generation waste,
> Thou shalt remain, in midst of other woe.

These lines predict Ike's omniscient and omnipotent presence in the next two stories, "Delta Autumn" and "Go Down, Moses," as an end of a beginning. As the end of "The Bear," these lines finally affirm the sacrifice of the "Fair youth, beneath the trees" bearing the cross as a gesture of ancient grace—"O Attic shape! Fair attitude!"—and one with the immortal existence of the Urn itself. Ike is metaphysically resurrected, which we cannot see because his sacrifice is beyond humanity, beyond man power. What we see is a mirror image of man—Boon is redeemed through suffering and repentance. As his image of the agonized lover of squirrels reminds us of the crucified son of God under the tree, we realize that Boon has suffered enough at last to attain God's truth—the truth of Love. Boon's last words are spoken in the form of "Cold Pastoral." Simple but crystal clear, the shepherd of squirrels delivers an ultimatum of beauty/truth/wisdom: The creatures in the woods are God's creations for man to keep, not to kill; the squirrels are his children.

Boon disappears after this scene. Boon's figure fades into the identity of Ike, through a not uncommon metafictive device, that is, fictive metamorphosis. Ike emerges as a Christ figure, as well as the immortal, youthful Greek lover in Keats' poem, invisibly but intelligibly, in silent form, who is to "remain in midst of other woe." Thus Ike's relinquishment is silently affirmed in the name of ideal love in negation of sexual love, in the mode of romantic love in negation of epic love.

If epic love is the capitalist mode of love, as I proposed in Chapter Three, then romantic love is a negation of the ideology of capitalism. Faulkner projects the model of romantic love as an antithesis to the epic. While epic love satisfies the desire for power and possession, romantic love touches the heart; it fulfills one's inner needs, spiritual well-being, and happiness with one's self. Ike's relinquishment of a sinful inheritance is not only a denial of slavery, but a revolt against capitalism with its private ownership of property. When Faulkner was writing the novel, slavery had been abolished a long time before, but the socialist movement was fervent in the spirit of the age. The failure of Ike's marriage presents no compromise between the two types of ideology implied in the two different modes of novelistic love. Faulkner resolutely repudiates the dominant mode of epic love, and he relies on the power of romantic love to provide an immutable critique of his culture and history.

Writing in Tory tradition, Faulkner tends to view female power as identical to the rise of the bourgeoisie, so that the white woman in Faulkner is often unfortunately portrayed as a representative of that social power. Thus Ike's wife's desire is cast in the mode of epic love. In an interview, Faulkner tells us his idea of casting her in such a role:

> She—from her background, her tradition, sex was something evil, that it had to be justified by acquiring property. She was ethically a prostitute. Sexually she was frigid. I think that . . . he

[Ike] knew that there was no warmth that he would ever find from her, no understanding, no chance ever to accept love or return love because she was incapable of it.[18]

To call a perfect legal wife "ethically a prostitute" is a radical subversion of a value system; it is romantic and revolutionary indeed. Faulkner offers a radical condemnation of the Pamela syndrome. He does it even harsher and cruder than did Fielding. Considering the audience of his domestic world, where Ike's wife's value system prevails, the most effective rhetorical strategy once again lies in a Socratic "love story." To deliver his radical critique of the Pamela syndrome, he stages the bedroom scene in a Hollywood style, with such sensational and stark naked violence that his novelistic idea surely will impress his audience.

Faulkner conceives the ideological implication of Ike's wife's desire as the evil of the bourgeois establishment itself; moreover, he identifies economic gains in marriage as equivocal to the practice of prostitution. In this respect, Faulkner is in line with the cultural critique of Karl Marx that capitalism has drowned innocent love between husband and wife. Ike dares to accept death in a bourgeois marriage, where love is bound by capitalist economy and the female body is installed in the bedroom to be used as machinery of productivity. Faulkner had the wisdom to sense the doom of such a system as the end of love, the system personified in the body of Ike's wife. We see from the bedroom scene that she is lost for the value that she presents and projects to her husband, her love, while he preserves himself by self-control, and does not grieve for the loss of her love (see *GD,M* 314). For the true lover, there is a higher stage of love way beyond the mode of epic love, that is, romantic love from the "unheard melodies" of Keats's poem:

More happy love! more happy, happy love!
Forever warm and still to be enjoyed,
Forever panting, and forever young;
All breathing human passion far above.

Ike chooses to be the romantic lover, and he identifies himself with the immortal Greek lover in the poem. Brooks once remarked on Faulkner's immortal romantic passion: "Faulkner, as we have observed, began as a romantic and a romantic he remained to the end, though a reformed or foiled or chastened romantic."[19] Although I am not sure if it is adequate to call Faulkner a romantic, I certainly see Faulkner's romantic passion "reformed or foiled or chastened" in the end when novelistic love under his pen becomes Platonic. His use of Keats's "Grecian Urn" deals with a specific local historical condition, which in effect goes far beyond the aesthetic interest of Keats, or, I would rather say, beyond the limitations of New Critical interpretations of Keats and of Faulkner as well. In *Go Down, Moses*, Faulkner's romantic love is "reformed" to embrace his political ideology and "chastened" to transcend the personal and psychological, even the lyric and pure aesthetic. It reaches a state of philosophical profundity, almost a religious piety—near the still point of Socrates' mystic gaze in Plato's *Symposium* that I described in Chapter Two.

Romantic love in Faulkner is one with the love of God. However, one must understand that in Faulkner the word "God" may or may not be the Christian God alone. As Faulkner says in an interview: "No one is without Christianity, if we agree on what we mean by the word."[20] The word "God" functions in his text as an omniscient and omnipotent phallic sign, as universal as Love, which exists beyond Christendom. As I mentioned in Chapter One, if art was a religion during the modernist movement, Love in a larger sense, beyond sensual pleasure and toward communion, has virtually become a postmodern religion. A modernist artist turned into a postmodernist metafictionist, Faulkner treats the subject of Love as a displacement of the sign of God. Once this is understood, the concluding statement of "The Bear" ought not to be interpreted in terms of Christian humanism. Faulkner is neither a nihilist nor a pacifist. In fact, he believes that there is a difference between just wars and injust wars —war in defense of one's own country and against a superpower is time honored. In the middle of "The Bear," he makes a philosophical statement about war. He asserts that no one could have declared a war against a power with ten times the area and a hundred times the men and a thousand times the resources, except men who could believe that all necessary to conduct a successful war was not acumen nor shrewdness nor politics nor diplomacy nor money nor even integrity and simple arithmetic, but just love of land and courage (*GD, M* 288-89). During war, what counts is not mere power, but the control of power and the testimony of horsemanship, for what endure are not missiles and bombs but land force, not rhetoric and eloquence before the Security Council or on the TV screen, but the spirit of life and death in the battlefields. Ike is superior not because of his blood lineage, but because of the education he has received from an Indian woodsman, whom Faulkner crowns as his unblemished and gallant ancestry, Sam Fathers, who taught the boy how to hunt in the woods, when to shoot and when not to shoot, and most importantly, if one kills a deer or a bear, what to do with it afterward.

Faulkner is not a pacifist. Ike does kill. He kills a deer as a ritual so as to be initiated into the woods. In contrast, Roth Edmonds misfires and kills a doe—his sweetheart personified. To say the least, he is a bad hunter. He is, in fact, the illegitimate lover and incompetent ruler. As a consequence of his "misfire," he kills his own heart, his progeny, and his Love. The injustice he has done to himself is probably more fatal than he has done to his beloved, for the woman will go north with the silver horn in her hand, the symbol of a legacy in the future, which Ike passes down to her; and as Ike expects of her, she will marry someone of her kind. But Roth is left, as far as the story goes, an unwed widower. Does he have another son? Is he ever "happy happy" afterward? In contrast, the married widower Ike McCaslin is possibly a happier one, never need to grieve.

More Happy, Happy Love: Plato's Man, Lion, and Monster

Happiness is a philosophical concept that Faulkner employs to measure the achievement of human potential and human responsibility in every action his characters perform throughout the novel. I have just discussed Boon's grief and Ike's peace of mind as a contrasting consequence of human actions—a contrast that Faulkner presents for philosophical speculation. The philosophical implication of Faulkner's Idea can be traced to Plato's notion of happiness. In the chapter on "Imperfect Societies" in *The Republic,* Plato projects four types of imperfect societies: timarchy, oligarchy, democracy, tyranny; he imaginatively describes the character of the rulers in each society; and he measures "their degrees of Happiness" and the happiness of each society.[21] Faulkner read Plato when a boy, and it must be a significant part of his "education in the woods." [22] In *Go Down, Moses,* he is exploring race relations and power relations in American society; Plato's critique of "Imperfect Societies" surprisingly parallels the structure and characterology in his novel, and Faulkner's "love stories" are dramatizations of Plato's philosophy, as well as his own cultural criticism. Before I give a detailed reading of Faulkner's adaptation of Plato, let me give an account of Plato's idea of happiness.

Plato begins with a brief "Recapitulation" of the perfect state, where the Philosopher Ruler assumes his role as the king. He proceeds by an analysis of four imperfect types of society and the character of their representative rulers: the timarchic, the oligarchic, the democratic and the tyrannical rulers. Plato is mainly concerned with the degeneration of character in these rulers. The problem of degeneration in the ruler results from the lack of proper education, the kind of education he has proposed for the Philosopher Ruler in the previous chapter. He describes the problem by telling a story of generic decay in a house that has ruled at least for three generations from timarchy through oligarchy to democracy, passing its legacy from father to son. As if telling a family history, Plato predicts the relative happiness and unhappiness of each ruler and of each society that he rules, in measurements of harmony, pleasure, and economy. Even though the last ruler, the tyrant, is not necessarily son of the ruling family, but elected under democracy by the majority of people, yet because these people "are more interested in their private enterprise than in government and politics," their election will not guarantee the excellence of leadership and happiness of society.

Plato explores both social and psychological cause and effect in the transformation of character. For Plato, happiness is a dialectical concept, so his basic method is to contrast the worst type of rulers with the best (which is also Faulkner's method in *Go Down, Moses*). When he ranks them by degree of their Happiness, he calculates in numerical terms that each ruler is less happy than his predecessor, though he could be richer in wealth and power. The last of the four, the Tyrannical character, in Plato's intriguing calculation, proves to be "729 times more unhappy" than the ideal ruler, the Philosopher King.

Since each ruler is portrayed as the bearer of the character of the type of society he rules, the degeneration of character is also conceived as a consequence of a dynastic social transformation. Correspondingly, the society ruled by the most unhappy ruler is the most unhappy, characterized by a high criminal rate, foreign debts, domestic bankruptcy, political turmoil, economic depression, and a constant need for war. Its people fight abroad as mercenary troops during war, and during peace they commit crimes at their liberty.

Plato's ideology mainly presupposes that mere accumulation of wealth and power will not lead a country toward a happy state, if the essential human needs are not happily fulfilled. These needs include man's love for justice, peace, friendship, freedom, and happiness in private life. On the other hand, if the popular mind has lost its respect for goodness—truth/ beauty/wisdom—in one, then even the most powerful person will not have peace and happiness in mind. He will be surrounded by a bad company, have no friends he can trust. His bodyguards are the drones that swarm to him from abroad, admire him very much, though all decent men detest and avoid him. His followers are parasites, his mistresses whores. After they have gained enough profit from him, they will either leave him or betray him. So he is actually the most wretched slave of his own power (R 390).

In order to argue convincingly that just and unjust conduct affects the happiness of its author, Plato does not limit himself on ethical grounds only. He offers a psychological analysis of a human being possessed with power. He constructs a model of the human personality as a three-dimensional entity; and he fabricates an imaginary creature to illustrate his theory. The creature he draws is at once possessed with the potential of a Man, the power of a Lion, and the lust of a Monster—Chimaera, or Sylla, or Cerberus. Plato's model of the human personality wears the external appearance of only one of the three dimensions, that of a Man, "so that to eyes unable to see anything beneath the outer shell it looks like a single creature, a man" (R 416). Deep down the Man is only the size of a boy; whereas "the many-headed creature is by far the largest, and the Lion the next largest" (R 416).

In such a construct, it is not hard to recognize that Plat's concept of "Man" in "the size of a boy" only stands for the a little human potential to be civilized; the Monster is an uncultivated force in human nature—lust; but the Lion is a neutral power that can be developed into either a positive or negative force, depending upon the power balance of the two other parties. If the Monster rules, war and violence are bound to take place, and the Lion will be unleashed as a killing force—"to gratify the beast's greed and love of money, they school the lion to put up with insults and turn it into an ape" (R 418). Will an "ape" be happy? Will the Man be happy? (Think of Boon now.) Psychologically, when internal turmoil grows, the person has no peace, and therefore he will not be happy.

On the other hand, happiness can be attained if the "little boy" be brought up properly

> to strengthen the Man within us, so that he can look after the many-headed beast like a farmer, nursing and cultivating its tamer elements and preventing the wilder ones growing, while he makes an ally of the lion and look after the common interests of all by reconciling them with each other and with himself. (R 416-17)

Thus, under the control of the civilized Man, the Lion can be turned into a constructive force. He may serve as a police force to maintain peace and harmony within the power structure of the human personality. Imaginably, power is only a neutral force; it can bring either happiness or misery to its possessor, depending upon the upper hand that handles it.

Therefore, it is necessary to form a character in which "self control and justice and understanding are combined," Plato believes, because a person with such a character"won't be dazzled by popular ideas of happiness and make endless troubles for himself by piling up a fortune. . . . We shall always find him attuning his body to match the harmony of his mind and character" (R 419). But, as Plato further explains, the good man has no place in all four types of imperfect societies because imperfect societies can neither recognize the goodness of such a man, nor have use for him. The good man's place is not in the center of the existing social order, but rather beyond death and destruction in the happy state, which he projects on theoretical ground—a utopia in which, he believes the good man will be the ruler.

On the conceptual level, Faulkner's creation of the good man Ike McCaslin is identical with Plato's idea of the Philosopher Ruler: The philosopher is in love with truth, that is, not with the changing world of sensation, which is the object of opinion, but with the unchanging Reality which is the object of knowledge. The Urn, the woods, and Sam Fathers are embodiments of such knowledge. Ike is an idealist, loves truth in a philosophical sense and beauty with aesthetic distance. He is not interested in wealth, property, and possessions, but liberty and justice. Always attuning his body to match the harmony of his mind and character, he displays incredible self-control of lust in his relinquishment.

Faulkner's presentation of the most crucial action in the novel—the killing of the bear—is constructed in the Platonic tradition through a "love making" scene (*see GD,M* 240-41). In this scene Faulkner also enacts a three-dimensional statuary—man, dog, and bear—to tell a wonderful "love story." We see the bear, in the moment of destruction, act like a benevolent and brave lover. Being attacked by the hunting dog Lion sent by Boon, it does not choose to fight or struggle with the dog as beasts do; instead, it catches the dog in both arms, embraces it almost loverlike; and the two fell down together. Lion is underneath the bear in the position of a woman. The bear is in perfect control of his supreme power; death and destruction do not destroy its dignity, composure, and might. While Lion is still clinging to its throat, the bear is strong enough to strike one of the hounds with one paw and hurl it five or six feet. At the same time, it is capable of making love to the dog in its arms. Slowly, it rises and stands half erect, rising and rising as though it would never stop and rakes at Lion's belly with its forepaws.

Boon comes into the scene with the rapacious power of man. The love scene turns into a rape scene. Boon comes running, leaping among the hounds, hurdling them and kicking them aside as he runs. With the gleam of the blade in his hand, he flings himself astride the bear, his legs locked around the bear's belly, his left arm under the bear's throat where Lion clings. The glint of his knife rises and falls in and out of the bear's throat. There is neither love nor self-love in his action. If Boon's pure physical strength is capable of raping and destroying the bear, his violent action does not gain him the power as man over the bear, or even the position of a lover. Tragicomically, in that physically entangled posistion, Boon is still underneath the bear, in the position of a woman—his legs locked around the bear's belly.

The bear is portrayed as a heroic tragic lover, almost like a man. Destroyed by man's blind actions, it is still loving, still caring, still carrying in its bosom the burden of man's self-destruction. We see the bear pulled over backward by Boon's weight. With Boon's blade buried in its throat, it still has the might to surge erect, and more, raising with it the man and the dog too. Then it takes steps towards the woods, walking on its hind feet as a man would have walked. When it falls, Faulkner tells us that it does not collapse, or crumple. The bear, the man, and the dog fall all of a piece, like a tree, like a piece of statuary.

The hierarchical structure Faulkner casts into this still moment of statuary scene contains a Platonic metaphor of power struggle and power balance in Faulkner's fictive universe. When all the worldly forces are brought in alliance against the bear, we see clearly that it is the work of man done in the hands of Boon the plebeian, who in a desperate effort to rescue Lion, brings down the bear, the dog, and man himself in total destruction. This brilliantly structured scene may offer a reflection of the power struggle between Plato's Lion and the Monster. Sadly enough, the civilized part of man, the enlightened man, the boy, is not there, only his shadow—Boon the scapegoat, sacrificed, humiliated, survives to suffer.

Faulkner's marble statuary is bigger than Plato's portrait. It represents not merely a human personality, but humanity in a fast-developing but self-destructive capitalist society—what is being destroyed is Melville's unspeakable, unspoken letter "H—."[23] It is a society envisioned through the eyes of Plato's good old philosopher. When the killing takes place, Ike is not participating in the game, but watches the death of Old Ben from a distance. "This is rotten, I don't like it, I can't do anything about it, but at least I will not participate in it myself, I will go off into a cave or climb a pillar to sit on," as Faulkner explains to us Ike's mind.[24] The good man has no place in Faulkner's social world. Nevertheless, he has the best view that enables him to tell us the story. Like Ishmael, he is the only one who "did survive the wreck."

Faulkner could well conceive himself in such a marginal position in the 1930s when his reputation suffered considerably.[25] Or as he later pronounced:

> The artist in America really has no place in our economy, which is an economy based on success rather than on any quality of the human spirit. . . we haven't found yet that we need the artist, the philosopher.[26]

Only in fiction he is free to create such a character as Ike McCaslin and bring him to the center, to testify social reality and project the reality of absence. Ike's social status manifest itself in the self-conscious but disjoined narrative form: He is at once an insider and an outsider of the narrative world. Such a position is inscribed in the narrative consciousness itself. The presence of Ike's consciousness is alienated but encompassing, distanced but ever-present. It flows in and out of time and history, backward and forward. His voice is sometimes mute, and his freedom of speech is broken and repressed. In spite of the difficulties of expression, he has a firm grasp of "heart's truth."

From the beginning of the novel, the narrative framework is set from the perspective of the good old Philosopher Ruler, repudiated, ruled out, but still judging the imperfections of his world. The narrator is no more the modernist artist as Joyce assumes, "refined out of existence, indifferent, paring his fingernails,"[27] but rather a postmodern Sylvan historian, committed to his land, with endured love and a deep apprehension, watching the progress of his kind—"Isaac McCaslin, 'Uncle Ike,' past seventy and nearer eighty than he ever corroborated anymore, a widower now and uncle to half a county and father to no one"—a gigantic immortal figure (GD,M 3). His life holds both the beginning and the end—the beginning of Reconstruction and the end of Segregation. He is born in the year of 1867 into the coffin of Reconstruction and Repudiation of Andrew Johnson, and "dies" in 1947, as he himself puts it, "after Hitler gets through with it. Or Smith or Jones or Roosevelt or Wilkie or whatever he will call himself in this country" (GD,M 338). Ike survives the first publication of Go Down, Moses by seven years. Thus at the end of the book, he must be somewhere up there, witnessing the burial of Butch and the wrath of Molly's mourning, endlessly rocking in his cradle, foreboding the Second Coming of the civil rights movement. In a way he is Faulkner's soothsayer, Moses.

The little boy of Plato's idea, who is the potential of human civilization, is amplified to the magnitude of a mythic character. As big and ancient as the bear, chaste and immortal as the Urn, and wise as already an old man, Ike alone is in control of the heart's truth and heart's complexity of the history not only of his family, but also of His land. He speaks of the land as though it were the land of God, and he conceives himself as though he were God. The land was originally his. Without possessing it, it is still his. He still lives on it. He looks over it from the woods as a shepherd, brooding over his tale in silent form—the cold pastoral.

His consciousness serves as a Last Judgment of all actions. The author who plays the pipe—the hand in control of his writing—drives Ike's critical intelligence to the center of the fictive universe he creates, far above and beyond the narrative actions. Then like the hushed appearance, or apparition, of the bear, his conscious judgment is there, somewhere and everywhere. So even if in some parts of the novel—"The Fire and the Hearth," "Pantaloon in Black," and "Go Down, Moses"—Ike does not partake in the narrative actions, I should think, it is still Ike's story.

By appearance, Faulkner's novel is "loosely" structured, without a coherent order of chronology or explicit statement of genealogy. Such incoherence is by itself self-conscious and self-reflective of the broken human bondage and irretrievable curse in the McCaslin genealogy. On the one hand, the textual irrationality must be viewed as a carnivalesque social protest on the author's part to dismantle the linguistic patriarchy and to unearth the buried truth in "history." On the other, its rationale can still be pursued on the ideological level through a reading of the "love stories." The seven tales are intelligibly structured in the same order as Plato's presentation of "Imperfect Societies." Love stands as a controlling idea, an absolute principle, measuring the degree of happiness in each regime.

The operational structure of Faulkner's novel is mythic; the mythic structure, as Levi-Strauss perceives, is a "spiral wise," discontinuous pattern rendered apparent through varied repetition. So does Faulkner portray the dynastic decay of a society from love's comedy to tragedy "spiral wise," and with historical discontinuity, plunging downward from a happy state into human misery. The repetition of his "love stories" entails and unfolds his historical vision, rendering apparent truth/beauty, that is probably all we "need to know" in this "Sylvan history."

In fact, the seven tales can be read as a "symposium" of "love stories" of sorts—Faulkner's novelistic dramatization of Plato's political ideology. If we focus on love as a measurement of happiness and examine Faulkner's treatment of the subject of love in each tale, we may discern a thematic unity of love's decay from things as it *was* to the death of love in

"Go Down, Moses." In each tale there is the idea of a "love story" of sorts. We have courtship and marriage in "Was"; divorce and reunion in "The Fire and the Hearth"; bereavement and alienation in "Pantaloon in Black"; adultery and miscegenation in "The Old People"; denial and castration in "The Bear"; true love and deprivation in "Delta Autumn"; and death of love and progeny in "Go Down, Moses."

By proposing such a thematic unity, I hope, first, to reveal the presence of the above-stated mythic structure rendered apparent through varied repetitions of "love stories"; and second, to point out such a structure in a downward spiral narrative movement that parallels Plato's account of the "Imperfect Societies." Last but not the least, I hope to reach the bottom line of the entire novel that contains "the heart's truth and the heart's complexities"—Faulkner's social and historical vision. I believe what the good man Ike McCaslin fails to articulate explicitly in a rational public discourse can be read through the feminine fiction of Faulkner's "love stories." In the following pages, I shall provide a reading, or a re-reading, of Faulkner's "flowery tale."

Forever Wilt Thou Love, and She Be Fair!: Love in Race Relations

"Was"

The first story in *Go Down, Moses*, "Was," as the title suggests, is a recapitulation of a historical condition, which is portrayed as a kind of fictional timarchy. According to Plato's model, in a timarchy, the men and women share the same education and same occupations both in peace and war, governed by those who are best at philosophy and war. The rulers possess nothing, no private quarters, but everything is common to all. They are to train for war and act as Guardians over the community, devote themselves to the care of their fellow Guardians and the whole state. The twin brothers are Timarchic rulers, sportive and well mannered; they act as guardians, having little self-interest whatever games they play. One has a Greek name, Theophilus, the other a Latin name, Amodeus, both meaning the love of God. They rule with a spirit of kindred love and diplomatic gaiety. Slavery is but a historical condition they unfortunately inherited from the past; "they by instinct knew that slavery was wrong but they didn't know quite what to do about it."[28] In order to preserve their freedom from bondage, they lock up their slaves in the big house, while they themselves live in a cabin away from the house. When a slave runs away, under feudal obligation, it is but their duty to find him, even at the risk of war with their neighbors.

Whatever disputes they have to settle with their neighbors, they fight as they are trained under the honor code of chivalry. When they catch their slave, their "quarry," they do not punish him, but treat him "with the same respect that the bear or the deer would" have had from them—"a chance for life." "They wouldn't have betrayed him, tricked him, they wouldn't have built a deadfall for him." Faulkner conceives a slight difference between Buck and Buddy in their ruling strategies. Buck, who tries to lay his hands on Turl, the run away slave, fails and loses his control—the "bear" escapes him and laughs at him. Buddy, on the contrary, has the manner not to touch the slave when "Tomey's Turl's saddle-colored hands came into the light and took up the deck and dealt" (*GD, M* 27). The beauty of his action is enhanced by the comic outcome that Turl "stacks the deck" to help him win![29] The wisdom of Buddy's ruling strategy can be only understood in that poetic metaphor Faulkner repeatedly presents through dramatic actions: "Forever wilt thou love, and she be fair!" The mode is already inscribed in that comic scene.

Remarkably, Buck and Buddy fight not to gain back the slave, but to get rid of their bondage. Women also have a share in their game. Sophonsiba is hand in glove with her brother to intrigue Buck into her bedroom, and her maid, Tennie, is with her lover, Tomey's Turl, when he goes into hiding. But Faulkner makes it a point that the rulers fight not for the possession of women, but rather to help each other escape marriage. They also play their poker game on behalf of their runaway slave and win the girl he wants to marry so that he won't run away again. In other words, the good rulers fight for their people, and they recognize that their duty is to see to the happiness of their subjects.

They are also competent rulers. Because the rulers have an ideal love for personal freedom and liberty and little interest in possessions, and also because they maintain a chivalric honor code playing their games and preserve a sense of justice in dealing with their inferiors as well as their equals, they succeed in solving all their problems happily. Peace is negotiated and restored through a kind of "ping-pong diplomacy." The story begins with courtship and ends with a happy marriage between Tomey's Turl and Tennie Beauchamp, which is what the slave wanted and which is the cause of war now solved for good. As for the twins, Buck is rescued by his brother from an unwanted marriage with Sophonsiba; and Buddy, who has the least self-interest in the whole affair, turns out to be the most competent gamer and successful ruler. He exemplifies Plato's philosophy that "the only men to get power should be men who do not love it, otherwise we shall have rivals' quarrels." (Imagine what could have been had the twins both wanted Tennie or Sophonsiba!) So what we have in "Was" is not a perfect state, but it *was* a tolerably *happy* state.

"The Fire and the Hearth"

The second story, "The Fire and the Hearth," presents a society undergoing the transition from timarchy to oligarchy. The Edmonds are oligarchic rulers, appointed by their elders, less capable than their predecessors, but wealthy with inherited private property. Accordingly, their relationship to their subjects changes. As Plato presumes, when the oligarchic rulers have problems with their subjects, they distribute property to make compromises in order to stop violence. This takes place when Lucas challenges the authority of Zack and Roth. The former gives him back his wife; the latter lets him have his way to pawn the mule under his name. But even in such actions, it is only fair to observe that there is a great deal of human understanding on the ruler's part and proper respect for the ruled.

The focus of Faulkner's idea in this story is still on the importance of Love in power relations: "Forever wilt thou love, and she be fair!" Between Zack and Lucas, the infantile bondage is never completely broken, so that even though they once fought to solve their problems—Lucas wanted to know if Zack had used his wife and Zack denied it—their fight is described as a sibling's fight (*GD, M* 56-57); one never meant to kill the other: "'You thought I wouldn't, didn't you?' Lucas said . . . they met over the center of the bed"—the two did sleep in the same bed and hunt together when young—Lucas clasped the other "almost like an embrace" and then Zack heard his "miss-fire" (*GD, M* 56-57). The misspelled word "miss-fire" is a carnivalesque word, which indicates that it wasn't really a "misfire." The unpronounced truth is, as I hear it, that violence is avoided when the upper hand knows its limit.

Faulkner also gives Zack a chance to show his self-control in return. When his son, Roth, is unhappy with the way Lucas treats his "masters," Zack tells him: "You let me and Lucas settle how he is to treat me, and I'll let you and him settle how he is to treat you" (*GD, M* 115). This kind of manner is not a sentimental gesture or hypocritical modesty, but a far-sighted, wise, long-range ruling tactic developed through experience and knowledge. Zack knows Lucas means no harm, so that he can relinquish his power before Lucas—his "bear" he respects and well trusts. The kind of trust in Lucas Zack shows his son becomes a decisive factor in settling disputes even later on when his son becomes the ruler.

The day comes when his son Roth has to represent Molly before the court of justice to file a divorce against Lucas. Lucas shows equal trust in Roth in a comic scene. The chancellor is ready to pass the bill "in due form and order" in approval when Lucas shows up and stops it: "We dont want no voce. Roth Edmonds knows what I mean" (*GD, M* 128). This is all he has to say, and all he needs to say for Roth to withdraw the bill. Even his wife, Molly, has no idea what he means. But Roth gets it. He takes his word and withdraws the case. He feels good, even proud of himself, when he can tell Molly: "Didn't you hear Lucas tell the judge that Roth Edmonds knows what he means?" (*GD, M* 129) He gets it perfectly in fact—that Lucas means what he says: He'll accept the condition Roth proposed to him the day before; he'll give up the gold-digging machine to save his marriage. Although Lucas doesn't say it before the judge, and Roth doesn't have to make him say it in the courtroom either, such a textual silence can be read as an indication that the presence of natural understanding between the white and the black is completely absent in the public discourse; it has no place in ordinary language. In the public language of the court clerk, sort of a bastard "ruler," Lucas is an "uppity" and a "nigger." But in the private ear of Roth Edmonds, Lucas's broken, black English is as good as a gentleman's honor.

As it turns out, that night Lucas comes to see Roth and turns in his "divining machine":

> It was clean of mud now; it looked as though it had been polished, at once compact and complex and efficient looking with its bright cryptic dials and gleaming knobs. (*GD,M* 130)

That gold-digging machine is another symbol of phallic power, but like the Lion in Plato's paradigm, it is a neutral power. Now that it is so well handled by the civilized force of man, while the monster and the greed that lured in Lucas have surrendered and become subdued, the tool itself shines with glory, pride, and phallic efficiency. Roth is boss again over Lucas. It is this sort of honor code that he maintains with Lucas and his understanding of him that makes Roth a competent ruler, up to this point in the novel at least.

That's why when he loses his manner in "Delta Autumn," Ike questions nothing but his sense of honor (GD, M 356).

Even more important than his honor is the bondage of Love that supports and sustains his power to be a successful ruler. His action is well motivated by a good will to not allow the

> breaking up after forty-five years the home of the woman who had been the only mother he, Edmonds, ever knew, who had raised him, fed him from her own breast as she was actually doing her own child, who had surrounded him always with care for his physical body and for his spirit too, teaching him his manners and behavior. (GD,M 117)

Faulkner himself probably had been raised this way in the hands of his Mammy, Caroline Barr, "who was born in slavery and who gave to my family a fidelity without stint or calculation of recompense and to my childhood an immeasurable devotion and love" (the book is dedicated to her).[30] Faulkner's bondage of love with his black mammy had nurtured his spirit of liberalism as a white Southerner. Molly, the center of "the Fire and Hearth," maintains the spirit of Love in the black and in the white family, as well as peace and harmony between the two races. Therefore, she holds the truth/beauty/wisdom of ruling ethics. The "manners" that Molly teaches Roth comprise the honorable behavior for masters, for rulers:

> —to be gentle with his inferiors, honorable with his equals, generous to the weak and considerate of the aged, courteous, truthful and brave to all— . . . without stint or expectation of reward that constant and abiding devotion of love. (GD,M 117)

These words, in essence, are Faulkner's "Princely Lore," the learning he has programmed for "the education of Roth," the proper conduct for "natural aristocracy." A "plebeian" like Boon Hogganbeck, equipped with mere physical power and modern efficiency without the knowledge of history and philosophy, may not understand how important such "manners" are in power relations. He puts on airs before the Negroes and wastes his bullets to scare black ladies. What Faulkner proposes is a civilized way of ruling and seeking peaceful solution to any human conflict. As long as there is a bondage of love, mere dominance and subjugation are not occasion enough to split a human relationship, whether it is between the black and white or husband and wife. Only when the ruler loses his manner will hatred grow in the ruled. I think this is why Faulkner's critics are given to understand in racial conflict that "it is on the white man . . . that the blame must ultimately rest."[31] Faulkner himself says in a public speech:

> It is our white ma's shame that in our present southern economy, the Negro must not have economic equality; our double shame that we fear that giving him more social equality will jeopardize his present economic status; our triple shame that even then, to justify ourselves, we must becloud the issue with the purity of white blood.[32]

In "The Fire and the Hearth," thanks to the bondage of love that still exists among most of these characters, the "love story" remains a humorous comedy. Although the relationship between "husband and wife" becomes complicated with Molly's demand for divorce and Lucas's greed for gold, the old couple ends with a dramatic reunion. Out of the courtroom, Lucas "puts into Molly's hand" a sack of candy—"a nickel's worth." "Here," he says, "You aint got no teeth left but you can still gum it" (*GD,M* 130). Melting candies are "sweet," gummed candies are "sweeter." The lady didn't ask for a divorce out of her own selfish desire, since she "aint got no teeth left," but for the well-being of her husband. Therefore, she wins her case. She remains at the center of "the fire and the hearth," holding the native bondage between the two families together as though

> husband and wife did not need to speak words to one another, not just for the old habit of living together but because in that one long-ago instant at least out of the long and shabby stretch of their human lives, even though they knew at the time it wouldn't and couldn't last, they had touched and become as God when they voluntarily and in advance forgave one another for all that each knew the other could never be. (*GD,M* 107-108)

Faulkner suggests that domestic quarrels, whether between husband and wife or between black and white, are natural and inevitable. Any society has its disputes and domestic problems. If the problems can be settled within the family by "the fire and the hearth" instead of foreign interference, either by law or by force, then not only peace, but also (and more important), Love can be happily restored. Otherwise, the risk may involve mutual destruction. Faulkner must have believed that in a family dispute, if one party is to invite a foreign power to use force or law against the other, its risk may very well involve the danger of mutual destruction in the end. In this case, however, even the love between Roth and Lucas, which was once lost when Roth was a child, is happily repaired.

"Pantaloon in Black"

What would have become of Lucas had he lost the love of his wife? This is the idea and a natural question to be explored in the next story, "Pantaloon in Black." "Pantaloon in Black" has always been a problem for Faulkner's critics place it within the structure of the novel as a whole. Not until we can envision Faulkner's conceptual framework of race relations in the metaphor of marriage does this story find its logical place in the thematic development of the seven tales. Rider's death is a reiteration and reinforcement of the conclusion reached at the end of "The Fire and the Hearth": How can a black man live in this world without his wife, without domestic love?

Rider, a black man, a tenant on the estate of Carothers Edmonds, lost his wife after only six months of marriage. After the burial of his wife, Rider is a lost soul. "I am snakebit and bound to die" (*GD,M* 152). He gets drunk and wanders into a white company. Looking for comfort, only to be insulted, he starts a quarrel with a white man. They fight. This time, the fight is not in the center of McCaslin's bed, "the two of them squatting, facing each other above the dice and the money." The white man draws a pistol:

> before the half-drawn pistol exploded he actually struck at the white man's throat not with the blade but with a sweeping blow of his fist, following through in the same motion so that not even the first jet of blood touched his hand or arm. (*GD,M* 154)

The reader is given to know that it is the white man who draws his pistol first. Faulkner's depiction of this fatal action holds the white man responsible from a legal point of view. What follows is a presentation of the legal justice in conducting the case. The next day, the sheriff comes into Rider's house, arrests him, puts him in jail, and within a few hours, without court trial or legal proceedings, he is lynched to death by a group of white men's "hired niggers."

Before his death, Rider is portrayed as the most powerful warrior in all of Faulkner's stories. Even during the lynching scene, he is presented, as a student of mine observed, like a football champion on a slow-motion movie screen; he is physically a "superman." Rider's story is real, and it is also surreal. Faulkner's presentation of the most powerful yet tragic moment of his death is far beyond realism:

> Ketcham went in and begun peeling away niggers until he could
> see him laying there under the pile of them, laughing, with tears
> big as glass marbles running across his face and down past his
> ears and making a kind of popping sound on the floor like
> somebody dropping bird eggs, laughing and laughing and saying,
> "Hit look lack Ah just cant quit thinking. Look lack Ah just cant
> quit." (*GD,M* 159)

The cruelty of lynching is real; but the scene is surreal with the hallucination of Rider's dying words, the grotesque laughter of black humor. Those tears "making a kind of popping sound on the floor" are Shakespearean "pearls." When Rider dies, he still has the heart to say, "Look lack Ah just cant quit." Later, in Chapter 3 of "The Bear," when Sam Fathers dies after the killing of the Bear, we are told that his heart fails and he just quits. He no longer wish to serve the white men in their bloody game. The time span in between these two episodes can only be speculated metaphorically within the fictional universe Faulkner creates. What Faulkner presents at this stage of generic decay is the unfortunate destruction of the phallic power on the land, that is, the black power. The story is entitled "Pantaloon in Black": "Pantaloon" is a buffoon in pantomimes; but it is also a piece of garment, man's wide breeches, said to be a popular costume in England during the reign of Charles II, a once-dethroned prince. In either case, the word signifies a dressed-up stage character. "Pantaloon" is very possibly a sign of the Robe. Its significance is undeniably there. The first line of the story draws the reader's attention to Rider's "Robe": "He stood in the worn, faded clean overalls which Mannie herself had washed only a week ago, and heard the first clod stride the pine box" (*GD,M* 135). This is not the only place in the novel the "overalls" are used as a garment of princely identity. In "The Bear," when Faulkner crowns Sam Fathers as a prince of natural aristocracy, he describes him in the battered and faded overalls and the frayed five cent straw hat which had been the badge of the Negro's slavery and was now the regalia of his freedom. Such theatrical device entertains the kind of audience who can appreciate the characters beyond the color of their skin.

At any rate, the emotional power of love in the black man being so strong and authentic, its depression or deprivation naturally causes its explosion and leads to violence and terror. Critics have called Rider "Faulkner's Prince Hamlet." I think, as the story begins with the burial scene, he also plays the role of the grave digger. He is the grave digger of a better time, though the time at the end of "The Fire and the Hearth," where peace and love are still preserved. His bird-egg tears are shed not for his own end, but for the end of a regime.

The role of the grave digger is in effect innocent. He is not responsible for what is dead inside "the pine box" (*GD,M* 135), be it Ophelia or Mannie. The cause of violence and destruction still lies in the lack of love in the power relationship, the alienation between the black and the white, the ruler and the ruled, the husband and the wife. The structure of the story itself conveys such a sense of alienation. The same story is told twice, in two totally alienated discourses and from completely disjointed opposite viewpoints; one dwells within Rider's consciousness, the other outside of it from the white sheriff's dumb point of view and a numb conscience.

At the same time, Faulkner presents two opposing marriage scenes. In the black family, the bereaved husband bemoans his wife, seeing her spirit and talking to her as though she were alive.

> "Den lemme go wid you, honey." But she was going. She was going fast now, he could actually feel between them the insuperable barrier of that very strength which could handle alone a log which would have taken any two other men to handle, of the blood and bones and flesh too strong, invincible for life, having learned at least once with his own eyes how tough, even in sudden and violent death, not a young man's bones and flesh perhaps but the will of that bone and flesh to remain alive, actually was.
>
> Then she was gone. (*GD,M* 141)

This kind of love is now dead, although the dead is still tragically alive. In the white family, love is absent during the whole scene, as though the living were comically dead now. It is mealtime; the white sheriff is telling Rider's story to his wife. As he speaks all the way through in the form of a monologue, his wife makes no response to whatever he says. So he's practically talking into a vacuum. She is not even there, she is in the next room. When the husband finishes his story with the horrible death of Rider, he asks: "And what do you think of that?"

> "I think if you eat any supper in this house you'll do it in the next five minutes," his wife said from the dining room. "I'm going to clear this table then and I'm going to the picture show." (*GD,M* 159)

The wife's indifference is only too well matched by the husband's bloody ignorance of the very subject of which he is speaking:

> "Them damn niggers," he said. "I swear to godfrey, it's a wonder we have as little trouble with them as we do. Because why? Because they aint human. They look like a man and they walk on their hind legs like a man, and they can talk and you can understand them and you think they are understanding you, at least now and then. But when it comes to the normal human feelings and sentiments of human beings, they might just as well be a damn herd of wild buffaloes." (*GD,M* 154)

Faulkner exposes the sheriff as an unfeeling man and his wife an insensitive woman. The dramatic irony is so rich and profound in the words of the sheriff just quoted that whatever he says turns into a perfect satire upon himself. Here is Faulkner's brilliant criticism of racial prejudice and the white man's racism grown out of a pure ignorance, ignorance not only of the Other, but also of himself, of marital love itself. Power in the hands of such white "running dogs," who "look like a man and they walk on their hind legs like a man," is nothing but doom.

The later rulers in *Go Down, Moses*, such as the white sheriff in "Pantaloon in Black" and Cass and Major de Spain in "The Bear," who "have got one foot straddled into a farm and the other foot straddled into a bank" (*GD,M* 250), gradually become indifferent bureaucrats in a democracy. When the spirit of Love, or benevolence, is lost in the ruler, racial tension and racial conflict naturally intensify. According to Plato's theory, in a democracy, law and legislation are introduced to protect the rights and privilege of the nouveau riche, while the poor are not even represented by the two parties. One represents the remnants of oligarchy, and the other is full of hired politicians on behalf of the rising upper-middle class. "The Bear" is a close examination of democracy with an apocalyptic vision. The love story of Ike's marriage, as I discussed before, is a comic tragedy, that reinforces the theme of the impotence of love between husband and wife in the white family as seen in in "Pantaloon in Black."

"The Old People"

"The Old People" can be read as a Preface to "The Bear." Short as it is, the social relations, the doom of the wildness, and the actions that eventually take place in "The Bear" are all preconceived and predetermined in "The Old People." The "love story" in "The Old People" tells about the adultery and miscegenation of an Indian chief, which offers a counterpart of "Imperfect Societies" in the Indian tribe. It is with the same pattern of curse and generic decay that Faulkner reinforces Plato's ideology. According to Plato, generic decay results from indiscreet and inopportune marriages; the children from such marriages "will be neither gifted nor lucky." In the family of the Indian chief, the first generation were good hunters; when Sam Fathers saw the Bear, he saluted him: "'Oleh, Chief,' Sam said. 'Grandfather'" (*GD,M* 184). But the throne of "the ancient immortal Umpire" (another carnivalesque word) was usurped by Issetibbeha's sister's son, Ikkemotubbe, "who had named himself Doom." Doom is an oligarchic ruler ruined by luxury and bribery. In his youth, he

> had run away to New Orleans and returned seven years later with a French companion calling himself the Chevalier Soeur Blond de Vitry, who must have been the Ikkemotubbe of his family too and who was already addressing Ikkemotubbe as Du Homme; —returned, came home again, with his foreign Aramis and the quadroon slave woman who was to be Sam's mother, and a gold-laced hat and coat and a wicker wine-hamper containing a litter of month-old puppies and a gold snuff-box filled with a white powder resembling fine sugar. (*GD,M* 165-66)

I have quoted the above passage in order to show the dubious identity of Doom's "foreign Aramis" entangled in the middle of the syntax that ends up with mixed stuff of luxury, drugs, infants, poison, and false appearance of "fine sugar." As Faulkner tells us, "Sam Fathers" in the Indian language means "having two fathers." The question remains: Which two are his real fathers? Doom and the slave, or Doom and his "French companion"? The original curse may have to be traced beyond the spoiled Indian chief to the "white powder" in the "gold snuff-box."

At any rate, the curse will accomplish its own revenge in the end. Doom marries his pregnant mistress to a slave he inherited—exactly the same way, as Ike discovers from the family ledger, that his grandfather Lucius Quintus Carothers McCaslin (1722-1837) did to Eunice; and years later, Doom sold his land together with the slaves to his white neighbors the McCaslins. Plato did mention that when a ruler brings himself to sell his own son or daughter as a slave, he degenerates into a Tyrannical character. Doom's curse shall eventually befall the shoulders of Roth Edmonds in the last two tales—in "Delta Autumn" when he lets his own son go with his Negro mistress unmarried or to marry someone else; and in "Go Down, Moses," too, when his "only mother," Molly Worsham Beauchamp, accuses him: "Roth Edmonds sold my Benjamin. Sold him to Pharaoh. Sold him in Egypt and now he dead" (*GD,M* 380-81). Go down, Moses . . .

"Delta Autumn"

Roth plays a prolonged double role as the son of the timarchy and the oligarchy that Plato has portrayed in his text. Plato predicts that the son of the timarch sees his father's failure in battle or in administration with "a wrong sense of shame"; as he is brought up in his father's "narrow economic way," he tends to indulge himself in pleasure when he grows up. At the same time, he "will be harsh to the slaves, because his imperfect education has left him without a proper sense of his superiority to them" (R 359-76). This applies perfectly to Faulkner's characterization of Roth Edmonds. In "The Fire and the Hearth," Roth sees his father, Zack Edmonds, as a failure of a ruler, who tries to preserve the feudal tradition of plantation life, but is unable to rule over Lucas. Then one day, with his "haughty ancestral pride based not on any value but on an accident of geography, stemmed not from courage and honor but from wrong and shame" (*GD,M* 111), Roth turned away from the black family who raised him.

In "Delta Autumn," Roth is reduced from an oligarchic to a democratic ruler. He has lost his honor code altogether, indulges himself in his expenditure and pleasure. "Haven't you discovered," he asks Ike, "that women and children are one thing there's never any scarcity of?" (*GD,M* 339). So he gives himself a good time, spending six weeks with his sweetheart in Mexico, leaves her pregnant, and then in a good old-fashioned way, uses money to pay her off. "This is all of it. Tell her I said No" (*GD,M* 356). He asks Ike to give his last payment to his mistress, knowing she's coming to see him in the deer hunters' tent. With bad luck, he has to face the "Last Judgment" of his "Maker"—Ike McCaslin: "'What did you promise her that you haven't the courage to face her and retract?' 'Nothing!' the other said. 'Nothing!' . . . He was gone" (*GD,M* 356). But he cannot fool the old man, the "Philosopher Ruler," who will find out that Roth has lied.

The night before, when the hunters were having a "men's talk" (*GD,M* 345-48) in the tent, Ike already discerned that things went wrong with Roth, who looks sullen, moody, harsh, and unhappy. His spirit is out.

The phrase "He was gone" follows him repeatedly (*GD,M* 348, 356) as though he were "dead." That was the night Roth made his final choice—what he wanted in his life and how he would live the rest of his life—which completely departed from Ike's expectations. He made at least two clear statements in his rejection of Ike's romantic idealism. First, he is subdued by the social pressure that conditions him as a social animal. He admits that a man lives under the eyes of his neighbor and also the pressure of his own social "badge." "A man in a blue coat, with a badge on it watching him. Maybe just the badge." Ike tries to make him see that it is the little human potential that distinguishes man from circumstances, "that now and then, maybe most of the time, man is a little better than the net result of his and his neighbors' doings, when he gets the chance to be" (*GD,M* 346). Roth won't even listen; he fails to face the challenge. A moment later, Ike brings up the topic again to say that God has created man to live in a better world, an ideal world, "the kind of world he would have wanted to live in if He had been a man." In other words, he is saying that man ought to live in the eye of God, the image of his ideal self, instead of the eyes of his neighbors. When asked what kind of a world God would have wanted, and how man ever gets to know or to see such a world, Ike is even more assured than Plato in his projection of the ideal world. He simply points to the door of love. He believes that it is through love that man sees his ideal image, teaches himself about the world God promised him, and makes himself God. This is the moment when he makes that immortal outcry of love:

> "I think that every man and woman, at the instant when it dont even matter whether they marry or not, I think that whether they marry then or afterward or dont never, at that instant the two of them together were God." (*GD,M* 348)

Roth, whose education is not completed in the woods, lacks the quality to be initiated into the ultimate reality of life in this world, that is, the attainment of Truth beyond ordinary reality in the ideal world. He is so determined that he cannot afford love for all the worth of his wealth and status quo. So he'd rather deny it: "'Then there are some Gods in this world I wouldn't want to touch, and with a damn long stick,' Edmonds said. .... 'I am going to bed.' He was gone" (*GD,M* 348). His ear is shut and his door closed. But Ike has a sleepless night.

Ike keeps seeing the shadow of a Negro looming at his window (*GD,M* 351-52). When the dawn comes, he discovers: "It was not the negro, it was his kinsman"—Roth Edmonds. Such a montage technique is used to suggest that subconsciously Ike must have a very low opinion of his "kinsman." The difference between a "man" and a "nigger" in Faulkner's text is never "skin-deep." Faulkner has a very ironic use of the word "nigger"; it functions as a subversive signifier. In *The Sound and the Fury*, Quentin realizes that "a nigger is not a person so much as a form of behavior; [it is] a sort of obverse reflection of the white people he lives among." [33] In "Barn Burning," Caddy calls Jason a "nigger." The word "nigger" is often used as an "obverse reflection," a shadow, a mirror image of white men's behavior. The contrast between a "nigger" and its opposite is formed through Faulkner's subversive writing beyond its social and racial distinction to mark the distinction of character. The difference lies often in being a "man" and being a "nigger." Again, as Morris tells us, in Mississippi the word "nigger" can also be applied to a white man whose personal quality and character are degenerated. "Behaving like a nigger" was to stay out at all hours and to have several wives or husbands. "Nigger talk" was filled with lies and superstition. A "white nigger store" was owned by a white man who went after the "nigger trade."[34]

Roth in his misbehavior is characterized with all these listed "distinctions": sensual indulgence, lying, paying off his girlfriend with money—"the nigger trade." Ike seems to have already made up his mind about Roth even before he takes his blame from Roth's mistress: "I could have made a man of him. He's not a man yet. You spoiled him. You, and Uncle Lucas and Aunt Mollie. But mostly you" (*GD,M* 360). Ike, in his renunciation of the McCaslin heritage, leaves Roth a slave to his title—a "nigger."

In Ike's philosophy, the man who denies love denies God, the man who betrays love betrays himself. And it follows that he who does not have love is deprived; he who is deprived is a slave. In the name of romantic love, the ordinary concept of slave and freeman, is completely reversed. The ethics of romantic love functions as a strong rhetoric, an interrogative and persuasive power in the narrative, that negates the existing order of social superiority and inferiority. In the scene when Ike encounters Roth's mistress, the "doe" Roth kills, the stereotype of race and even gender shall be provocatively challenged and subverted in the name of love.

In a way, the "love story" proper functions as lyric. As in lyric, subjectivity is the personal expression of a personal emotion imaginatively phrased; it partakes of ecstasy. Faulkner's historical vision of race relations is imaginatively phrased in the narrative conscious of Ike's subjectivity, situated in Ike's personal emotions and response to the tragic love story that he witnesses and the ecstasy he experiences. When Ike finds out that Roth's mistress has not come for money, but for love, for him it is a cultural shock, beyond his cultural understanding, as well as his personal experience. "'Then what do you want?' he said. 'What do you want? What do you expect?' 'Yes,' she said. 'I would have made a man of him. He's not a man yet'" (*GD,M* 359-60). The woman did not come to ask Roth to marry her, as most critics arbitrarily assume. She says: "He didn't have to. I didn't ask him to. I knew what I was doing. . . . I believed myself" (*GD,M* 358-59). There was an agreement of love, a gentleman's agreement, a word of honor, that's "all of it." The woman will not bear Roth a grudge even after she learns that Roth has betrayed her. It is a surprise, a cultural shock, as one might say, that such generosity and gallantry—manly love—should come from a woman. Ike, who is content to remain a romantic lover holding his ideal for a lifetime, at last sees what love is.

A similar moment one may recall from Henry James's *The Ambassadors*, when Strether is impressed by Madame de Vionnet's devoted love to Chad Newsome. He remarks: "A creature so fine could be, by mysterious forces, a creature so exploited." Seeing Vionnet's true love touches his Puritan conscience so deeply that he chastises Chad: "You'll be a brute, you know—you'll be guilty of the last infamy—if you ever forsake her."[35] This is the same embarrassing truth that Ike would have said to Roth Edmonds; but he is not free to do so, because instead of a French lady, Faulkner's heroine is a "nigger" woman. Racial difference makes all the difference in freedom of speech. Ike, or Faulkner in the 1940s, was not free to express his admiration for a black woman and condemn Roth Edmonds, the head of a white patriarchy, openly in a public discourse. Both Faulkner and James are writing against a common cultural heritage that is obsessed with economic interest and biological productivity in matters of love and marriage; whereas, romantic love does not have legacy in it. However, what James discovers as an absence in his native culture, Faulkner reveals to us, a denied presence.

Romantic love, which is free of social, economic interest, is what Ike fails to have from his wife—a domesticated petit bourgeois woman. Faulkner calls her "ethically a prostitute" because she uses her sexual power to bargain for the McCaslin estate. "Delta Autumn," which comes shortly after the bedroom scene in "The Bear," completes Ike's story. His knowledge of this woman properly negates his deprivation in "The Bear," saves him from despair. It turns out to be his salvation, his "Resurrection."

The appearance of this woman has significantly changed Ike's idea about women. The night before he sees this woman, Ike thought of women in a mean spirit:

> But women hope for so much. They never live too long to still
> believe that anything within the scope of their passionate wanting
> is likewise within the range of their passionate hope. (*GD,M* 352)

Without knowing this one, Ike only knows, from his own cultural background, his own limited life experience, that women hope for "possession." Now the hope of this woman, also "passionate" and "wanting," convinces Ike that women hope not for money or possession, but for Love itself. It is an experience for Ike, a crossover. Ike's knowledge of her changes even the meaning of "hope" itself.

"Delta Autumn" is still Ike's story, a tragicomic story of his Platonic love and spiritual marriage. After years of chastity, Ike is ready for a religious feeling of love, a higher stage of love, the stage when one is to be initiated into the mystery of love. Ike's love is to be fulfilled in a religious, missionary sense, in a desire that is repressed in reality, as well as in the rational discourse of language.

Set in the romantic world of the hunters' tent, Ike's desire for love is metaphysically consummated in a moment of ecstasy, the moment when he delivers his horn. Because of the spiritual quality and spiritual experience involved in Ike's touch with this woman, his depiction of the touch, the gaze, the striptease, and the echo is mystical, ambivalent, surreal.

The touch: When Ike hands the woman Roth's money, he momentarily touches her hand. It is a sensational touch before he even sees the baby.

> He put out his hand. But sitting, he could not complete the reach
> until she moved her hand, the single hand which held the money,
> until he touched it. He didn't grasp it, he merely touched it—the
> gnarled, bloodless, bone-light bone-dry old man's fingers
> touching for a second the smooth young flesh where the strong
> old blood ran after its long lost journey back to home. (*GD,M*
> 362)

The word "touch" is repeated three times in the above passage. Moreover, the tender soft touches form a distinctive contrast with the physical violence with which Faulkner stages the bedroom scene in "The Bear."

The gaze: Then he sees the baby in her arms, "It's a boy, I reckon. They usually are, except that one that was its own mother too" (*GD,M* 362). The woman, with "the Son" in her arms, is transformed, in a moment of epiphany, into the image of the unwed Mary. She is mother of a race sacrificed, deprived, as Ike recalls involuntarily, "that was its own mother too." Behind her there is a line of her kind—Eunice and her daughter. Ike's mind is not focused on the baby, but the mother. Strangely, the scene becomes increasingly sensual and darkly intimate. As it continues, we have *the Striptease:*

> When once more he said Wait and moved beneath the blanket. "Turn your back," he said. "I am going to get up. I aint got my pants on." Then he could not get up. He sat in the huddled blanket, shaking, while again she turned and looked down at him in dark interrogation. (*GD,M* 362)

One wonders what happens to the old man. Why is he shaking and unable to get up? Why does Faulkner call our attention to his nakedness? What is the naked truth beneath the blanket?

The striptease, I should suggest, is a desperate textual strategy, used as a bold print, to emphasize the symbolic significance of dramatic actions. Faulkner must have his unspeakable heart's truth embedded, hidden beneath the blanket (Ike's blanket is a repeated metaphor in the story). He is telling a "love story" covered by his "blanket," a dividing sheet between Ike's enlightened vision gazing toward the sun/son and the darksome reality in Plato's cave—the here and now, between the surface of words and the depth of truth/beauty. The man above the cave, in order to avoid mob violence, avoid the fate of being stoned by the crowd in the cave for what he has to say, tells a "love story" with the rhetorical strategy of a fake, a drama, a gap. The telling of divine truth tragically, comically, relies on the strategy of a "striptease."

The truth is that the night before the woman came to his tent, Ike recalled "first time and last time" (*GD,M* 351) that he had always wanted to see his wife "naked because he loved her and he wanted to see her looking at him naked because he loved her" (*GD,M* 313). Now Ike is under the critical gaze of this woman—"in dark interrogation." The power of her love touches him to the quick so that he loses his defence against women. He could let himself go, now he is ready to yield completely to his passion. One may assume that in the presence of this woman, romantic love personified, Ike surrenders his masculine power—exposing himself naked.

Bernhard Radloff, in an article titled "The Fate of Demonism in William Faulkner," offers a superb interpretation of Faulkner's notion of love as a metaphor in dealing with heritage:

> Love or friendship do not calculate effects in advance in terms of

a pre-conceived design. They necessarily place themselves in the open, risk the unexpected, and leaving themselves open to negation, first become free for what has never been before. By the same measure, a heritage still has a future when those who carry the past—Ike or Quentin, for example—let the past go, leave the accumulated past be, in order to free themselves for those as yet unrealized possibilities inherent in the heritage.[36]

Ike, being willing to take the blame from the woman, the blame of letting Roth have the family inheritance, accepts the negation of his past. Thus he frees himself from the past and seizes the "yet unrealized possibilities inherent in the heritage." To Ike, this woman, who descends from the dark side of Ike's family, the Beauchamps, who have never had a legacy, presents "an unrealized possibility inherent in his heritage."

The Echo: In spite of his feelings, Ike's voice is still harsh and commanding. In reality there is no language available, "not yet," in Faulkner's words, for a white man raised in an Anglo-Protestant culture to give up his control and yield to the power of a "nigger" woman. It is even illegal to acknowledge a white man's love for a black woman, either sexual or ideal. The subject is suppressed and repressed in the public discourse just as it is forbidden by law. How can Ike, or Faulkner in 1940, express his deep admiration for a "nigger" woman and denounce Roth Edmonds in a public discourse that privileges the dignity and respect of a white patriarchy? The difficulty of speaking his "heart's truth" is delivered in the "naked truth" he has shown. What is not said is expressed in Ike's symbolic action.

> "There," he said harshly, in the thin and shaking old man's voice.
> "On the nail there. The tent-pole."
> "What?" She said.
> "The horn!" he said harshly. "The horn." (*GD,M* 362)

The horn he gives her is the last phallic symbol that ever is to appear in the novel. Its legacy, in all its authenticity, belongs to Ike himself. By handing it over to her, he hands over his self and all the love and hope he has to the last of his days. It is, once again, a repetition, a gesture of relinquishment before the bear. Like the bear, the woman is also possessed with composure and grace in her distress, in her destruction. Ike must be convinced that the kind of spirit shown in this woman is worthy of the sacrifice and solitude he has endured in a bachelor's life before he hands her the horn. Her presence recalls the Keatsian reference in "The Bear": "She cannot fade, though thou hast not thy bliss" (*GD,M* 297). He feels pity for her, but is also sorry for Roth.

While Keats's "Ode on a Grecian Urn" is directly quoted in "The Bear," "Delta Autumn" entails the indirect but suggestive "unheard melodies" of Keats's poem. The setting, the mood, the tone of "Delta Autumn" are all cast in the mode of "Ode to a Nightingale":

> My heart aches, and a drowsy numbness pains
> My sense, as though of hemlock I had drunk,
>
>   . . . .
>
> Here, where men sit and hear each other groan;
> Where palsy shakes a few, sad, last gray hairs,
> Where youth grows pale, and specter-thin, and dies;
> Where but to think is to be full of sorrow
> And Leaden-eyed despairs,
> Where Beauty cannot keep her lustrous eyes,
> Or new Love pine at them beyond tomorrow.

These "unheard melodies" best describe Ike's mood, his "heart ache" in "Delta Autumn."

"Delta Autumn" is Faulkner's fictional "Ode to a Delta Woodpecker." The metaphor of the nightingale is transformed into a Delta woodpecker; its allegorical figure of the biblical Ruth restored to an old legacy of the unwed Mary. I refer to stanza 7 in "Ode to a Nightingale":

> Perhaps the selfsame song that found a path
> Through the sad heart of Ruth when, sick for home,
> She stood in tears amid the alien corn.
> Charmed magic casements, opening on the foam
> Of perilous seas, in faery lands forlorn.

One can envision the image of the woman, college educated, free and modern, come back to the rural South, unwilling to leave; she is "sick for home . . . in faery lands forlorn." Ike sees her as a different type from the ordinary rural woman in the South—a "Delta peckerwoods," as he says to her:

> "You sound like you have been to college even. You sound almost like a Northerner even, not like the draggle-tailed women of these Delta peckerwoods. Yet you meet a man on the street one afternoon just because a box of groceries happened to fall out of a boat. And a month later you go off with him and live with him until he got a child on you: and then, by your own

statement you sat there while he took his hat and said goodbye
and walked out. Even a Delta peckerwood would look after even
a draggle-tail better than that." (*GD,M* 360)

"Peckerwood" is an inversion of "woodpecker." The word is a twentieth-century slang used disparagingly for a rural white Southerner. The woman in Ike's opinion is not a "peckerwood"; therefore, the negation of that word negates the stereotype that word stands for, the norm of the ordinary type. Thus Ike's vision reverses the image of that word to its opposite—a free spirit, the spirit of the woods, a "Delta woodpecker." A woodpecker is a native of the woods, undomesticated, the natural companion to woodsmen. In Ike's vision, she is not a "nigger," but a sign of liberty.

Idealist as he is, the old man is not a sentimental romantic fool in handing over his horn. He has enough wisdom in predicting the woman's competency in handling it, in exercising her power. Her honor is testified on the spot. Horn in hand, she displays noble virtue—benevolence, self-control, and a forgiving nature in handling her power—the legacy of chivalry. Ike challenges her with the idea of revenge, suggesting that she could get even with Roth by marrying a black man, a real man, "if it's revenge you want."

"Old man," she said, "have you lived so long and forgotten so
much that you dont remember anything you ever knew or felt or
even heard about love?" (*GD,M* 363)

The woman's question is again a Socratic fake, a rhetorical question, that carries the weight of undeniable truth. Not without a sense of humiliation, Ike accepts the truth she speaks, that is, the white civilization in its advancement of capitalism has lost its value, its spirit, and its sense of love.

After all, these are the very words Ike has been dying to hear for a lifetime. He is as happily inspired by her words as Keats is by a nightingale: "Forlorn! The very word is like a bell\ To toll me back from thee to my sole self!" These lines are the "unheard melodies" when Ike delivers his horn—"the gnarled, bloodless, bone-light bone-dry old man's fingers touching for a second the smooth young flesh where the strong old blood ran after its long lost journey back to home" (*GD,M* 362). In spirit, he is one with the woman. His heart is filled with a kindred warmth, sensation, and fertility that he had sensed when he first came "entering the Delta" to watch the last game (*GD,M* 335), just as Faulkner's language is erotic, intoxicated, and orgiastic.

The spirit of love kindles Ike's romantic youthful dream, long buried: "Was it a vision, or a waking dream?/ Fled is that music: —Do I wake or sleep?" The resounding echo of these "unheard melodies" from Keats, which the reader may recall from memory, fills the air of Ike's last dream, awakening his life long repressed desire for love. The immortal lover, who pursues not wealth, power, and fame, but truth, beauty, and love, hears his "wedding bell."

The woman's question is the ultimate outcry of love in the novel. After that, we shall hear no more. Hers is the cry of the nightingale. Ike's state of mind is cast in silent form. His emotional and mental response to the woman's question is played out in an intertextual symphony, through the trace of lyricism of Keats's poem. Stanza 6 articulates Ike's heart's truth as though it were Ike's own voice:

> Darkling I listen; and for many a time
> I have been half in love with easeful Death,
> Called him soft names in many a mused rhyme,
> To take into the air my quiet breath;
> Now more than ever seems it rich to die,
> To cease upon the midnight with no pain,
> While thou art pouring forth thy soul abroad
> In such an ecstasy!
> Still wouldst thou sing, and I have ears in vain—
> To thy high requiem become a sod.

Evoked by love's last powerful cry, Ike is lost in a mood that is darksome and mysterious. "Then she was gone too. The waft of light and the murmur of the constant rain flowed into the tent" (GD,M 363). Ike is caught in a strangely mixed mood of fertility, love, despair, and sorrow. He is seen "lying back once more, trembling, panting," like the immortal lover on "the Grecian Urn" that he remembers in "The Bear," "forever panting, forever young." Like Moses, "the blanket huddled to his chin and his hands crossed his breast," he is in a gesture of praying. With a dying heart, "He listened to the pop and snarl, the mounting then fading whine of the motor until it died away. . . the destructive and self-destructive forces of ill-controlled mechanic engine . . . and once again the tent held only silence and the sound of rain" (GD,M 364). The silence that follows, the mixed feelings and dark mood that flow in the air, the train of thoughts in which Ike expresses his final vision of the world all reveal, all reinforce, backward and forward, the significance of his action.

It has been always taken for granted among Faulkner critics that the horn is the McCaslin family legacy Ike gives her as a recognition of kinship, but intended to pass on to Roth's son.[37] Though Faulkner critics have expressed a great deal of admiration for the character of this woman, few have ever considered or acknowledged her legitimacy, her title to Ike's horn. But if we consider the symbolic value of that horn and the symbolic meaning of Ike's action, such an easy assumption apparently undoes Faulkner's poetic justice, vulgarizes Faulkner's theme. Now that the old man's "love story" is revealed, truth takes on a different light. There is no plausible reason why Ike at this stage would have any hope or faith in Roth's son as he could have in this woman herself.

Either he is in the cast of Moses or of the Philosopher Ruler, Ike is not a family man, nor meant to be. The McCaslin estate Ike has long repudiated and relinquished. For Ike, the McCaslin family heritage is a burden, a repeated curse of incest and miscegenation. Now in "Delta Autumn," the curse repeats itself in Roth Edmonds. Considering what has happened before, it is hard to imagine and hard to explain that Ike would want to "spoil" Roth's illegitimate son by giving him another "family" legacy, which the child would neither be able to claim nor deserve.

The horn does not belong to the McCaslin family at all. It is neither the badge of its family name nor the treasure of its estate. The horn comes from General Compson. In his will, he left it to Ike for the fond memory of Ike's "education in the woods." Ike's interaction with General Compson is briefly related in "The Bear," so that the value of the horn must be traced to that scene, that fond memory. General Compson appears in Chapter 4 of the "The Bear" when Sam Fathers is dying. Ike wants to stay in the woods; but Cass Edmonds (father of Roth, then guardian to Ike) insists he go home and be ready for school on Monday. There Compson abruptly snaps away the legacy of Cass's guardianship and gives Ike license to stay in the woods. Compson gives Ike license of absence from school because he trusts the boy, admires his wisdom and character: "This boy was already an old man long before you damned Sartorises and Edmondses invented farms and banks to keep yourselves from having to find out what this boy was born knowing and fearing too" (*GD,M* 250). Ike was a wise good boy, having been initiated into the woods. The legacy of the hunting horn is the legacy of woodsmanship, which is Ike's diploma from his education in the woods. It cannot be given to another child who has not been initiated into the woods yet and whose character is unknown.

Besides, what "great expectation" could Ike have from the son of Roth Edmonds? Even though it might be an old man's last hope, where is the sign of hope? At best, he would grow up to be another Tennie's Jim; and at worst, he might end up in jail in Chicago, as Faulkner shows us to be the fate of another black issue, Butch, Molly's grandson, in the following story, "Go Down, Moses." In that bleak funeral scene, which ends the novel, the future of a black son is sealed in the coffin. Faulkner completely cancels the illusion, or false hopes, if any, created in "Delta Autumn."

After all, the horn is not given, but "taken." When he hands the horn to the woman, Ike says: "It's his. Take it" (*GD,M* 363). Logically, Roth is the "heir apparent" to whatever Ike has left in his possession; so the horn would have been his. In the narrative, Ike has already used the phrase "take it" several times to refer to the money Roth wants him to give the woman, so "take it" is subconsciously and rhetorically linked with whatever comes from Roth. The woman accepts it unquestioningly, without the baby in mind, without showing the baby once again. The child only appears once in the text to complete her image as Mary, as I showed above. Created as an unself-conscious character, she takes it as a souvenir from Roth, which seems to be the way Ike wants her to believe, and which, under the circumstance, is the only thing the old man may do for her. It is a gesture of Ike's last-ditch effort to save himself, however symbolically, to preserve the faith of love in her and in himself.

The horn is a "Sylvan" legacy, which Ike has failed to pass on to Roth—his spirit and ideality—and which he sees akin to the very femininity of this woman. The legacy she holds is the love of God; with which the nameless woman is ordained a namesake with Buck and Buddy, Theophilus and Amodeus, meaning "the love of God" in Greek and Latin, respectively. She is the promise of God. That is what Ike had tried in vain to make Roth understand—the better life that God intended for man to live, romantic love.

She is Ike's idea, not unlike Plato's "miracle," the ideal future state that the good man who wishes can see it and find it in his own heart. Ike has it now. As Plato has said: "It doesn't matter whether it exists or ever will exist, in it alone and in no other society, could he [the good man] take part in public affairs." So in Ike's heart of hearts, where the court of his last judgement is held, this mulatto woman, neither black nor white, not a man but so akin to him, educated free, whose love shall nurture a future generation of the human race, is "the legitimate lover and rightful ruler" of the future.

The horn, "covered with the unbroken skin from a buck's shank and bound with" not gold but "silver"—a genuine feminine color—is a negation of that soiled handkerchief wrapped with Roth's dirty money, the masculine power. Ideally, that phallic power melt in the silver spirit of feminine love is the only hope for a happy state. In her wonderful discussion of Faulkner's idealism, Blanche Gelfant remarks that a recurrent motif in Faulkner's work is the combination of masculinity with spiritual beauty, which is linked to the existence of a Platonic world.[38] Gelfant suggests that Faulkner wanted his contemporaries to look within it, as had the Romantic poets, for the material of their art. I should like to add that Faulkner's artistic world is not without historical context; Faulkner wanted his contemporaries to look into it and see the Reality of race relations that they choose to ignore. Nothing does a better job than a flowery tale, a "love story" of sorts.

In the fictive art of romantic love, power is shifted to right the wrong, and the traditional social hierarchy of class, race, and gender is turned upside down. Faulkner's writing strategy, from a postmodern theoretical perspective, is exactly as Lynda Hutcheon observes in her discussion of the postmodern historiographic metafiction: It "manages to legitimize culture even as it subverts it."[39] *Go Down, Moses* is certainly a postmodern historiographic metafiction. It can be said that Faulkner retrieves the historical legacy of chivalry, the legacy of Confederate soldiers and Southern squirearchy—the Compsons, that existed before the legacy of the bankers, the legacy of money and power, the legacy of capitalism, that rules the land at present—the Edmonds, who are corrupted. More significantly, by taking it away from the white male patriarchy and placing it gently in the soft hands of a liberated woman, and a mulatto woman, Faulkner poetically undoes the curse of its cultural legitimacy, that has passed down from generation to generation in a white male patriarchy. This symbolic gesture of privileging a black woman breaks a cultural taboo, and it reinvents, in our imaginary, a new legacy, the legacy of the land-free, property-free, and family-marriage-name-free—free souls, half black, half white, neither black nor white.

Technically, however, such transformation of power is not real but ideal, "not yet," as Ike says, not in Faulkner's time. In reality, it does not happen. Ike will not rule the land because, according to Plato's theory, a goodman is not wanted in imperfect societies unless a "miracle" takes place. Neither will the woman rule. If she would, blessed the land. Unfortunately, the land is for the moment doomed, North or South, as we will see in the next story. In the meanwhile, she is the land itself—"This Delta. *This land which man has deswamped and denuded and delivered in two generations*" (*GD,M* 364), which at present is carelessly trampled and trodden, just as Ike's legacy of power is abused in the hands of Roth Edmonds and his horn soiled with money. The hope Ike sees in her lies in the future:

"*Maybe in a thousand or two thousand years in America*, he

thought. *But not now! Not now!* He cried, not loud, in a voice
of amazement, pity, and outrage: "You're a nigger!" (*GD,M* 361)

This ironic revelation of her identity is Ike's ironic love cry. After all, we
know what the word "nigger" signifies by now. In Ike's view, the present
is hopeless and loveless and therefore cursed, because "*white men live like
niggers and niggers crop on shares and live like animals . . . until no man
has time to say which one is which nor cares*" (*GD,M* 364).

Faulkner cared. He fought with Ike McCaslin's hunting horn, his
"penmight," as Joyce did in *Finnegans Wake*. The avant-garde artist is also
a cultural avant-garde. But throughout five decades of Faulkner criticism, the
easy acceptance of an arbitrary critical interpretation reveals a presence/
absence of a cultural consensus, which is male oriented, male chauvinistic,
racially biased, and bound by a narrow-minded bourgeois value of family
property and a feudal inheritance law. Ironically, all of this is what Ike
McCaslin repudiated and Faulkner artistically subverted.

The story of romantic love between Roth and his mistress is staged
to readdress the power balance in race relations in the South. Charged with
the emotional power of romantic love, Faulkner's narrative evokes the
reader's sympathy for the forlorn woman—the sexually exploited,
historically wronged, socially underprivileged underdog. In the measure of
human capacity for love, Faulkner repositions the superiority and inferiority
of race and gender. The ethics of romantic love functions as a strong
rhetoric, an interrogative and persuasive power in the narrative, that negates
the existing order of cultural legacy. Thus reality can be preserved and
presented in the form of a poetic truth, which is timeless. It is timeless
because philosophical truth is ahistorical and timeless. The philosophical
truth implied in romantic poetry—"She cannot fade, though thou hast not thy
bliss"—is as timeless as truth itself. Simple as it is, this truth answers a series
of questions plotted throughout the dramatic actions in the novel that cannot
be answered in the logic of capitalism—why thou shalt not kill. Truth is
one, truth is simple: The possession of power without the spirit of Love and
self-control is self-destructive—the killer only kills, degenerates, "denudes"
his beloved, but he deprives himself.

In spite of the sad ending and the failure of Roth Edmonds, "Delta
Autumn" is a happy chapter in Faulkner's "Sylvan history." Ike reaches for
a moment the ideal state. With the birth of a child, the endurance of feminine
love, the fertility of water and rain pouring on the Delta, and the departure
of the mulatto woman, horn in hand, going North, symbolically carrying the
torch of liberty, Ike seems to see some hope ahead of his time. Once the

promise of future is made, the Sylvan historian finishes his book with a final view of the present state of affairs upon the land.

"Go Down, Moses"

In the last story, "Go Down, Moses," political power is transferred to the hands of the census taker in the city jail of Chicago. He has even more power than expected over the life and death of a "freed" Negro. But Faulkner leaves a great ambiguity in conceiving Sam Beauchamp's commitment of murder:

> "Samuel Worsham Beauchamp. Twenty-six. Born in the country near Jefferson, Mississippi. No family. No—"
> "Wait." The census taker wrote rapidly. "That's not the name you were—lived under in Chicago."
> The other [an armed guard, a counterpart of the sheriff in "Pantaloon in Black"] snapped the ash from the cigar. "No. It was another guy killed the cop."
> "All right. Occupation—" (*GD,M* 369-70)

The census taker goes on indifferently. A key word left over from the last tale is "care." The census taker, the representative of bureaucrats, the "caretaker" of the people, could have cared when he *sensed* that the prisoner is not the man "*sen(t/entenced)*" for killing the cop. Very likely Sam Beauchamp is suspected because he is, as the next line suggests, "getting rich too fast" and has no occupation.

The caretaker of the land and of the McCaslin family business is a hired attorney, Gavin Stevens, "Phi Beta Kappa, Harvard, Ph.D. Heidelberg" (*GD,M* 371). He proves utterly ineffective in using his power even to take care of Molly Beauchamp, the good old woman. He fails to cover the "family scandal" from media publicity. He handled his case contrary to the wish of his client. What he succeeds in doing is nothing but using Lucas's money "to bring a dead nigger home. It's for Miss Worshman" (*GD,M* 378). Faulkner's mood is increasingly bitter toward the end of the novel.

Stevens is the failure of the last democratic ruler before tyranny sets in over the land. As he "undertakes" his care, he is reduced from the status of a caretaker to that of an undertaker. That's why the end of the novel is a funeral scene with Stevens riding in the car behind the hearse,

circling the Confederate monument and the courthouse while the
merchants and clerks and barbers and professional men who had
given Stevens the dollars and half-dollars and quarters and the
ones who had not, watched quietly from doors and upstairs
windows, swinging then into the street which at the edge of town
would become the country road leading to the destination
seventeen miles away, already picking up speed again and
followed still by the two cars containing the four people—the
high-headed erect white woman, the old Negress, the designated
paladin of justice and truth and right, the Heidelberg Ph.D.—in
formal component complement to the Negro murderer's
catafalque: the slain wolf. (*GD,M* 382)

The symbol of ruling power—"the designated paladin of justice and truth
and right," the glorious badge of the highest academic honor, "the
Heidelberg Ph.D.," all juxtaposed with the "Negro murderer's catafalque,"
swiftly fades into an ill omen. The domestic center of the country, which
once had a "fire and hearth," is now dimmed into the gray hair of "the
high-headed erect white woman" and the desperate and heart-broken "old
Negress," whose love for Roth Edmonds, the son she raised and cared as if
her own, is now dead.

> "Roth Edmonds sold him," the old Negress said. She
> swayed back and forth in the chair. "Sold my Benjamin."
> . . . .
> "Sold my Benjamin," she said. "Sold him in Egypt."
> "Sold him in Egypt," Worsham said.
> "Roth Edmonds sold my Benjamin."
> "Sold him to Pharaoh."
> "Sold him to Pharaoh and now he dead." (*GD,M*
> 380-81).

Roth Edmonds is not even present at the funeral. He "is completely gone."
The love between Molly and Roth is dead. To be cursed in public by the
"only mother" he has and cares for is probably the most unfortunate fate,
because such a curse is beyond redemption.

The question remains to be seen if Molly's accusation can be
justified. Unfortunately, Gavin Stevens knows it is true; it is through the
attorney's judicious judgment that Faulkner holds Roth Edmonds
responsible:

> But then, according to her, Edmonds had already refused to have anything to do with it. . . . Now he [Stevens] comprehended what the old Negress had meant. He remembered now that it was Edmonds who had actually sent the boy to Jefferson in the first place: he had caught him off the place and forbidden him ever to return. *And not the sheriff, the police, he thought. Something broader, quicker in scope.* (*GD,M* 373)

Roth, as the ruler of the present regime, takes the ultimate blame. As the supreme ruler in the "White House" of the McCaslins, he is above "the sheriff, the police." He is the head of a system, a machinery "broader, quicker in scope." He has virtually reduced to Plato's tyrant—he has sold his own people as slave.[40]

If Faulkner sounds cynical toward Gavin Stevens's "twenty-two-year-old unfinished translation of the Old Testament back into classic Greek" (*GD,M* 371), in writing *Go Down, Moses*, he himself had undertaken that project, and had finished it. This is the role of a serious fictionist, whose vocation does justice to the world, as lawyers and politicians may not. What Aunt Molly asks in the end, instead of to cover up the unhappy story, which may bring disgrace to her family, is but to get the bad news out: "I wants hit all in de paper. All of hit . . . . You put hit in the paper. All of hit" (*GD,M* 383). Faulkner has done it for her; the novel is written in her name. In order to include what has been conventionally excluded in reading Faulkner, I have written a long chapter so that Molly's curse be heard.

Molly's curse is bad news, but to "put it in the paper" is to tell the world what is true. If the historian fails to tell the world what is true, the novelist does it by telling a "love story" or two. Novelistic love, as Plato exemplifies in Socrates' panegyric that I have disseminated, is the summit of the idealism of romantic love, the "Pregnant Invert" of aesthetic love, the mystic Indian cave of philosophical love, and the tragicomedy of Socrates' "love story," which is Platonic Love in its dramatic form. Surprisingly, Faulkner has transformed the romantic love of his youthful passion, his aesthetic love of Keats's poem, and his philosophical love of Plato into an expressive form of novelistic love. Writing "love stories" of sorts, he has overcome the difficulties in delivering the heart's truth of his historical vision, his political ideal, and his cultural criticism. He wrote his Sylvan history with a philosophy that will survive the forces of destruction, only because it is true. Philosophical truth survives history. "When old age shall this generation waste," the moonlight of his novelistic love shall "remain amidst other woe."

Notes

1. Plato, *The Republic*, trans. Desmond Lee, 2nd ed. (London: Penguin, 1987), 412.

2. Andre Blekasten, "For/Against an Ideological Reading," *Faulkner and Idealism: Perspectives from Paris*, ed. Michel Gresset and Patrick Samway (Jackson: University Press of Mississippi, 1983), 30.

3. See Williams, *The Whig Supremacy*.

4. Carolyn Porter, "Faulkner's America," in *Seeing and Being: The Plight of the Participant Observer in Emerson, James, Adams, and Faulkner* (Middletown CT: Wesleyan University Press, 1981), 222-26.

5. John M. Muste, "The Failure of Love in *Go Down, Moses*," *Modern Fiction Studies* 10, no 4 (Winter 1964-65): 366-78.

6. Walter F. Taylor Jr. "Let My People Go: The White Man's Heritage in *Go Down, Moses*," *South Atlantic Quarterly*, 58 (Winter 1959): 21.

7. Charles D. Peavy, *Go Slow Now: Faulkner and the Race Question* (Eugene: University of Oregon Press, 1971), Introduction.

8. Sidney Lanier, "The Symphony," *Sidney Lanier: Poems*, Centennial Edition, vol. 1, ed. Charles R. Anderson (Baltimore: Johns Hopkins University Press, 1945), 46-56, 53.

9. See Cleanth Brooks, *On the Prejudices, Predilections, and Firm Beliefs of William Faulkner* (Baton Rouge: Louisiana University Press, 1987), 13. See also Albert Gelpi's discussion on John Crowe Ransom's love poems in *A Coherent Splendor: The American Poetic Renaissance, 1910-1950* (New York: Cambridge University Press, 1987), 32-43.

10. Willie Morris, "Growing Up in Mississippi," *North Toward Home* (Boston: Houghton Mifflin Co., 1967); reprinted in *Critical Essays on William Faulkner: The McCaslin Family*, ed. Arthur F. Kinney (Boston: G. K. Hall & Co., 1990), 113.

11. Even Eric J. Sundquist is rather "doubtful" speculating upon the possibility of love between the white man and the black woman: "That love—doubtful at best, a mockery at worst, and in any event fruitless beside the agony it entails—defines both the limits and the ramifying contours of Ike's repudiation" (Eric J. Sundquist, *Faulkner: The House Divided* [Baltimore: Johns Hopkins University Press, 1983], 157).

12. *Faulkner in the University*, ed. F. L. Gwynn and J. L. Blotner (Charlottesville: University of Virginia Press, 1977), 162.

13. When Warren Beck pointed out to Faulkner some implications in *Go Down, Moses* he had missed, Faulkner replied: "I wish that I had consciously intended them; I will certainly believe I did it subconsciously and not by accident" (*Selected Letters of William Faulkner*, ed. Joseph Blotner [London: The Scholar Press, 1977], 142).

14. John Keats, "Ode on a Grecian Urn," *Keats: Poetical Works*, ed. H. W. Garrod (London: Oxford University Press, 1966), 209.

15. See *Selected Letters of William Faulkner*, 144.

16. Morris Beja, *Epiphany in the Modern Novel* (Seattle: University of Washington Press, 1971), 190-91.

17. Around the time he was publishing *Go Down, Moses* Faulkner explained his concerns: "I have been writing all the time about honor, truth, pity, consideration, the capacity to endure well grief and misfortune and injustice and then endure again, in terms of individuals who observed and adhered to them not for reward but for virtue's own sake, not even merely because they are admirable in themselves, but in order to live with oneself and die peacefully with oneself when the time comes. I don't mean that the devil will snatch every liar and rogue and hypocrite shrieking from his deathbed. I think liars and hypocrites and rogues die peacefully every day in the door of what he calls sanctity. I am not talking about him. I'm not writing for him" (*Selected Letters of William Faulkner*, 142).

18. *Faulkner in the University*, ed. Gwynn and Blotner, 275.

19. Cleanth Brooks, "Early Romantic Prose," in *William Faulkner: Toward Yoknapatawpha and Beyond* (New Haven, CT: Yale University Press, 1978), 51.

20. *Lion in the Garden: Interviews with William Faulkner, 1926-1962*, ed. James B. Meriwether and Michael Millgate (Lincoln: University of Nebraska Press, 1980), 246.

21. Plato, "Imperfect Societies," *The Republic*, 356-420. Subsequent references will be indicated as R.

22. Faulkner read Catullus, Euripides, Plato, and Sophocles, too, and he absorbed the essence of classic literature. Speaking on the influence of classic literature on Faulkner, F. R. Karl observes, "much of this material, coming from so many cultural directions and historical eras, proved nourishing for Faulkner's imagination. . . . Yet no single book, or even group of books, influenced him; he absorbed, as any autodidact does, what was important to him, discarding along the way what fails to fit. . . . Faulkner might have gained a sense of a mature writer completely in command of his material, and that confidence in self and material would have sufficed. Influence, as such, can be as fleeting as that." (Frederick Karl, *William Faulkner: American Writer* [New York: Weidenfeld & Nicolson, 1989], 186-87).

23. I am referring to my discussion of Melville's presentation of the letter H— in *Moby-Dick* in the beginning of Chapter One.

24. See *Faulkner in the University*, ed. Gwynn and Blotner, 246.

25. Cowley believes this is the accurate picture of Faulkner's reputation in 1945: "His early novels, when not condemned, were overpraised for the wrong reasons; his later and in many ways better novels have been ridiculed or simply neglected; and in 1945 all his seventeen books were effectively out of print, with some of them unobtainable in the secondhand book-shops. . . . Even his warm

admirers, of whom there are many—no author has a higher standing among his fellow novelists—have shown a rather vague idea of what he is trying to do; and Faulkner himself has never explained. He holds a curious attitude towards the public that appears to be lofty indifference. . . but really comes closer to being a mixture of skittery distrust and pure unconsciousness that the public exists. . . . He said in a letter, 'I think I have written a lot and sent it off to print before I actually realized strangers might read it.' Others might say that Faulkner, at least in those early days, was not so much composing stories for the public as telling them to himself" (Malcolm Cowley,"William Faulkner: An Introduction and Interpretation," *Portable Faulkner* [New York: Barnes & Noble, 1963], xxi).

26. *Faulkner in the University*, ed. Gwynn and Blotner, 166.

27. James Joyce, *A Portrait of the Artist as a Young Man*, ed. Chester G. Anderson (New York: Penguin, 1986), 215.

28. See Faulkner's own comment on the twins and their ruling strategy in *Faulkner in the University*, ed. Gwynn and Blotner, 39-40.

29. Ibid., 40.

30. Faulkn's *Go Down, Moses* is dedicated to his black mammy, Caroline Barr, Mississippi (1840-1940). See Dedication in the book and his epigraph.

31. Taylor, "Let My People Go," 20-32.

32. William Faulkner, *The Segregation Decisions: Papers Read at a Session of the Twenty-First Annual Meeting of the Southern Historical Association, Memphis, Tennessee, November 10, 1955* (Atlanta, GA: Southern Regional Council, 1956), 11.

33. William Faulkner, *The Sound and the Fury*, Norton Critical Edition (New York: W. W. Norton & Co., 1994), 55.

34. Morris, "Growing Up in Mississippi," 114.

35. Henry James, *The Ambassadors*, Norton Critical Edition, ed. S. P. Rosenbaum (New York: W. W. Norton & Co., 1964), bk. 12, 332, 335.

36. Bernhard Radloff, "The Fate of Demonism in William Faulkner," *Arizona Quarterly* 46, no. 1 (Spring 1990): 46.

37. See Cleanth Brooks's interpretation in *William Faulkner: The Yoknapatawpha Country* (Baton Rouge: Louisiana State University Press, 1990), 272.

38. Blanche H. Gelfant, "Faulkner and Keats: The Ideality of Art in 'The Bear,'" *Southern Literary Journal* (Fall 1969): 48.

39. Lynda Hutcheon, *The Politics of Postmodernism* (New York: Routledge, 1989) 14-15.

40. Faulkner says in a public speech: "We don't need to sell them on America and freedom because they are already sold; even when ignorant from inferior or no education, even despite the record and history of inequality, they still believe in our concepts of freedom and democracy" (*The Segregation Decisions*, 11).

SELECTED BIBLIOGRAPHY

Primary Sources

Barth, John. *Chimera.* New York: Fawcett Crest, 1972.
———. *Lost in the Funhouse.* New York: Doubleday, 1988.
Barthelme, Donald. *Snow White.* New York: Atheneum, 1986.
Beckett, Samuel. *Molloy, Malone Dies, The Unnamable: Three Novels.* New York: Grove Press, 1965.
Bronte, Emily. *Wuthering Heights.* Norton Critical Edition. 2nd ed. Ed. William M. Sale Jr. New York: W. W. Norton & Co., 1972.
Calvino, Italo. *Cosmicomics.* Trans. William Weaver. New York: Harcourt, 1968.
Conrad, Joseph. *Heart of Darkness.* Norton Critical Edition. 2nd ed. Ed. Robert Kimbrough. New York: W. W. Norton & Co., 1971.
———. *Under Western Eyes.* London: Penguin, 1987.
Coover, Robert. *Pricksongs & Descants.* New York: New American Library, 1969.
Defoe, Daniel. *The Fortunes and Misfortunes of Moll Flanders.* New York: New American Library, 1964.
———. *The Fortunate Mistress: Roxana.* Ed. David Blewett. London: Penguin, 1988.
Dickinson, Emily. *The Complete Poems of Emily Dickinson.* Ed. Thomas H. Johnson. Boston: Little Brown, 1960.
Eliot, T. S. *The Complete Poems and Plays, 1909-50.* New York:

193

Harcourt Brace & World, 1971.

Ellison, Ralph. *Invisible Man*. New York: Random House, 1952; New York: Vintage Books, 1981.

Emerson, Ralph. "Friendship." *Selected Writings of Emerson*. Ed. Donald McQuade. New York: Random House, 1981.

——. "Plato; Or the Philosopher." *Ralph Waldo Emerson: Representative Selections*. Ed. Frederic I. Carpenter (New York: American Book Co., 1934), 231-32.

Faulkner, William. *Go Down Moses*. New York: Random House, 1973.

Federman, Raymond. *Smiles on Washington Square: A Love Story of Sorts*. New York: Thunder's Mouth Press, 1985.

Fielding, Henry. *The History of Tom Jones, A Foundling*. Ed. Fredson Bowers. Introduction by Martin C. Battestin. Wesleyan Edition. Oxford: Clarendon Press, 1974. Also, Norton Critical Edition. Ed. Sheridan Baker. New York: W. W. Norton & Co., 1973.

——. *The True Patriot: The History of Our Own Times*. An annotated edition by M. A. Locke. Birmingham: University of Alabama Press, 1964.

Fitzgerald, F. Scott. *The Great Gatsby*. New York: Charles Scribner's Sons, 1953.

Forster, E. M. *A Passage to India*. New York: Harcourt, 1952.

Goethe, Johann Wolfgang Von. *Elective Affinities*. Trans. R. J. Hollingdale. London: Penguin, 1986.

Hardy, Thomas. *Jude the Obscure*. Norton Critical Edition. Ed. Norman Page. New York: W. W. Norton & Co., 1978.

Hawkes, John. *Travesty*. New York: New Directions Books, 1976.

Hemingway, Ernest. *The Sun Also Rises*. New York: Charles Scribner's Sons, 1970.

James, Henry. *The Ambassadors*. Norton Critical Edition. Ed. S. P. Rosenbaum. New York: W. W. Norton Co., 1964.

Joyce, James. *Finnegans Wake*. New York: Penguin, 1984.

——. *A Portrait of the Artist as a Young Man: Text, Criticism, and Notes*. Ed. Chester G. Anderson. New York: Penguin, 1986.

——. *Ulysses*. Ed. Hans Walter Gabler. New York: Random House, 1986.

Keats, John. *Keats: Poetical Works*. Ed. H. W. Garrod. London: Oxford University Press, 1966.

Kingston, Maxine Hong. *China Men*. New York: Vintage International, 1980.

———. *Tripmaster Monkey*. New York: Vintage International, 1987.

Lanier, Sidney. *Sidney Lanier: Poems*. Centennial Edition. Vol 1. Ed. Charles R. Anderson. Baltimore: Johns Hopkins University Press, 1945.

Lawrence, D. H. *Women in Love*. London: Penguin, 1987.

Lewis, Matthew. *The Monk*. Ed. Howard Anderson. New York: Oxford University Press, 1988.

Melville, Herman. *Moby-Dick*. Norton Critical Edition. Ed. Harrison Hayford and hershel parker. New York: W. W. Norton & Co., 1967.

Mishima, Yukio. "Patriotism." *The Norton Anthology of Short Fiction*. 3rd ed. Ed. R.V.Cassill. New York: W. W. Norton, 1978, 1062-81.

Nabokov, Vladimir. *The Annotated Lolita*. Ed. Alfred Appel Jr. New York: McGraw-Hill, 1970.

Plato. *The Republic*. 2nd ed. Trans. Desmond Lee. London: Penguin, 1987.

———. *The Symposium*. Trans. Walter Hamilton. London: Penguin, 1987.

Proust, Marcel. *Remembrance of Things Past*. Trans. S. K. Scott Moncrieff and Terence Kilmartin. New York: Random House, 1982.

Pynchon, Thomas. *The Crying of Lot 49*. New York: Harper & Row, 1986.

Richardson, Samuel. *Clarissa or the History of a Young Lady*. Ed. Angus Ross. London: Penguin, 1985.

———. *Pamela*. New York: W. W. Norton & Co., 1958.

Sterne, Laurence. *Tristram Shandy*. Norton Critical Edition. Ed. Howard Anderson. New York: W. W. Norton, & Co., 1980.

Swift, Jonathan. "Cadenus and Vanessa." *Jonathan Swift: The Complete Poems*. Ed. Pat Rogers. New Haven, CT: Yale University Press, 1983.

———. *A Tale of a Tub*. Ed. Angus Ross and David Woolley. New York: Oxford University Press, 1986.

William Shakespeare. *The Complete Works*. Ed. G. B. Harrison. New York: Harcourt, 1952.

Tillotson, G. et al., eds. *Eighteenth Century English Literature*. San Francisco: Harcourt, 1969.

Vonnegut, Kurt. *Slaughterhouse-Five*. New York: Dell Publishing Co., 1969.

Secondary Sources

Adams, Hazard, and Leroy Searle, ed. *Critical Theory Since 1965.* Tallahassee: Florida State University Press, 1986.

Adams, Robert M. *James Joyce: Common Sense and Beyond.* New York: Random House, 1966.

Adorno, Theodor W. and Max Horkheimer. "The Culture Industry: Enlightenment as Mass Deception." *Dialectic of Enlightenment.* Trans. John Cumming. New York: Continuum, 1969.

Baker, Sheridan. "Bridget Allworthy: The Creative Pressures of Fielding's Plot." Reprinted in the Norton Critical Edition of *Tom Jones*, 961. (See Fielding)

Bakhtin, M. M. *The Dialogic Imagination.* Ed. Michael Holquist. Trans. Caryl Emerson and Michael Hoquist. Austin: University of Texas Press, 1981.

Barthes, Roland. *A Lover's Discourse: Fragments.* Trans. Richard Howard. New York: Hill & Wang, 1978.

——. *Mythologies.* Trans. Annette Lavers. New York: Hill & Wang, 1972.

——. *The Pleasure of the Text.* Trans. Richard Miller. New York: Hill & Wang, 1975.

——. *S/Z.* Trans. Richard Miller. New York: Hill and Wang, 1974.

Bassett, John Earl. *Faulkner: An Annotated Checklist of Recent Criticism.* Kent, OH: Kent State University Press, 1983.

Battestin, Martin C. "Tom Jones and 'His Egyptian Majesty': Fielding's Parable of Government." PMLA 82 (1967): 68-77.

——. "Fielding's Definition of Wisdom: Some Functions of Ambiguity and Emblem in Tom Jones." ELH 35 (1968): 188-217.

Bayles, Martha. "The Problem with Post-Racism." *Rereading America.* Ed. Cary Colombo et al. New York: St. Martin's Press, 1989, 615-21.

Blekasten, Andre. "For/Against an Ideological Reading." *Faulkner and Idealism: Perspectives from Paris.* Ed. Michel Gresset and Patrick Samway. Jackson: University Press of Mississippi, 1983.

Bloom, Harold, et al., eds. *Deconstruction and Criticism.* New York: Continuum, 1986.

Blotner, Joseph. *Faulkner: A Biography.* New York: Random House,

1984.

——, ed. *Selected Letters of William Faulkner*. London: Scholar Press, 1977.

Bongie, L. *The Love of a Prince: Bonnie Prince Charlie in France, 1744-48*. Vancouver, Canada: British Columbia University Press, 1986.

Bowen, David Warren. *Andrew Johnson and the Negro*. Knoxville: University of Tennessee Press, 1989.

Bradbury, Malcolm, and James McFarlane, eds. *Modernism*. London: Penguin, 1976.

Brodsky, L. "Faulkner and the Racial Crisis, 1956." *Southern Review* 24 (Autumn 1988): 791-807.

Brooks, Cleanth. *First Encounters*. Baton Rouge: Louisiana State University Press, 1987.

——. *William Faulkner: Toward Yoknapatawpha and Beyond*. New Haven, CT: Yale University Press, 1978.

——. *William Faulkner: The Yoknapatawpha Country*. Baton Rouge: Louisiana State University Press, 1963.

——. *On the Prejudices, Predilections, and Firm Beliefs of William Faulkner*. Baton Rouge: Louisiana State University Press, 1987.

——. *The Well Wrought Urn: Studies in the Structure of Poetry*. New York: Reynal & Hitchcock, 1947.

Campbell, Joseph and Henry Morton Robinson. *A Skeleton Key to Finnegans Wake*. New York: Harcourt, 1944.

Carlton, Peter J. "The Mitigated Truth: Tom Jones's Double Heroism." *Studies in the Novel* 19 (Winter 1989): 397-409.

——. "Tom Jones and the '45' Once Again." *Studies in the Novel* 20 (Winter 1988): 361-73.

Castel, Albert. *The Presidency of Andrew Johnson*. Lawrence: Regents Press of Kansas, 1979.

Chomsky, Noam. *Necessary Illusions: Thought Control in Democratic Societies*. Boston: South End Press, 1989.

Clayton, Jay. *Romantic Vision and the Novel*. New York: Cambridge University Press, 1987.

Cleary, Thomas R. *Henry Fielding: Political Writer*. Waterloo, Ont. Canada: Wilfrid Laurier University Press, 1984.

Cockshut, A. O. J. *Man and Woman: A Study of Love and the Novel (1740-1940)*. London: Collins, 1977.

Cowley, Malcolm. "William Faulkner: An Introduction and Interpretation." *Portable Faulkner*. New York: Barnes & Noble, 1963.

———. *The Faulkner-Cowley File: Letters and Memories, 1944-62*. New York: Viking Press, 1966.

Cross, Wilbur L. *The History of Henry Fielding*. New York: Russell & Russell, 1963.

Daniel, Bradford, ed. *Black, White and Gray: Twenty-one Points of View on the Race Question*. New York: Sheed & Ward, 1964.

Davis, Thadious M. *Faulkner's "Negro": Art and the Southern Context*. Baton Rouge: Louisiana State University Press, 1983.

Derrida, Jacques. *Dissemination*. Trans. Barbara Johnson. Chicago: University of Chicago Press, 1981.

———. *Of Grammatology*. Trans. Gayatri Chakravorty Spivak. Baltimore: Johns Hopkins University Press, 1976.

Dudden, F. Homes. *Henry Fielding: His Life, Works, and Times*. Hamden, CT: Anchon Books, 1966.

Ellman, Richard. *James Joyce*. New York: Oxford University Press, 1959.

Empson, William. "Tom Jones." *Kenyon Review* 20 (1958): 249.

Faulkner, William. *The Segregation Decisions: Papers Read at a Session of the Twenty-first Annual Meeting of the Southern Historical Association, Memphis, Tennessee, November 10, 1955*. Atlanta, GA: Southern Regional Council, 1956.

Federman, Raymond, ed. *Surfiction: Fiction Now and Tomorrow*. 2nd ed. Chicago: Swallow Press, 1981.

———. "Fiction in American Today or the Unreality of Reality." *Indian Journal of American Studies* (January 1984): 5-16.

Fiedler, Leslie A. *Love and Death in the American Novel*. Rev. ed. New York: Scarborough House, 1982.

Finney, Arthur F. *Critical Essays on William Faulkner: The McCaslin Family*. Boston: G. K. Hall & Co., 1990.

Fitzgerald, F. Scott. *The Crack-up*. New York: New Directions Books, 1956.

Foucault, Michel. *The Archeology of Knowledge: The Discourse on Language*. Trans. A. M. Sheridan Smith. New York: Pantheon Books, 1972.

———. *The Use of Pleasure*. Trans. Robert Hurley. New York: Random House, 1986.

Fowler, Doreen. "Idealism Denounced: *Go Down, Moses*." *Faulkner's Changing Vision: From Outrage to Affirmation*. Ed. Doreen Fowler. Ann Arbor, MI: UMI Research Press, 1983, 47-52.

———. *Faulkner and the Craft of Fiction: Faulkner and Yoknapatawpha*,

1987. Jackson: University Press of Mississippi, 1989.

———. *Faulkner and Humor: Faulkner and Yoknapatawpha, 1984.* Jackson: University Press of Mississippi, 1986.

Gelfant, Blanche H. "Faulkner and Keats: The Ideality of Art in 'The Bear.'" *Southern Literary Journal* 2 (Fall 1969): 43-65.

Gelpi, Albert. *A Coherent Splendor: The American Poetic Renaissance, 1910-1950.* New York: Cambridge University Press, 1987.

Glicksberg, Charles I. *The Sexual Revolution in Modern American Literature.* The Hague, Netherlands: Martinus Nijhoff, 1971.

Godden, G. M. *Henry Fielding: A Memoir.* London: S. Low, Marston, 1910.

Goldgar, Bertrand A. "Myth and History in Fielding's Journey from This World to the Next." *Modern Language Quarterly* 47, no. 3 (1990): 235-52.

Grimwood, Michael. *Heart in Conflict: Faulkner's Struggles with Vocation.* Athens: University of Georgia Press, 1987.

Gwynn, F. L., and J. L. Blotner, eds. *Faulkner in the University: Class Conferences at the University of Virginia, 1957-1958.* Charlottesville, Virginia: University of Virginia Press, 1977.

Harari, Josue V., ed. *Textual Strategies: Perspectives in Post-Structuralist Criticism.* Ithaca, NY: Cornell University Press, 1979.

Harries, Karsten. "Metaphor and Transcendence." *On Metaphor.* Ed. Sheldon Sacks. Chicago: University of Chicago Press, 1978.

Hoffman, Frederic John and Olga W. Vickery, eds. *William Faulkner: Three Decades of Criticism.* Michigan State University Press, 1960.

Holman, C. Hugh. "The Reconciliation of Ishmael: *Moby-Dick* and the Book of Job." *Modern Fiction Studies.*157, no. 4 (Autumn 1958): 477-541.

Hovde, Carl F. "Faulkner's Democratic Rhetoric." *Southern Atlantic Quarterly.* 63, no. 4 (Autumn 1964): 530-41.

Hume, Kathryn. "Science and Imagination in Calvino's *Cosmicomics.*" *Mosaic* 5 (December 1982): 47-48.

Husserl, Edmund. "The Acquisition of Pure Generalities by the Method of Essential Seeing." *Experience and Judgment: Investigations in a Genealogy of Logic.* Trans. James S. Churchill and Karl Ameriks. Evanston, IL: Northwestern University Press, 1973.

Hutcheon, Linda. *The Politics of Postmodernism.* New York: Routledge, 1989.

Jameson, Fredric. *The Ideologies of Theory, Essays, 1971-1986. Vol. 2: Syntax of History.* Minneaplois: University of Minnesota Press, 1988.

Jehlen, Myra. *Class and Character in Faulkner's South*. New York: Columbia University Press, 1976.

Jenkins, Lee. "Go Down, Moses." *Faulkner and Black-White Relations: A Psychoanalytical Approach*. New York: Columbia University Press, 1981.

Karl, Frederick. *William Faulkner: American Writer, A Biography*. New York: Weidenfeld & Nicolson, 1989.

Kinney, Arthur F., ed. *Critical Essays on William Faulkner: The McCaslin Family*. Boston: G. K. Hall & Co., 1990.

Klosko, George. *The Development of Plato's Political Theory*. New York: Methuen, 1986.

Koreman, Joan S. "Faulkner's Grecian Urn." *Southern Literary Journal*. 7 (1964): 3-23.

Kousser, J. Morgan, and James M. McPherson, eds. *Region, Race, and Reconstruction: Essays in Honor of C. Vann Woodward*. New York: Oxford University Press, 1982.

Kristeva, Julia. *Desire in Language: A Semiotic Approach to Literature and Art*. Ed. Leon S. Roudiez. Trans. Thomas Gora, Alice Jardine, and Leon S. Roudiez. New York: Columbia University Press, 1980.

Kropf, Carl R. "Judgment and Character: Evidence and the Law in *Tom Jones*." *Studies in the Novel* 21 (Winter 1989): 357-66.

Kybet, Susan M. *Bonnie Prince Charlie: A Biography of Charles Edward Stuart*. New York: Dodd, Mead & Co., 1988.

Lacan, Jacques. *Ecrits*. Trans. Alan Sheridan. New York: W. W. Norton & Co., 1977.

Lanier, Sidney. The English Novel. Centennial Edition. Vol. 4. Ed. Clarence Cohdes and Kemp Malone. Baltimore: Johns Hopkins University Press, 1945.

Leaver, Florence. "Faulkner: The Word as Principle and Power." Modern Fiction Studies. 57 (Autumn 1958): 464-75.

Lee, Desmond. "Translator's Introduction." In Plato's *The Republic*. (See Plato.)

Lernout, Green. *The French Joyce*. Ann Arbor: University of Michigan Press, 1990.

Levi-Strauss, Claude. "The Structural Study of Myth." *Critical Theory Since 1965*, 809-23. (See Adams and Searle.)

Lewis P. Simpson, ed. *I'll Take My Stand: The South and the Agrarian Tradition by Twelve Southerners*. Baton Rouge: Louisiana State University Press, 1977.

Lindboe, B. R. "'O' Shakespeare, Had I Thy Pen!: Fielding's Use of

Shakespeare in *Tom Jones.*" *Studies in the Novel* 14 (Winter 1982): 303-15.

Locke, M. A. "Henry Fielding and the Historical Background of the 'Forty-Five.'" *The True Patriot: The History of Our Own Times.* (See Fielding.)

Lynch, James. *Henry Fielding and the Heliodoran Novel: Romance, Epic, and Fielding's New Province of Writing.* Rutherford, NJ: Fairleigh Dickinson University Press, 1986.

Lyon, Harvey T. *Keats' Well-Read Urn.* New York: Henry Holt, 1958.

Mace, Nancy A. "Henry Fielding's Classical Learning." *Modern Philology* (February 1991): 243-60.

Manganiello, Dominic. *Joyce's Politics.* London: Routledge, 1980.

Mao, Tsetung. *Poems.* Bei Jin: Foreign Languages Press, 1976.

———. *Selected Readings from the Works of Mao Tsetung.* Beijing: Foreign Languages Press, 1971.

Marx, Karl, and Frederick Engels. *The Communist Manifesto.* 28th Printing. New York: International Publishers, 1989.

———. *The Economic and Philosophic Manuscripts of 1844.* Ed. Dirk J. Struik. Trans. Martin Milligan. New York: International Publishers, 1964.

McCaffery, Larry, ed. *Postmodern Fiction: A Bio-Bibliographical Guide.* New York: Greenwood Press, 1986.

McCrea, Brian. *Henry Fielding and the Politics of Mid-Eighteenth Century England.* Athens: University of Georgia Press, 1981.

McHugh, Roland. *Annotations to Finnegans Wake.* Baltimore: Johns Hopkins University Press, 1980.

McKeon, Michael. *The Origins of the English Novel: 1600-1740.* Baltimore: Johns Hopkins University Press, 1987.

Meriwether, James B., and Michael Millagate, eds. *Lion in the Garden: Interviews with William Faulkner, 1926-1962.* Lincoln: University of Nebraska Press, 1980.

Miller, Henry Knight. *Henry Fielding's Tom Jones and the Romance Tradition.* Victoria British Columbia: University of Victoria, 1976.

Miller, Randall M., and John David Smith, ed. *Dictionary of Afro-American Slavery.* New York: Greenwood Press, 1988.

Millgate, Michael. *The Achievement of William Faulkner.* New York: Random House, 1966.

Minter, David. *William Faulkner: His Life and Work.* Baltimore: Johns Hopkins University Press, 1980.

Moreland, Richard C. *Faulkner and Modernism: Rereading and Rewriting.*

Madison: University of Wisconsin Press, 1990.

Morrison, Toni. "Unspeakable Things Unspoken: The Afro-American Presence in American Literature." *Michigan Quarterly Review* 28, no. 1 (Winter 1989): 1-34.

Moses, W. R. "Where History Crosses Myth: Another Reading of 'The Bear'." *Accent* 13 (Winter 1953): 21-23.

Muste, John M. "The Failure of Love in *Go Down, Moses.*" *Modern Fiction Studies* 10, no. 4 (Winter 1964-65): 366-78.

Nabokov, Vladimir. Interview by *Wisconsin Studies.* (See Nabokov, *The Annotated Lolita*, 327.)

Nietzsche, Friedrich. "The Will to Power in Art." (See Rader, *A Modern Book of Esthetics*, 103.)

O'Shea, Michael J. *James Joyce and Heraldry.* Albany, NY: SUNY Press, 1986.

Peavy, Charles . *Go Slow Now: Faulkner and the Race Question.* Eugene: University of Oregon Press, 1971.

Perkins, Hoke. "'Ah Just Cant Quit Thinking': Faulkner's Black Razor Murderers." *Faulkner and Race: Faulkner and Yoknapatawpha, 1986.* Ed. Doreen Fowler and Ann J. Abadie. Jackson: University Press of Mississippi, 1987, 222-35.

Porter, Carolyn. *Seeing and Beeing: The Plight of the Participant Observer in Emerson, James, Adams, and Faulkner.* Middletown, CT: Wesleyan University Press, 1981.

Rader, Melvin, ed. *A Modern Book of Esthetics.* 5th ed. New York: Holt & Rinehart & Winston, 1979.

Radloff, Bernhard. "The Fate of Demonism in William Faulkner." *Arizona Quarterly* 46, no. 1 (Spring 1990): 27-50.

Ragan, David Paul. "The Evolution of Roth Edmonds in *Go Down, Moses.*" *Mississippi Quarterly* 38 (Summer 1985): 295-309.

Rexroth, Kenneth. "Tom Jones." *Saturday Review,* July 1, 1967, 13.

Roller, David C., and Robert W. Twyman, eds. *The Encyclopedia of Southern History.* Baton Rouge: Lousiana State University Press, 1990.

Rougemont, Denis de. *Love in the Western World.* Trans. Montgomery Belgion. Princeton, NJ: Princeton University Press, 1983.

Roussel, Roy. *The Metaphysics of Darkness.* Baltimore: Johns Hopkins University Press, 1971.

———. *Conversation between Sexes.* New York: Oxford University Press, 1986.

Ryan, Michael. *Marxism and Deconstruction: A Critical Articulation.*

Baltimore: Johns Hopkins University Press, 1986.

Saussure, Ferdinand de. "Course in General Linguistics." *Critical Theory Since 1965*, 649. (See Adams and Searle.)

Schmitz, Neil. *Of Huck and Alice*. Minneapolis: University of Minnesota Press, 1983.

———. "Tall Tale, Tall Talk: Pursuing the Lie in Jacksonian Literature." *American Literature* 48 (January 1977): 471-91.

Schwarts, Lawrence H. *Creating Faulkner's Reputation: The Politics of Modern Literary Criticism*. Knoxville: University of Tennessee Press, 1988.

Sharpe, Kevin, and Steven N. Zwicker, eds. *Politics of Discourse: The Literature and History of the Seventeenth-Century England*. Berkeley: University of California Press, 1987.

Singer, Irving. *The Nature of Love*. Chicago: University of Chicago Press, 1988.

Skei, Hans H. *William Faulkner: The Short Story Career, an Outline of Faulkner's Short Story Writing from 1919-1962*. Oslo, Norway: The American Institute University of Oslo, 1981.

Sleeth, Irene Lynn. "William Faulkner: A Bibliography of Criticism." *Twentieth Century Literature*. April 1962-January 1963. New York: Kraus Reprint Corporation, 1966.

Songtag, Susan. "Beauty." *Seventy-Five Readings: An Anthology*. New York: McGraw-Hill, 1991.

Spacks, Patricia Meyer. *Gossip*. New York: Alfred A. Knopf, 1985.

Stampp, Kenneth M. *The Era of Reconstruction, 1865-1877*. New York: Alfred A. Knopf, 1966.

Starobinski, Jean. *The Invention of Liberty, 1700-1789*. Cleveland, OH: The World Publishing Co., 1964.

Stone, William B. "Ike McCaslin and the Grecian Urn." *Studies in Short Fiction* 10 (Winter 1974): 93-94.

Stryker, Lloyd Paul. *Andrew Johnson: A Study in Courage*. New York: Macmillan, 1929.

Sundquist, Eric J. *Faulkner: The House Divided*. Baltimore: Johns Hopkins University Press, 1983.

Sussman, Henry. *Afterimages of Modernity*. Baltimore: Johns Hopkins University Press, 1990.

———. *The Hegelian Aftermath: Readings in Hegel, Kierkegaard, Freud, Proust, and James*. Baltimore: John Hopkins University Press, 1982.

———. *High Resolution: Critical Theory and the Problem of Literacy*. New

York: Oxford University Press, 1989.

Tangum, Marion. "Rhetorical Clues to *Go Down, Moses*: 'Who Is Talking to Whom?'" *Heir and Prototype: Original and Derived Characterizations in Faulkner*. Ed. Dan Ford. Conway: University of Central Arkansas Press, 1987, 8-22.

Taylor, Mark, ed. *Deconstruction in Context: Literature and Philosophy*. Chicago: University of Chicago Press, 1986.

Taylor Jr., Walter F. "Let My People Go: The White Man's Heritage in *Go Down, Moses*." *South Atlantic Quarterly* 58 (Winter 1959): 30-32.

Taylor, William R. *Cavalier and Yankee: The Old South and American National Character*. New York: George Braziller, Inc. 1961.

Thornbury, Ethel Margaret. "Henry Fielding's Theory of the Comic Prose Epic." *University of Wisconsin Studies* 30 (1931): 140.

Tillyard. E. M. W. *The Epic Strain in the English Novel*. London: Chatto & Windus, 1963.

Tindall, George Brown. *The Emergence of the New South, 1913-45*. Baton Rouge: Louisiana State University Press, 1967, 650-56, 696-71. (On Faulkner in 1930s).

Trefousse, Hans L. *Andrew Johnson: A Biography*. New York: W. W. Norton & Co., 1989.

Unsworth, John. "Tom Jones: The Comedy of Knowledge." *Modern Language Quarterly* 48 (September 1987): 242-53.

Utley, F. et al., eds. *Bear, Man, and God: Eight Approaches to William Faulkner's "The Bear."* 2nd ed. New York: Random House, 1971.

Vance, "Love's Concordance." *Diacritics*. Spring 1975.

Valency, Maurice. *In Praise of Love: An Introduction to the Love-Poetry of Renaissance*. New York: Shocken Books, 1982.

Warner, William B. "Realist Literary History: Mckeon's New Origins of the Novel." *Diacritics* (Spring 1989): 62-81.

Warren, Robert Penn. "William Faulkner and His South." Unpublished lecture. University of Virginia, 1951.

Watson, J. Steven. *The Reign of George III, 1760-1815*. Oxford: Clarendon Press, 1960.

Watt, Ian. *The Rise of the Novel: Studies in Defoe, Richardson, and Fielding*. Berkeley: University of California Press, 1957.

William C. Dowling. *The Epistolary Moment: The Poetics of the Eighteenth Century Verse Epistle*. Princeton, NJ: Princeton University Press, 1991.

Williams, Basil. *The Whig Supremacy*. Oxford History of England

Series. Ed. G. N. Clark. Oxford: Clarendon Press, 1939.

Winston, Robert W. *Andrew Johnson: Plebeian and Patriot.* New York: Henry Holt, 1928.

Woodward, C. Vann. *Origins of the New South, 1877-1913.* Baton Rouge: Lousiana State University Press, 1951.

———. *The Burden of Southern History.* Baton Rouge: Lousiana State University Press, 1960.

Zwicker, Steven N. *Politics and Language in Dryden's Poetry: The Arts of Disguise.* Princeton, NJ: Princeton University Press, 1984.

Index

in *Remembrance of Things Past*, 33
in *The Symposium*, 32, 33;
  love as mediator, 40–41
Lolita, 195;
  and the culture monopolies, 20
  pleasure as a weapon in, 9
  pluralistic modes of love, 63–64
Lost in the Funhouse, 30, 193
love, stages of, in Plato, 43–64
lover's discourse, xv, 11, 34;
  and Barthes, 11–12
  and Nietzsche, 34
  "raking up stories," 35–37

Melville, Herman, 3–4, 195
Moby-Dick. *See Moby-Dick*
metafiction, discourse in, 32–33
middle-class syndrome, 14–17;
  marriage and, 71–72
  Pamela syndrome, 67, 70–71,
    81–82
mimesis, 33, 36
mirror phase, and romantic love, 51.
    See also Penis envy
Mishima, Yukio, 12–13, 195
misogyny, question of, and Plato,
    37–38
Moby-Dick, 195;
  and *Go Down, Moses*, 4
  signifier of idea beyond the story,
    3–4
modernism:
  love, 46–47
  transition to postmodernism, 5–6
Moll Flanders, 76–77, 87

Nabokov, Vladimir, 9, 195;
  and novelistic love, 64
narcissism, 12–13
narrative structures, 31, 38–39. *See
    also* specific topics
"natural love," 34–35
novelistic love, 60–64;
  as healer/fertilizer, 63–64
  language as ultimate love power,
    61–62
  love as mediator, 40–41, 61

political agenda, 61

"orchestra," linguistic, and ideology,
    8–9, 11
Other, 11, 16, 52
"oversoul," and Plato's theory of
    philosophical love, 58

Pamela, and epic love, 67, 77, 81–82;
  virtue, 77, 81
Pamela syndrome. *See* Middle-class
    syndrome
"Patriotism," 12–13, 195
penis envy:
  and the middle classes, 14–17;
  exposure of in postmodernism,
    24
  identity, search for, 15–16;
  Phaedrus, in *The Symposium*,
    43–44
  publicity, anxiety for, 15, 17. *See
    also* Castration anxiety
sensual materialism, 16
philosophical love:
  achieving, 58–59
  contemplation of absolute beauty,
    56–57, 59
  in Eliot's "Four Quartets," 59
  indifference of love, 59–60
  and the Philosopher Ruler, 56–57
  self-sacrifice in, 56–57, 58
Plato, 195;
  misogyny, question of, and, 37–38
  and the Philosopher Ruler, 56–57,
    99, 109;
  in Faulkner's "The Bear," 158
  *See also The History of Tom Jones;
    The Republic; The
    Symposium*
Platonic love:
  attributes of, 38
  development of in *The Symposium*,
    42. *See also The Symposium*
pleasure:
  Barthes' "pleasure of the text," 56
  drive, and thanatos, 16–17
  and materialism, 16

About the Author

Jennie Wang is Assistant Professor of English at the University of Northern Iowa. She received her Ph.D. from the State University of New York at Buffalo in 1992 and her M.A. from Stanford University in 1984. She has published a number of articles on postmodern fiction including "The Player's Song of *Finnegans Wake*: Translating Sound Sense" (*Narrative Technique* 21), "To Wielderfight His Penisolate War: The Lover's Discourse in Postmodern Fiction (*Critique* 34), and "*Tripmaster Monkey*: Kingston's Postmodern Representation of a New China Man" (*MELUS* 20). Her Chinese translation of Raymond Federman's metafiction, *Smiles on Washington Square: A Love Story of Sorts*, is forthcoming from Shanghai Translation Publishing House. After several years of research, she is currently writing a book on Maxine Hong Kingston and American Orientalism.